Contemporary Jewish Civilization

Selected Syllabi

CONTINUING WORKSHOP ON
UNIVERSITY TEACHING OF CONTEMPORARY JEWISH CIVILIZATION

Academic Chairman of the Center: Prof. Moshe Davis

Director of the Center: Dr. Natan Lerner

Workshop Director: Dr. Gideon Shimoni

Advisory Committee:
Prof. Haim Avni, Israel
Prof. Doris Bensimon, France
Prof. Michael Brown, Canada
Prof. Deborah Dash Moore, USA
Prof. Sol Encel, Australia
Sally Frankental, South Africa
Prof. Samuel C. Heilman, USA
Lic. Judit Liwerant, Mexico
Prof. Mervin F. Verbit, USA

Contemporary Jewish Civilization

Selected Syllabi

Edited by Gideon Shimoni

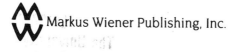Markus Wiener Publishing, Inc.

*Ongoing research for the series on Selected Syllabi
in University Teaching of Jewish Civilization
is made possible by grants from
Mr. and Mrs. Herbert Neuman
and
Mr. and Mrs. Richard H. Rubin*

ISBN 0-910129-28-2
Library of Congress Card Number: 85-040515

Printed in the United States of America

CONTENTS

Support for this publication has been given by the Joint Program for Jewish Education (State of Israel Ministry of Education and Culture – The Jewish Agency for Israel – World Zionist Organization) and the Memorial Foundation for Jewish Culture.

EDITOR'S PREFACE

This publication arises from a Workshop on the Teaching of Contemporary Jewish Civilization conducted in the summer of 1984 by a group of university teachers in a variety of disciplines and from various countries. The Workshop formed part of the activity of the International Center for University Teaching of Jewish Civilization established by Professor Moshe Davis.

The idea of conducting such a workshop emerged at a colloquium of interested university scholars which Professor Davis convened in conjunction with the Eighth World Congress of Jewish Studies, held in the summer of 1981. That colloquium issued in a series of workshop sessions. The first, held in 1982, undertook an examination and exchange of views on the problematics and needs of teaching in this area. A second session, held in 1983, focused on one particular area which impinges upon a wide range of teaching at universities throughout the world--"Israel: History, Society and Culture." This was followed by a third workshop session, the fruits of which are the subject of the present publication. Participants were invited to engage in a mutual exchange of courses given in their particular university teaching contexts and through the medium of their particular academic disciplines. The participants thus exposed their own conceptual frameworks, bibliographies and teaching experiences to the constructive criticism of colleagues.

(i)

It became evident that while the workshop participants were not in complete agreement as to any hard and fast definition of the term "contemporary," it was consensually understood to connote that part of the past which is covered by the experience of those who still live with us. This broad understanding of the term is compatible with a variety of more specific conceptions to be found in the literature. Thus, for practitioners of the historical discipline it provides an operative, if yet indeterminate, distinction between "modern" and "contemporary" as categories of periodization. At the same time it is not incompatible with a sociologically-centered view such as that of Marshall Sklare who has stated that "the field of scholarship known as contemporary Jewish studies is a specialty which utilizes the perspectives of social science to gain an understanding of the Jews of today and their immediate forebears."* By the same token, it may be regarded as subsuming the views of some who identify the term "contemporary" with particular events regarded as turning points in the twentieth century, such as the First World War, the Holocaust or the emergence of the State of Israel. Likewise, it is consonant with the pedagogically-oriented view which identifies a "contemporary" approach with the attempt to answer questions of existential importance for the present generation by methods of the social sciences and by enquiring as far as is relevant into the past.

Whatever differences remained over the definition of "contemporary Jewry," the exchange of views and experiences in the workshop left no doubt that courses such as those represented in the present publication

*Marshall Sklare (ed.), **The Jew in American Society** (New York, 1976), p. 1.

are proliferating at universities not only in Israel and North America, but also in other countries. They are being taught in a wide variety of contexts. The Institute of Contemporary Jewry at the Hebrew University is probably the most highly developed model; it embraces regional studies (e.g., American Jewry, Soviet Jewry, Latin American Jewry, Jewry in countries historically associated with the British Commonwealth); the different academic disciplines (e.g., history, sociology, social psychology, demography) and specific subjects (e.g., the Holocaust, Zionism). Courses in all of these fields are offered at M.A. level while a few are especially designed for B.A. students.

Another context in which courses in the area of Contemporary Jewry are taught is that provided by an interdepartmental program. An example of such a program may be found at Queens College of the City University of New York with its large Jewish student body. The Jewish Studies program at Queens College offers interdepartmental courses in areas such as Jewish intellectual and social history, sociology and folklore of the Jews. A number of these include a considerable "contemporary" dimension.

Other variants of courses in which Contemporary Jewish Civilization is taught are to be found in departments of Jewish studies, departments of religion, and at Jewish-sponsored institutes of higher learning such as Hebrew Union College and the Jewish Theological Seminary. At many universities courses are burgeoning within conventional academic disciplines such as history, literature, political science and sociology. Moreover, a growing desire is evident on the part of Jewish academics, who have hitherto not ventured out of the conventional subjects, to develop new options in the area of contemporary Jewry.

The purpose of the present publication is to indicate to a broader academic public what kinds of courses are being offered in various countries and university contexts and, in so doing, hopefully to stimulate even more academics to personally undertake the development of similar course options.

To be sure, these syllabi do not purport to be models of excellence for universal emulation; they are meant rather, simply to serve as examples of what is actually being done. Nor do they, as examples, pretend to be representative of every variant in the field. Indeed, barring one or two exceptions, the selection is limited, as was the workshop itself, to undergraduate courses given either at universities outside of Israel or in the special foreign language (i.e., non-Hebrew) programs offered by some Israeli universities to students from abroad.

The syllabi are here presented essentially as offered in practice, although in many cases the contributors have made improvements prompted by the exchange of ideas in the workshop. An attempt, however, was made to standardize the presentation with a view to optimal informativeness. Thus, the specific academic context for which the course has been designed is provided in each case. It succinctly describes the academic institution and department in which the course is offered and provides a profile of the students who take it. This is meant to indicate the considerations which influence the lecturer in defining his purposes, determining the scope of the course, compiling its contents and setting the assigned reading, bibliographies and requirements for grading. An outline of the course headings then follows with accompanying required and suggested reading. The last section of each syllabus presentation is a brief description of the "conceptual framework" of the course. This is intended to describe the main organizing ideas used in the course, the major questions raised and the way the themes and issues are developed.

Notwithstanding this standardized format, formulated by the workshop participants themselves, the autonomy of each contributor has been respected, allowing for varying degrees of detail in the presentation and for differences in course structure and methodology.

In the interests of multidisciplinary enrichment, and in conformity with the approach used in the workshop sessions, the syllabi in this publication have not been arranged according to academic discipline employed. Rather, it has been deemed more beneficial to divide them into three broad categories. The first is **Survey Courses in Contemporary Jewry,** encompassing some attempts at a multidisciplinary approach and others bound to a single academic discipline such as history or sociology. The common denominator of these courses is their relatively global scope. The second category is **Modern-Contemporary History.** The situation, world-wide, appears to be that many of the courses offered within the conventional framework of modern history actually incorporate a significant dimension of the contemporary. To separate for our purposes only the contemporary segments of such courses would be to disturb their natural integrity. We have therefore given their syllabi in full. The third category is **Thematic Courses in Contemporary Jewry.** The present selection is but a modest sample of the proliferating number of courses of this nature, especially on aspects of the Holocaust.

Some of the broader issues which have engaged the Workshop are reflected in introductory articles by Moshe Davis and Mervin Verbit. Behind the scenes, the preparation of this publication benefited from the invaluable work of Patricia Redifer, Matelle Bar-Chaim and Matthew Kalman.

Jerusalem, April 1985   Gideon Shimoni

THE GLOBAL EMPHASIS IN UNIVERSITY TEACHING OF JEWISH CIVILIZATIO

Moshe Davis

Academic Chairman,
International Center for University
Teaching of Jewish Civilization

Intellectual concern with contemporary problems is a long established tradition. Its placement within the university framework as part of the Humanities and Social Sciences came in the late 19th and early 20th centuries. And only in the mid-decades of this century, as change began to accelerate at whirlwind pace, were novel initiatives made through a variety of disciplinary, multidisciplinary and inter-disciplinary modes to create an integral academic entity of studies in contemporary civilization. Scholarly associations arose such as **Amicale** in France and the **Institut für Zeitgeschichte** in Germany. In addition, specialized university research centers were established in such departments as History and Religion, Political Science and Sociology. Most of these attempted to analyze the radical transformations in the contemporary world and to educate mankind towards its global responsibility in the rapidly advancing technological era.

Within these comprehensive frameworks, additional factors unique to the Jewish condition in the middle decades of our century made distinguished scholars aware of the need to put their talents to the service of the Jewish People and to study the present in anticipation of the future. Writing on the Jewish problem in 1942, before the total devastation of the Holocaust, the social philosopher Morris Ginsburg said: "The problem with which the Jews are confronted today is of a magnitude unparalleled in the long history of the Jewish People, for never before has it been worldwide in its significance. Never before have the Jews been threatened with destruction or disintegration in so many parts of the world at the same time. In short, the Jewish problem is worldwide in scope and deeply entangled in the major issues with which the world is now confronted."*

Geographically separated from the European maelstrom but deeply involved with the destiny of his People, Morris Raphael Cohen, the eminent American philosopher, stressed the urgency for awareness of our existing condition and better integration of available knowledge. He warned: "We are opposed by an enemy that has secured unexpected triumphs because his action has been based on thorough knowledge. Let us not fail through insufficient attention to the lessons of experience."**

These ideas--the compelling need for worldwide Jewry to cooperate in planning for its future and indispensable role of authentic scholarship in realizing that objective--were the basis of my personal conception when I was called to establish the Institute of Contemporary Jewry in 1959. Creation of solid foundations for the new field of contemporary Jewish civilization was the Institute's scholarly task; study of the present in light of both the precedented and unprecedented was its academic objective; forging a faculty and training teachers was its institutional responsibility. All of those involved in the Institute's formation firmly believed that the time was ripe for the

*Morris Ginsburg, "The Jewish Problem," Agenda (October 1942).

**Morris R. Cohen, Jewish Studies of Peace and Post-War Problems (including a Summary of the Activities of the Research Institute), Research Institute on Peace and Post-War Problems of the American Jewish Committee, 1943, p. 7.

State of Israel to serve the cause of world Jewish continuity by giving of its knowledge and creative resources to those Diaspora Jewries struggling for cultural integrity.

In presenting the programmatic framework of the Institute of Contemporary Jewry, my purpose is to submit a case illustration for the study of contemporary civilization. At the Hebrew University, distinguished scholars in the general disciplines joined with specialists in Jewish subjects to study the contemporary Jewish condition. The Institute grew through interdependent relationships between departments in the faculties of Humanities and Social Sciences within the University, and through cooperative activity with universities and research institutes in Europe, North and South America, and the British Commonwealth countries. Research, teaching and training programs were developed and linked with each other in conception and implementation. From the Institute's publications one can discern how findings in history, thought, literature, demography, sociology, political science and social psychology have been incorporated in basic research, university teaching and public education.

It must be underscored, however, that the Institute's program was not and could not be undertaken in Israel alone. The underlying principle of the entire enterprise was the conviction that the era of insular regional and even national preoccupations had passed in the Diaspora as well as in Israel. In the twentieth century, the Jews have become an interrelated world People. In many parts of the globe, they virtually share common problems, even within the varied contexts of specific Jewish communities. Thus contemporary Jewish studies deals with the ties and interdependence of the entire Jewish People as well as the study of particular Jewish communities throughout the world, including Israel.

It was this global conception which guided us as we proceeded to forge the program of the International Center for University Teaching of Jewish Civilization. At its very beginning, the Center embarked on a series of joint teaching projects in different parts of the world, not only in the field of contemporary Jewish civilization, but on the whole scale of Judaica. In addition, the International Center plans to publish university level curricular materials, including syllabi and pedagogic exposition in Jewish history, thought, language and culture. This material will be an outgrowth of the annual international workshops conducted in Jerusalem during the past few years. All of these activities can help overcome the serious problem of segmentation and compartmentalization in pedagogic literature; they guarantee an indispensable balance in the subject matter taught in universities.

This global orientation allows each of us to focus, from various regional situations, on the deeper socio-educational forces that motivated and shaped contemporary Jewry. Basically, however, this approach helps us to examine the Jewish condition from the perspective of our own times, and also systematically to study the salient issues confronting world society. Is there any more revealing example of how an entity functions in variegated settings than the global Jewish People?

TEACHING CONTEMPORARY JEWISH CIVILIZATION IN NORTH AMERICAN UNIVERSITIES: CURRENT STATUS AND NEEDS

Mervin F. Verbit
Member of the Workshop Advisory Committee
Director of the World Register of
University Courses in Jewish Civilization

At its outset, teaching of Contemporary Jewish Civilization confronted a problem that any new field of study is apt to encounter: the question of academic legitimacy. Contemporary Jewish Civilization or, as some prefer, Contemporary Jewry (here we shall use the two terms interchangeably), has faced that problem on two fronts. Among social scientists, the subject was often considered too specific--even, in universalistic rhetoric, parochial--for university study. Among scholars of Judaica, for whom classical materials tend to command higher esteem, it was widely considered too recent--even trivial--to merit serious attention. Fortunately, these problems have been surmounted. Social scientists, in part as a response to the growing popular acceptance of ethnicity, now recognize that the study of cultural groups is not only legitimate but essential to the development of general theories of behavior, provided that such study is done with conceptual and methodological sophistication. Similarly, most Judaica scholars have also come to appreciate the value of careful research on contemporary Jewish life and thought.

Precisely because Contemporary Jewry is now being taught in an already large and still growing number of institutions, and with the sophistication that characterizes other university subjects, new problems have arisen which need consideration. Since Contemporary Jewry is not a discipline, but rather a subject--or, more properly, a set of subjects--its disciplinary nature needs exploration.   Moreover, if any given aspect of contemporary Jewish life is to be put into the context of Contemporary Jewish Civilization generally, its comparative character needs to be specified.   Also, since Contemporary Jewish Civilization goes beyond academic interest to touch on matters of deep personal concern to both instructors and students, the need to combine academic dispassion with the kind of presentation that does not "lose the soul" of the material presents a challenge to anyone involved in a course in Contemporary Jewry.

In order to address these and related issues, the International Center for University Teaching of Jewish Civilization has convened a continuing Workshop on University Teaching of Contemporary Jewish Civilization.   This workshop brings together colleagues from various disciplines, from different kinds of academic settings, and from several countries, to consider these issues and to identify the kinds of materials that are needed to enhance the quality of university instruction in the field.

In this paper, we briefly summarize four sets of issues which confront the field: those involved, respectively, in defining it, in locating it in the academic structure, in conceptualizing it, and in motivating the instructors who offer the courses and the students who take them.

Defining the Field

As we come to understand more about the complexity and inter-connectedness of life, we appreciate more fully the difficulty, perhaps even the impossibility, of drawing neat borders around subject matters. No province of knowledge is self-contained or fully adequate to the interpretation of actual phenomena. Consequently, a field's definition is not so much a matter of boundaries as it is a matter of focus. With that in mind, we can consider "Contemporary Jewry" to be the study of "Jewish life and thought in the contemporary period."

That definition is not self-explanatory. Its three crucial terms all require some additional comment. The question of what is "Jewish" has two dimensions. One concerns the distinction between expressions of Jews which are self-consciously part of their Jewishness on the one hand and, on the other, those ideas and behavior patterns of Jews whose relationship to Jewishness is implicit or subconscious. Is Jewish art any art done by Jews or only art done as an expression of Jewishness, and, if the latter, how self-consciously Jewish must it be? Is Jewish political behavior whatever Jews do politically or only that part of their political behavior which is influenced by their Jewishness, and, again, how conscious does the influence need to be? To what extent are "Jewish" demographic patterns a consequence of Jewishness, and how consciously so?

The second dimension of the question of what is Jewish centers on the distinction between popular and official (or what Charles Liebman calls "folk" and "elite") Jewishness. Is Jewishness whatever Jews think and do, or is it a specific set of ideas, values, and behavior which can be ascertained by reading the major documents of Jewish history? The attempt to differentiate these two aspects of Jewish experience by using different terms for them--Jewishness and Judaism--

is a solution which, though available in some languages, is more semantic than real. These two facets of what is Jewish are interwoven. Indeed, the very nature of the interweaving is one of the more important areas of our investigation. Significantly, Hebrew uses one word (**yahadut**) for both.

Because spheres of behavior which are distinguishable from one another in analysis are usually interlocked in reality, we should examine both official and popular, both self-conscious and implicit, Jewish life and thought. Whichever may be our initial focus, we shall have to consider the others before our analysis can be adequate.

The phrase "life and thought" needs but little additional comment. Fortunately, life and thought are no longer seen as separable from one another, nor is either seen as clearly antecedent to the other. Both must be taken into account in any sound analysis of contemporary Jewish or any other, civilization.

Clearly, the time period implied by "Contemporary" cannot be sharp or precise; it will always be a matter of some contention. It is, however, the focus of investigation rather than the boundaries in time that defines the field. The study of Contemporary Jewry should have as its starting point the current conditions and issues of Jewish life. It should move back into history as far and as deeply as is necessary to understand those conditions and issues. The elements of the Jewish past do not all shape the current situation with equal force, nor does the influence necessarily weaken as we recede into the past. There are aspects of ancient Jewish life and thought which resonate far more loudly in Contemporary Jewry than do certain aspects of, say, the seventeenth century, or even the twentieth century. "Contemporary" defines where we begin our study; how far back we go and with what detail must depend on what we need to know in order to interpret the phenomena with which we start.

Locating the Field

The study of behavior can be organized either around disciplines or around substantive areas. While virtually all universities are organized around disciplines, institutions vary with regard to the extent to which substantive areas constitute the basis of academic units as well as the nature of those units. Substantive areas are represented sometimes by departments, sometimes by special programs drawing on faculty from several departments, sometimes by no formal structure at all. A student who wishes to give special attention to, say, Medieval Europe, the Orient, American Studies, urbanism, or Jewish Civilization, therefore, will, depending on the university attended, find a department, an organized program, a combination of the two, or random courses here and there in various disciplinary departments. There is no uniform pattern.

In most places, however, Jewish Civilization is not located in a separate unit. Certainly, Contemporary Jewry is not represented by a special unit. In this respect, the Hebrew University's Institute of Contemporary Jewry is unique. Elsewhere, Contemporary Jewry is taught by professors whose appointments place them in departments or programs of wider scope, and their teaching is likely to reflect their respective academic contexts, which, in turn, indicate their intellectual approaches and interpretive emphases.

Contemporary Jewish Civilization is likely to be taught by people trained and holding appointments in any of the following disciplines or subjects: sociology, history, social psychology, religion, literature, political science, Jewish Studies, or ethnic studies.   Ideally, a course in Contemporary Jewry would draw on all of these disciplines, using their respective methods to illuminate the various dimensions of Contemporary Jewish life and thought, as well as the relationships among them.   Realistically, even those professors who can mobilize more than one discipline will have primary training in one only.   The enrichment of courses in Contemporary Jewry, therefore, requires development of materials that will enable instructors to introduce the perspectives of fields in which they are not trained.

In addition to that general observation, each disciplinary frame- work poses its own peculiar issues.   When Contemporary Jewry is taught as a sociology course, for example, does the instructor use sociological theory and research to analyze the Jewish community, or is the Jewish community the case in point with which sociological theory and research are taught?   Similarly, does a course in contemporary Jewish literature use that literature as a window onto Jewish life and thought, or does it use that literature to train students in literary analysis?   Similar questions could be posed for all of the disciplinary contexts of Contemporary Jewry.   While these alternatives may seem to be matters of emphasis alone, they are more than that.   Different answers to the question lead to the selection of different materials for inclusion in the course.

Organizational context also implies intellectual context.   Will a Contemporary Jewry course in Jewish Studies draw on social and political factors as heavily as a course in sociology or political science? Will the latter give as much weight to the Judaic background of Contemporary Jewry as will the former? Will a Contemporary Jewry course in a department of religion emphasize the Jews as a religious group comparable to other religious groups, while a course in an ethnic studies program dwells more on those aspects of Jewish life that can be contrasted to comparable aspects of other ethnic groups? It is, of course, the proper balancing of the various sets of factors suggested by these contexts that constitutes sound analysis and, therefore, good teaching. Still, to recognize that fact is easy; to carry it over into teaching is less easy. Research can sometimes deal with one issue at a time; good teaching requires the constant integration of all relevant issues simultaneously.

What is true of courses in Contemporary Jewry is even more true of modules on Contemporary Jewry included in courses which cover other groups as well. On the one hand, inclusion of the Jews in such courses is to be encouraged. On the other hand, the risk of superficiality, with attendant dangers of misunderstanding, is heightened in such courses. Consequently, it is crucial that materials be prepared which will help instructors to cope with such difficulties.

Conceptualizing the Field

What are the Jews--a religious group, an ethnic group, a demographic category, a minority, a political factor, a socioeconomic element? They are none of these and all of these. Which set of theories, then, should be brought to bear on their behavior, and to whom should the Jews be compared?

In one sense, the Jews are unique. Then again, every group is unique. Still, without at least implicit comparison, understanding is impossible. To take perhaps the starkest example, even the uniqueness of the Holocaust becomes clear only when the Holocaust is compared to other destructions of populations. The essence of understanding is the ability to see both similarities and differences. The question—"What are Jews?"—and its corollary—"To whom should they be compared?"—must therefore, be answered.

Needless to say, the proper answer to that set of questions is complicated by the probability that what we have called the "location" of the field will carry its own operational answer. Also, the answer is likely to reflect the cultural definitions of the societies in which Contemporary Jewry is taught. What compounds the matter further is that the Jews themselves are influenced by the cultural definitions of the societies in which they live. In other words, Jewish self-definition is shaped in part by the social contexts in which Jews live, and that self-definition in turn shapes Jewish life and thought in those contexts.

The variety of Jewish self-definitions becomes especially problematic when Jewish life and thought is placed in the context of world Jewry. It is easy to argue that different analytic paradigms are needed for Israeli Jewry and the various Diaspora Jewries. However, we cannot teach about Contemporary Jewry globally unless we have a unifying paradigm with which to bring disparate patterns together.

All of this provides both an intellectual and an instructional challenge. The intellectual challenge is to develop conceptual frameworks for considering Contemporary Jewry in its various sociocultural situations.   The instructional challenge is to prepare materials through which the diversity of the contemporary Jewish condition can be made clear to students.

Motivation

Most of the students who enroll in courses in Contemporary Jewry, and some of those who teach such courses, do not do so because Contemporary Jewish Civilization is the field of their major interest. As has often been observed, they more frequently approach the subject as a way of clarifying their own Jewishness, at least subconsciously. There is nothing wrong with undertaking the study of a subject because its implications can have personal consequences, provided the study is sound and not distorted by prior assumptions and cherished commitments. Nevertheless, what is taught is likely to reflect the motivations of both instructors and students.   Three of the issues that arise in this regard can be mentioned here.

A review of courses in Contemporary Jewry makes it clear that they most often concern the local Jewish community.   In the United States, American Jewry is the likeliest topic; in France, French Jewry gets more attention; and so forth.   That fact is inevitable, and not particularly troublesome, as long as local Jewry is seen as part of World Jewry.   Since most instructors are likely to be relatively unfamiliar with Jewish communities other than their own, materials for teaching comparatively are urgently needed.

The second issue is more difficult. As has been widely recognized, courses concerning the Holocaust have become very popular with both students and donors of gifts to universities.   The growth of such courses has been criticized on the grounds that the Holocaust comes to occupy a disproportionate place in shaping Jewish self-understanding for the Jewish students who take those courses, but who do not take courses on other aspects of the historical Jewish experience.

The proper balance among courses in Jewish Civilization is a matter of no little controversy, and we do not offer a formula for its solution here.   Still, a few observations might be made.   To begin with, student registration is bound to be one potent factor in shaping a university's offerings, especially when budgets for higher education are tight.   However, no respectable university follows registration (the "election returns" as it were) alone.   Certain subjects must be taught, even if they attract few students, simply because they constitute a significant part of the human experience.   Finally, the very structure and content of the curriculum can themselves affect students' perceptions of what is important to know and how that knowledge fits into the total framework of understanding.   What all this means is that the people responsible for the teaching of Contemporary Jewry must develop offerings in the field according to some intellectually defensible plan.   While we may disagree over the nature of that plan, the development of courses in Contemporary Jewry should, where possible, not be left to chance.

The third issue that touches on the matter of motivation concerns courses on Israel and on the Arab-Israel conflict.   In these courses there is often a tendency for instructors to present the material in a way that supports their personal commitments and for students to want to hear material which they, in turn, find supportive of their views.

The meaning of academic objectivity is not at all clear as it relates to this matter. At a minimum, it means presenting the various sides of controversial issues as fully and as empathetically as possible. It does not mean, at least in this writer's opinion, that all sides are equally "right" or even that their claims are symmetric. Every instructor has commitments--left, right, or center (and let it be remembered that being in the "center" is also a position of commitment not necessarily more "neutral" than being "left" or "right"). A good teacher can present and explain positions other than his/her own, while avoiding the implication that all sincerely held positions are equally acceptable by criteria generally held to be valid in free, enlightened cultures. It is also the case, of course, that the university classroom is not the proper place for a political rally, with the result that advocacy is inappropriate there. With these general guidelines and with conviction in the justice of one's position, one can teach Israel and the Arab-Israel conflict in ways that are academically sound and personally responsible.

The implications of the various issues discussed above are evident in the syllabi in this volume. They show how some of the most accomplished people in the field select, organize, and present the material in their courses. It is our hope that making them available in this volume will prove helpful to others who teach Contemporary Jewish Civilization.

Syllabi in University Teaching of Contemporary Jewish Civilization

A. Survey Courses in Contemporary Jewry

I.   THE COURSE

WORLD JEWRY TODAY

Haim Avni*

Brandeis University, USA; Department of Near Eastern and Judaic Studies
One semester of 13 weeks, 3 hours per week, totalling 39 hours
Students are required to have completed a two semester course on Jewish
Civilization or other basic studies in modern Jewish history

II.   ACADEMIC CONTEXT OF THE COURSE
       This is an elective course in the Judaic studies program of the
Near Eastern and Judaic Studies Department, open to juniors, seniors
and graduate students of that and any other department. Since
Brandeis University does not have a stage-by-stage program
comprehending Contemporary Jewry, the students vary considerably in
their background and previous studies. The course is therefore planned
as a multi-level teaching experiment in which a common basis of class
work forms the starting point for each student to work individually
according to his/her own level of knowledge.

       The course is not intended to provide the student with detailed
information regarding each issue under discussion, but rather to
promote a general understanding of the nature of these issues.

       The course concentrates on the external factors which have shaped
the contemporary location and status of the Jewish people. Since the
existence of the State of Israel is one of the main influences on world

* Prof. Avni is on the faculty of the Institute of Contemporary Jewry,
the Hebrew University of Jerusalem. This course was offered by him as a
guest lecturer at Brandeis University.

Jewry, issues related to Israel have been assigned considerable attention. The specific cases of the various communities cannot be discussed in great detail because of the limited time available. Class work focuses therefore, on common problems which are illustrated through the widest possible range of community experiences. Here there is another limitation arising from the institutional framework: since the Contemporary Jewish Studies Course in the NEJS Department concentrates on the North American Jewish experience, it is deemed necessary to avoid overlapping. Hence the paucity of references to North American Jewry in this outline. If this course were taught elsewhere, the subjects covered, as well as the required reading material, would have to be amended to include North America.

In order to encourage a deeper acquaintance with specific communities, students are urged to write papers on two communities of their choice, analyzing the way in which the general issues raised in the course are reflected in the specific history and contemporary experience of these communities.

III. OUTLINE OF THE COURSE

1. Introduction: Definitions and approaches to the study of Contemporary Jewry.

   Required Reading:

   S. Lipset, "The Study of Jewish Communities in a Comparative Context," **Jewish Journal of Sociology** Vol. 5 No. 2 (Dec. 1963), pp. 157-166

   M. Davis, "Centers of Jewry in the Western Hemisphere, A Comparative Approach," **Jewish Journal of Sociology** Vol. 5 No. 1 (June 1963), pp. 4-26

PART ONE: The New Location

2. The new dispersion of the Jews: a century of emigration, Holocaust
   and aliya.

   Required Reading:

   A. Ruppin, **The Jewish Fate and Future**, (London: Macmillan,
   1940), pp. 25-60

   O. Schmeltz, "Demography," "Vital Statistics" and "Migrations,"
   Encyclopaedia Judaica (Jerusalem: Keter, 1972), Supplementary
   volume

3. The question of an open world: the dynamics of immigration policies
   as illustrated by the "Aliens Act" (Great Britain, 1906) and the
   "Displaced Persons Act" (USA, 1948).

   Required Reading:

   S. Adler-Rudel, "The Evian Conference on the Refugees Question,"
   Leo Baeck Institute Yearbook 13 (1968), pp. 235-273

   L. Holborn, **The International Refugee Organization, A Specialized
   Agency of the United Nations, Its History and Work, 1946-1952**
   (London/New York/Toronto, 1956), any 40 pages of the student's
   choosing

4. "The Law of Return" (Israel, 1950) and its impact on the trend of
   Jewish migration.

   Required Reading:

   H. Cohen, **Absorption Problems of Jews from Asia and Africa in
   Israel** (Jerusalem, 1974)

   D. Prital (ed.), **In Search of Self: the Soviet Jewish
   Intelligentsia and the Exodus** (Jerusalem: Mount Scopus, 1982),
   pp. 121-140

   D. Kass and S. Lipset, "Jewish Immigration to the U.S. from 1967 to
   the Present: Israelis and Others," in M. Sklare (ed.), **Understanding American Jewry** (New Brunswick/London, 1982), pp. 272-294

5. The formation of a Middle Class people: The contributions of emigration, aliya and the Holocaust to the new stratification of the Jewish people.

Required Reading:

A. Ruppin, **The Jewish Fate and Future** (London: Macmillan, 1940), pp. 119-192

S. Kuznets, "Economic Structure and Life of the Jews," in L. Finkelstein (ed.), **The Jews** (New York: Harper, 1960), pp. 1597-1604; 1634-1642; 1658-1661

6. The demographic results of migration, destruction and modernization.

Required Reading:

R. Bachi, **Population Trends of World Jewry** (Jerusalem, 1976), pp. 1-76

S. Della Pergola, "Quantitative Aspects of Jewish Assimilation," in B. Vago (ed.), **Jewish Assimilation in Modern Times** (Boulder, Colorado: Westview, 1981), pp. 185-205

PART TWO: The New Status

7. "Emancipation" or the legitimacy of being different.

Required Reading:

S. Baron, "The Modern Age" in **Great Ages and Ideas of the Jewish People** (New York, 1956)

D. Williamson, "Walther Rathenau: Patron Saint of the German Liberal Establishment 1922-1972," **Leo Baeck Institute Year Book** 20 (1975), pp. 207-222

B. Halpern, "Jewish Nationalism: Self Determination as a Human Right" in D. Sidorsky (ed.), **Essays on Human Rights** (Philadelphia: Jewish Publication Society, 1979), pp. 309-335

8. "The emergence from powerlessness."

    Required Reading:

    Y. Bauer, **The Jewish Emergence from Powerlessness** (Toronto: University of Toronto, 1979)

9. Old and new elements in the Jews' position among the nations: the religious aspect.

    Required Reading:

    N. Rotenstreich, "The Revival of the Fossil Remnant or Toynbee and Jewish Nationalism," **Jewish Social Studies** Vol. 24 No. 3 (July 1982), pp. 131-142

    J. Hershcopf Banki, **Vatican Council II's Statement on the Jews - Five Years Later** (New York: American Jewish Committee, 1971)

    M. Dubois, "The Catholic Church and the State of Israel after 25 Years," **Christian News from Israel** Vol. 23 No. 4 (12), (1973), pp. 216-224

    ibid., pp. 252-255: **The Declaration of the French Episcopal Commission for Relations with Judaism,** issued April 16, 1973

10. Old and new elements in the position of the Jews among the nations: the political aspect.

    Required Reading:

    N. Sagi, **German Reparations: A History of the Negotiations** (Jerusalem: Magnes, 1980), pp. 11-49

    I. Goldstein, **Brandeis University, Chapter of its Founding** (New York: Block, 1951), pp. 1-35

    G. Houseman, "Antisemitism in City Politics: The Separation Clause and the Indianapolis Nativity Scene Controversy, 1976-1977" **Jewish Social Studies** Vol. 42 (1980), pp. 21-36

11. Dual loyalty?   The cases of Great Britain, Argentina and South Africa.

    Required Reading:

    G. Shimoni, **Jews and Zionism: The South African Experience, 1910 - 1967** (Cape Town: Oxford University Press, 1980), pp. 305-353

    The Eichmann Case in the American Press (New York: American Jewish Committee, 1962)

PART THREE: Diaspora and Israel

12. The Jews and Eretz-Israel from World War I to the establishment of the State of Israel.

    Required Reading

    B. Halpern, **The Idea of the Jewish State** (Cambridge, Mass: Harvard University Press), Part 2: "Zionism and World Jewry", pp. 55-251

13. "Dialogues" and common endeavors between Diaspora Jewry and Israel before and after the Six Day War.

    Required Reading

    Charles Liebman, "Diaspora Influence on Israel: The Ben Gurion - Blaustein 'Exchange' and its Aftermath," **Jewish Social Studies** Vol. 36 Nos. 3-4 (1974), pp. 271-280

    A. Karpf, "The Reaction to Zionism and the State of Israel in the American Jewish Religious Community", **Jewish Journal of Sociology** Vol. 7 (1960), pp. 150-170

    Moshe Davis (ed.), **The Yom Kippur War, Israel and the Jewish People** (New York: Arno/Herzl, 1974):

       Saul Hayes and Irwin Cotler, "Canada - Overview," pp. 95-107;

       Emil Fackenheim, "Canada - Perspectives," pp. 107-123;

Ernest Krausz, "Great Britain, Oceania, South Africa – Overview," pp. 145-161;

Maurice Freedman and S. M. Schreter, "Great Britain – Perspectives," pp. 162-180

Additional Elective Reading:

Mark Wishnitzer, **To Dwell in Safety – The Story of Jewish Migration since 1800** (Philadelphia: Jewish Publication Society: 1948)

Source Book in Soviet Jewry (New York: American Jewish Committee, 1981)

William Korey, **The Soviet Cage: Anti-Semitism in Russia** (New York: Viking, 1973)

David Prital (ed.), **In Search of Self: The Soviet Jewish Intelligentsia and the Exodus** (Jerusalem: Mount Scopus, 1982)

Hayim Cohen, **The Jews of the Middle East, 1860-1972** (New York: Wiley, 1973)

Ruth Weintraub, **How Secure these Rights?** (New York: Doubleday, 1949)

Marshall Sklare, **America's Jews** (New York: Random House, 1971)

Marshall Sklare and B. Ringler, "A Study of Jewish Attitudes Toward the State of Israel" in M. Sklare (ed.), **The Jews: Social Patterns of an American Group** (Glencoe, Illinois: Free Press, 1967)

Daniel Elazar, **Community and Polity: the Organizational Dynamics of American Jewry** (Philadelphia: Jewish Publication Society: 1976)

S. Rosenberg, **The Jewish Community in Canada** 2 Vols. (McClelland and Stewart, 1971)

Peter Medding, **From Assimilation to Group Survival** (Melbourne, 1968)

Gideon Shimoni, **Jews and Zionism: The South African Experience
1910-1967** (Cape Town: Oxford University Press, 1980)

Haim Avni, "Argentine Jewry: Its Socio-Political Status and Organizational Patterns," **Dispersion and Unity** 12 (1971), pp. 128-
162; 13-14 (1971-72), pp. 161-208; 15 (1972-73), pp. 158-215

Judith Laikin Elkin, **Jews of the Latin American Republics**
(Chapel Hill: University of North Carolina, 1980)

Requirements of the Course for Grading:

1. Active participation in the discussion of the required reading.

2. Two papers of some 10 to 15 pages each in which the students
   either analyze more deeply some of the issues discussed in class
   or relate these issues specifically to two diaspora communities.
   The papers should be based upon some of the elective reading in
   addition to the required reading. Advanced students may write
   one extended monographic paper.

IV. CONCEPTUAL FRAMEWORK OF THE COURSE

Introduction. Emphasis is placed on conditions in the surrounding Gentile environment and their impact on contemporary Jewry, as
opposed to highlighting internal dynamics, and the suggestion that the
unity of world Jewry may be regarded as based on a shared set of
challenges and problems rather than on the similarity of local
responses and solutions.

It is explained that class discussion of the required reading is meant only to serve as an incentive and a starting point for the exploration of the issues involved; full exposition of these issues would require another type of course. However, advanced or particularly interested students are to be directed to amplify some of the issues in their papers.

The new dispersion. The map of the Jewish world on the eve of the destruction (as illustrated by Ruppin's comprehensive research) and the contemporary geographic location of the Jews; the factors which made emigration a vital necessity and those which determined its scope; the role of immigration policies.

The question of an open world. The Evian Conference (1938) and International Refugee Organization's (IRO) activities in 1945-48 as indicative of a world closed to Jewish emigration; opposition to immigration in Great Britain (1903) and in the United States (1945-48); the arguments and interests which shaped immigration policies.

The "Law of Return" and thereafter. The ideological and practical aims of the "Law of Return"; its immediate- and long-term effects as exemplified in: the absorption of Oriental immigrants on the one hand, and the options open to Russian Jewish immigrants on the other; Jewish migration in the last decades and the special case of emigration from Israel; the Jewish and non-Jewish factors which determine the scope and direction of Jewish migration today.

The formation of a middle-class people. The impact of immigration from under-developed areas in eastern Europe on expanding western economies; the destruction of Jewish poverty during the Holocaust as indicated by Arthur Ruppin's data; postwar economies and their effects on the strata in which Jews were heavily represented; the dynamics of immigration and modernization in Israel; the new socio-economic location of the Jewish people.

Demographic results. The problems of growth after destruction; biological and cultural losses; modernization as a multi-faceted factor.

"Emancipation" or the legitimacy of being different. Explicit and implicit conditions attached to the granting of equality by host societies; Walther Rathenau – subjective feelings versus "objective" realities; the fact of being different and the associated problem of acceptance.

The emergence from powerlessness. Jewish perceptions of Jewish power before and during the Holocaust; myths and realities concerning Jewish influence; the emergence of a Jewish fighting force and the limits of its abilities.

Old and new elements – the religious aspect. The cultural-historical and theological objections to the revival of the Jewish people; the new Christian perception of Jews; the status of Christians in a Jewish state; problems resulting from the new position.

Old and new elements in the position of the Jews - political aspects. The impact of guilt for the Holocaust upon the political position of world Jewry--as exemplified by the German Reparations agreements--a short- or long-term phenomenon? Some symbolic events attesting to the change in the status of American Jewry and evaluation of stable and changeable determining factors; the political status of other communities.

Dual loyalty? The possibility of a conflict between a vital Jewish interest and Government policy; the conclusions to be drawn from the Jewish fight against the 1939 British Government White Paper policies; the kidnapping of Eichmann; Israel's pro-Black stance in African racial disputes.

The Jews and Eretz Israel. Divisions and conformity in world Jewry regarding Eretz Israel before World War II; ideological and practical attitudes following the Holocaust; the role of world Jewry in the establishment of the State of Israel.

"Dialogues" and common endeavors between the Diaspora and Israel. The terms of the agreement reached immediately after the establishment of the State; their validity in the light of later developments; indications of continuity and of change since the Yom Kippur War.

I. THE COURSE

JUDAISM IN THE MODERN WESTERN WORLD

Arnold Eisen

Columbia University; Department of Religion

One Semester of 14 weeks, 3 hours per week, totalling 42 hours

Knowledge assumed: Some background in the history of Judaism

II. ACADEMIC CONTEXT OF THE COURSE

The course is offered to upper-level undergraduates, most of whom take it as an elective while pursuing majors in other disciplines. The students' backgrounds vary considerably. Courses in other periods of the history of Judaism are offered by the Department of Religion (including its allied department at Barnard College) and by the Department of History. It should be noted that the history of modern Jewry is covered by other courses. Hence the emphasis in this course is on religious thought and ritual: "Judaism" narrowly defined.

III. OUTLINE OF THE COURSE

A. Introduction: Modernity and the Jews

1. Historical and Sociological Introduction

Suggested Reading:

Selections from Jacob Katz, **Tradition & Crisis** (New York, 1971) and **Out of the Ghetto** (Cambridge, Mass., 1973) AND/OR

Joseph Blau, **Modern Varieties of Judaism** (New York, 1966), pp. 1-15.

2. Spinoza's Challenge to Jewish Identity & Faith

   Required Reading: Benedict de Spinoza, **Tractatus Theologico-Politicus** (New York, 1955), chap. 1.

B. Mendelssohn and His Heirs

   3. Mendelssohn's Redefinition of Judaism

   Required Reading: Mendelssohn, **Jerusalem** (Hanover, N.H., 1983), part two.

   Suggested Reading: Blau, pp. 16-27;

   Julius Guttmann, **Philosophies of Judaism** (Philadelphia, 1964), pp. 289-303.

C. The Rise of Reform, Neo-Orthodoxy & "Positive Historical Judaism"

   4. Wissenschaft des Judentums

   Required Reading: Michael A. Meyer, **Origins of the Modern Jew** (Detroit, 1967);

   W. Guenther Plaut, **Rise of Reform Judaism** (New York, 1965), pp. 11-26.

   Suggested Reading: Ismar Schorsch, "Ideology and History in the Age of Emancipation," in Heinrich Graetz, **The Structure of Jewish History and Other Essays** (New York, 1975), pp. 10-62.

   5. The Origins of Reform Judaism

   Required Reading: Plaut, pp. 112-124, 152-184;

   David Philipson, **The Reform Movement in Judaism** (New York, 1967), chap. 7;

   Paul Mendes-Flohr & Yehuda Reinharz, **The Jew in the Modern World** (New York, 1980), pp. 150-153 ("These Are the Words of the Covenant").

   Suggested Reading: Blau, chap. 2.

6. The Origins of Neo-Orthodoxy

   Required Reading: Samuel Raphael Hirsch, **Nineteen Letters on Judaism** (New York, 1960).

   Suggested Reading: Blau, chap. 3.

7. Positive-Historical Judaism

   Required Reading: Heinrich Graetz, **The Structure of Jewish History**;

   Mendes-Flohr, pp. 173-176 (Zechariah Frankel);

   Nachman Krochmal, "Guide for the Perplexed of the Time" in Michael A. Meyer, ed., **Ideas of Jewish History** (New York, 1974), pp. 189-214.

   Suggested Reading: Blau, chap. 4; Guttmann, 321-344.

D. The Origins of Modern Zionism and American Judaism

   8. The Zionist Forerunners and Founders

      Required Reading: Arthur Hertzberg, **The Zionist Idea** (New York, 1959), pp. 102-139, 224-226 (Herzl), 247-277 (Ahad Ha'am);

      Ahad Ha'am, **Selected Essays** (Philadelphia, 1912), pp. 41-45, 80-90, 171-194.

      Suggested Reading: Hertzberg, "Introduction."

   9. American Judaism to 1920

      Required Reading: Nathan Glazer, **American Judaism** (Chicago, 1972), pp. 1-42;

      Moshe Davis, **The Emergence of Conservative Judaism** (Philadelphia, 1965), pp. 151-165, 283-314;

      Kaufmann Kohler, **Jewish Theology** (New York, 1968), pp. 15-38, 323-330.

E. Modern Jewish Thought

   10. Rosenzweig and Buber

      Required Reading: Nahum Glatzer, (ed.), **Franz Rosenzweig Out of His Life and Thought** (New York, 1972), pp.190-208, 234-247, 278-303;

      Will Herberg, (ed.) **The Writings of Martin Buber** (New York, 1956), pp. 43-62, 239-250, 149-171, 293-299.

   11. Later Developments in Zionist Thought

      Required Reading: Hertzberg, pp. 368-395 (Gordon); 416-431 (Rav A.I. Kook); 606-620 (Ben Gurion).

   12. Later Developments in American Judaism

      Required Reading: Mordecai M. Kaplan, **Judaism as a Civilization**, pp. 173-224, and "The Columbus Platform," from **Yearbook of the Central Conference of American Rabbis, 1937;**

      Robert Gordis, **Conservative Judaism** (New York, 1945), selections.

   13. Contemporary Jewish Thought

      Required Reading: Emil Fackenheim, **God's Presence in History** (New York, 1972), selections;

      Abraham Joshua Heschel, **Man is Not Alone** (New York, 1966), selections;

      Joseph Soloveitchik, "The Lonely Man of Faith" in **Tradition,** Summer 1965, and **Halakhic Man** (Philadelphia, 1984), selections.

   14. Conclusion: Judaism Today

      Required Reading: Charles Liebman, **Aspects of the Religious Behavior of American Jews** (New York, 1974);

      Arnold Eisen, **The Chosen People in America** (Bloomington, Ind., 1983).

Requirements of the Course for Grading:

Students are expected to come to class prepared to discuss the assigned reading.

A midterm examination is set and a short paper (10 pages) is assigned to students on a thinker or a topic of their own choosing.

IV. CONCEPTUAL FRAMEWORK OF THE COURSE

1. The course opens with the assumption that it is impossible to discuss modern Jewish thought without familiarity with Jewish history in the modern period.   Acquaintance with parallel developments in Christianity is also helpful, the better to understand that faith in general comes under siege in the modern West, with particular challenges to Jewish faith and Jewish existence. An attempt is made to understand the course material against the background of broader social and intellectual changes.

2. The course demonstrates how Spinoza set the fundamental challenges. He denied that there was any place for a corporate Jewish group (kehillah) in the European political order which he correctly saw emerging. And, having denied the existence of a personal God of providence who had special plans for the Jewish people, and having adopted modern criticism of the Bible, Spinoza concluded that Jewish faith no longer had any continuing validity or relevance. His challenges had to be answered.

3. Mendelssohn came to the defense of Judaism with its redefinition as "revealed legislation," religion as such--essential beliefs about the nature of God and human obligation--being declared accessible to all human beings, through reason. The commandments were presented as a

"ceremonial script" designed to lead Jews to, and remind them of, truths in principle available to all by other means.

4-7. In succeeding generations Jewish thinkers carried further the efforts at integrating Jewish and European cultures pioneered by Mendelssohn. They also continued the two conflicting directions of his teaching. Reformers focused attention on Judaism's creedal essence, shared with Christianity, and repudiated elements of the "ceremonial script" which no longer served to advance adherence to Judaism's core beliefs. Samson Raphael Hirsch defended the symbol as essential to religious and moral life, and ingeniously found new meaning for the commandments called into question by contemporaries. The Positive Historical School sought middle ground: "organic" change in keeping with the general character of past Jewish religious life, rather than in conformity to a creedal statement of principles. The Science of Judaism aided in all three efforts, by tracing the development--and underlining the value--of Jewish life and thought.

8-9. Here the course's concern shifts to the two new centers of Jewish life in the modern period, Israel and America, tracing the definition of Judaism as religion in the latter and as nationality in the former (both streams being seen as continuous with the developments surveyed in previous weeks). The principal schools of Zionist thought (cultural, political, religious) are introduced through their leading thinkers. The emphasis in America is on continuity with the tradition and its European reformulation, side by side with adaptation to the new--and unique--American setting. In weeks 11-12 attention turns to more recent developments: the working out of political, cultural and religious Zionism in the Yishuv and the reborn State; the change in American Jewish thought during the formative years of the "second generation."

10, 13-14. The other topic in the second half of the course is modern Jewish thought as we have come to know it, created under the influence of European developments such as neo-Kantianism and existentialism. In conclusion the course looks at the twin continuing challenges of secularism and the Holocaust, in the shadow of which contemporary Jewish thought proceeds. The final lecture is devoted to America because the students are American; teachers in other Diaspora countries might prefer to devote it to developments closer to home.

I. THE COURSE

THE JEWS IN CONTEMPORARY SOCIETY

Sol Encel

University of New South Wales, Australia; Department of Sociology
Two Semesters (28 weeks), 2 hours per week, totalling 56 hours
Knowledge assumed: At least one year of academic study in history or
the social sciences, and some Jewish background, evaluated by
interview

II. ACADEMIC CONTEXT OF THE COURSE

The University of New South Wales offers B.A., M.A. and Ph.D. degrees in a wide range of disciplines, including sociology. Students with sociology as their major subject may take it over a period of three years for the B.A. (Ordinary) degree, or four years for the B.A. (Honors) degree. In their third year, the sociology program consists of a range of electives, of which this course is one. With the permission of the instructor, second-year students of sociology may also take the course. In addition, non-degree or 'miscellaneous' students may be admitted to the class with the instructor's permission.

As an elective in sociology, the course shares the general aims and objectives of teaching in that discipline. This means, among other things, that emphasis is placed on individual research by the student. Since the course was introduced, students have completed a variety of projects, including studies of immigrant groups (e.g., from South Africa, the U.S.S.R. and Asia), welfare services for aged persons, and the nature of Jewish identification within the student body at the university. In addition, the course examines theoretical issues connected with anti-Jewish prejudice, the historical role of Jews in economic development, and the evidence concerning Jewish political allegiance.

III. OUTLINE OF THE COURSE

1. Historical Background – a brief review of some major themes in recent Jewish history

A.L. Sachar, **A History of the Jews,** 5th edition (New York: 1975).

S. Grayzel, **A History of the Jews,** 2nd edition (New York, 1970).

H.M. Sachar, **The Course of Modern Jewish History** (New York: 1958).

H.M. Sachar, **A History of Israel** (New York: 1979).

2. The Debate on Jewish Identity

Max Weber, **The Sociology of Religion** (London, 1966)

M. Sklare & J. Greenblum, **Jewish Identity on the Suburban Frontier,** 2nd edition (Chicago, 1979).

D. Sidorsky (ed.), **The Future of the Jewish Community in America** (New York, 1973).

Karl Kautsky, **Are the Jews a Race?** (New York, 1934).

G. Friedmann, **The End of the Jewish People?** (New York, 1968).

Simon Herman, **Jewish Identity** (Beverly Hills, 1977).

3. Marxism and the Jews

Karl Marx, **On the Jewish Question** (New York, 1964).

Karl Marx, **The Holy Family** (Moscow, 1956)

A. Leon, **The Jewish Question** (New York, 1970).

J. Carlebach, **Karl Marx and the Radical Critique of Judaism** (London, 1978).

Isaiah Berlin, **Karl Marx,** 4th edition (Oxford, 1978).

4. Soviet Communism and the Jews

   Paul Lendvai, **Anti-Semitism in Eastern Europe** (London, 1972)

   S.M. Dubnow, **History of the Jews in Russia and Poland**, vol. 3 (New York, 1975)

   L. Kochan (ed.), **Jews in Soviet Russia since 1917**, 3rd edition (London, 1978)

   Z. Gitelman, **Jewish Nationality & Soviet Politics** (Princeton, 1972)

   Victor Zaslavsky & Robert J. Brym, **Soviet Jewish Emigration & Nationality Policy** (New York, 1983)

5. Jewish Society in Israel

   S.N. Eisenstadt, **Israeli Society**, 2nd edition (London, 1984)

   S. Smooha, **Israel: Pluralism & Conflict** (London, 1978)

   Amos Elon, **The Israelis** (London, 1971)

   M. Rodinson, **Israel** (New York, 1973)

   M. Curtis & M. Chertoff (eds.), **Israel: Social Structure and Change** (New York, 1972)

   Yoram Peri, **Between Battles & Ballots** (Jerusalem, 1982)

   E. Krausz (ed.), **The Sociology of the Kibbutz** (London, 1983)

   D. Weintraub, M. Lissak, Y. Atzmon, **Moshava, Kibbutz & Moshav** (Ithaca, 1969)

6. Israel and the Diaspora

   S. Avineri, **The Making of Modern Zionism** (New York, 1981)

   G. Friedmann, **The End of the Jewish People** (New York, 1967)

   H. Arendt, **Eichmann in Jerusalem** (New York, 1963)

J. Robinson, **And the Crooked Shall be Made Straight** (New York, 1974)

M. Sklare (ed.), **The Jewish Community in America** (New York, 1974)

D. Sidorsky, **The Future of the Jewish Community in America** (New York, 1973)

P. Medding (ed.), **Jews in Australian Society** (Melbourne, 1973)

Requirements of the Course for Grading:

1) Students are required to lead discussions in class on topics which have been selected from the course outline, and to hand in written versions for marking.

2) One prescribed essay is to be completed each semester.

3) A longer paper dealing with an approved topic in depth, based either on research or reading.

IV. CONCEPTUAL FRAMEWORK OF THE COURSE

Sociological theory includes a number of key questions relating to the Jewish people. According to Marx, the acquisitive spirit of capitalism was derived from Judaism by way of Christianity, and the essence of the Jewish religion was its worship of money. The 'Jewish question' would disappear when capitalism was overthrown. The debate engendered by this violently anti-Jewish polemic has continued to the present day. It was continued in the first decade of the 20th century by two leading German writers, Max Weber and Werner Sombart. Weber's famous essay, 'The Protestant Ethic and the Spirit of Capitalism' argued that the development of capitalism rested upon a system of values and beliefs which became dominant in Europe at the time of the Protestant Reformation, but were ultimately traceable to Jewish tradition and Jewish precepts. Sombart, a close friend and contemporary of Weber, extended this argument in his book, **The Jews and Modern Capitalism.** Recent research on the economic history of the Jews has revived interest in the debate between Weber and Sombart.

Similarly, the role of Jews in anti-capitalist and revolutionary movements has fascinated a succession of writers, including sympathetic critics as well as anti-Semites. An important variety of 20th century anti-Semitism revolved around the alleged affinity between Jews and revolutionary radicalism, and has stimulated the growth of an extensive literature which is concerned, e.g., with the role of Jews in the Russian revolution and their subsequent vicissitudes in Soviet society.

The nature of anti-Semitism, and by extension, of racial and religious prejudice in general, is a major preoccupation of both psychology and sociology. A number of Jewish writers have made classic contributions to this inquiry, from Freud onwards, and their work has become central to the vast literature on the subject of prejudice. The influence of Freud is obvious in the findings of investigations like those recorded in **The Authoritarian Personality,** first published in 1950 and still a landmark in the history of the subject.

One of the objectives of the course is to introduce students to these long-standing topics of sociological debate. A second objective is to explore the question of Jewish identity, both in terms of the long-standing debate among Jews themselves, and in relation to recent arguments and inquiries concerning the meaning of 'ethnicity'. The third and final objective is to review the current situation of some of the world's principal Jewish communities as well as the Australian Jewish community. This includes the complex questions arising from the relationship between Israel and the Diaspora.

I. THE COURSE

WORLD JEWRY SINCE 1945

Deborah Dash Moore
Vassar College, USA; Department of Religion
Two 75 minute periods per week for 13 weeks, totalling 32 hours
There are no pre-requisites for students taking the course

II. ACADEMIC CONTEXT OF THE COURSE

Vassar College is an elite liberal arts college that stresses excellence and independence in choice of study. The department of religion, a small department with 4 full-time members and 3 part-time faculty, offers a major for students who wish to concentrate on the study of religion. However, most students choose only to take one or two courses in the department. There is no major or minor in Jewish studies at Vassar, but students interested in a concentration can major in religion emphasizing Judaism or create an independent major which must be multi-disciplinary. Most students choose to take only one or two courses on Jews and Judaism. The introductory course thus faces the challenge of one-time study by most of the enrolled students.

In addition, the course attracts students from all classes, from freshman to senior, the latter only finding time at the very end of their college career to study Jews and Judaism. The typical student enrolling in such a course is exceptionally bright with a good background in the liberal arts but is woefully ignorant of any but the most superficial aspects of Jewish culture. Given the lack of background, the course materials must be accessible and simple; given the intellectual ability the readings must also be sophisticated and provocative. These students may also bring varied personal agendas to their study of Jewish culture, but this factor is no more prominent than in many other religion courses.

III. OUTLINE OF THE COURSE

Introduction

The scope of the course and the approach to the readings; the relationship of contemporary Jewry to major themes of Jewish history and religion in the modern era.

1. The Character of Contemporary Jewry

A definition of contemporary Jewry as post-Holocaust and of the era of the State of Israel; basic demographic trends and features of contemporary Jewry.

2. In the Wake of the Holocaust

The response of the survivors, the response of the world, the response of the Jews. The latter is divided into two sections, one focusing on the issue of the appropriateness of Jewish actions during the Holocaust, the second on the theological problems raised including the existence of God, the problem of evil, the meaning of Jewish history, and the role of the State of Israel. The discussion of the response of the survivors looks at the year immediately after the defeat of Germany when the survivors developed a vision of a new world and a program of action. The persistence of antisemitism despite the excesses revealed in the concentration camps is the crux of the discussion of the world's response.

Required Reading:

Irving Heymont, **Among the Survivors of** the Holocaust, (Cincinnati, 1983)

Hannah Arendt, **Eichmann in Jerusalem,**(New York: Viking Press, 1963)

Eliezer Berkovits, **Faith After the Holocaust,** (New York: Ktav, 1973)

Additional Reading:

Yehuda Bauer, **Flight and Rescue,** (New York: Random House, 1970)

Leonard Dinnerstein, **America and the Survivors of the Holocaust,** (New York: Columbia, 1982)

Leo Schwarz, **The Redeemers,** (New York: Farrar, Straus and Young, 1953)

Karl Jaspers, **The Question of German Guilt,** [reprint of 1947 ed.] (LC: Greenwood, 1978)

Abram Sachar, **The Redemption of the Unwanted,** (New York: St. Martin's/Marek, 1983)

Jacob Robinson, **And the Crooked Shall be Made Straight,** (New York: MacMillan, 1965)

Gershom Scholem, "On Eichmann", in **On Jews and Judaism in Crisis,** (New York: Schocken, 1978)

Eva Fleishner (ed.), **After Auschwitz,** (New York: Ktav, 1972)

Emil Fackenheim, **God's Presence in History,** (New York: Harper and Row, 1972)

Richard Rubinstein, **After Auschwitz,** (New York: Bobbs-Merrill, 1966)

3. The Jewish State: Ideology and Action

Zionism and the Second Generation. Attitudes towards issues facing Israel today. The discussion of Zionism as an ideology and a program of action emphasizes the early years of state-building, the absorption of immigrants, and the search for social consensus. The problems of the second generation are analyzed with reference to frontier societies, the limits and demands of nationalism, the difficulties of sustaining ideology and the compromises of the half-way covenant. The third aspect of contemporary Israeli society emphasizes the tensions within it, the wide range of attitudes towards basic values, the conflict with the Arabs, and the ambivalent relationship with Diaspora Jews.

Required Reading:

Amos Elon, **Israelis: Founders and Sons,** (New York: Weidenfeld and Nicolson, 1971)

Amos Oz, **In the Land of Israel,** (London: Chatto and Windus, 1983)

Additional Reading

Walter Laqueur, **A History of Zionism,** (New York: Schocken, 1976)

Howard Sachar, **A History of Israel From the Rise of Zionism to Our Time,** (New York: Knopf, 1976)

Melford Spiro, **The Kibbutz: Venture in Utopia,** (New York: Schocken, 1971)

J.L.Talmon, **Israel Among the Nations,** (New York: MacMillan, 1971)

Naamani, Rudavsky and Katsh (eds.), **Israel: Its Politics and Philosophy,** [revised ed.] (New York: Behrman House, 1974)

Charles Liebman and Eliezer Don Yehiya, **Civil Religion in Israel,** (Berkeley: University of California, 1983)

Dan Segre, **A Crisis of Identity,** (Oxford: Oxford University Press, 1980)

Paul Mendes-Flohr (ed.), **A Land of Two Peoples,** (New York: Oxford University Press, 1983)

Arthur Goren (ed.), **Dissenter in Zion,** (Cambridge, Mass: Harvard, 1982)

Kevin Avruch, **American Immigrants in Israel,** (Chicago: University of Chicago, 1981)

4. The Almost Promised Land: American Jews and Judaism

As the largest and most prosperous Diaspora Jewish community with an ideology of its uniqueness and exceptional character in Jewish history, American Jewry receives separate treatment from other Diaspora communities. The discussion of the changes that have occurred among American Jews since 1945 draws upon the experiences of the students, emphasizing generational patterns. American Judaism receives sociological treatment and attention is paid to ideology and the growth of an American Jewish civil religion emphasizing the centrality of Israel within a framework of symbolic ethnicity.

Required Reading:

Steven M. Cohen, **American Modernity and Jewish Identity**, (New York: Tavistock, 1983)

Additional Reading:

Chaim Waxman, **American Jews in Transition**, (Philadelphia: Temple University, 1983)

Marshall Sklare, **America's Jews**, (New York: Random House, 1971)

Ben Halpern, **The American Jew**, (New York: Herzl, 1956)

Daniel Elazar, **Community and Polity**, (Philadelphia: Jewish Publication Society, 1976)

Joseph Blau, **Judaism in America**, (Chicago: University of Chicago, 1976)

Nathan Glazer, **American Judaism**, (Chicago: University of Chicago, 1957)

Charles Liebman, **The Ambivalent American Jew**, (Philadelphia: Jewish Publication Society, 1973)

5. Diaspora Jewry: Identity and Community

Discussion of Diaspora Jewish communities looks at those elements they share in order to highlight the diversity of Jewish communal organization and the varieties of Jewish identity. Major Jewries in the Soviet Union and Europe with continuous traditions of settlement are contrasted with the new Jewries of South America, Australia and South Africa. Among the common themes characterizing the latter is the influence of frontier societies on Jewish life; among the differences are the role of the culture of the majority society and the place of origin of immigrants to the countries. The question of continuity of Jewish identity and antisemitism forms the focal points of discussion of European and Russian Jewries. The experience of North African Jews is contrasted to the others.

Required Reading:

Dominique Schnapper, **Jewish Identities in France: An Analysis of Contemporary French Jewry,** (Chicago: University of Chicago, 1983)

Julius Gould (ed.), **Jewish Life in Modern Britain,** (London: Routledge and Kegan Paul, 1964)

Lionel Kochan (ed.), **Soviet Jewry Since 1917,** (New York: Oxford University Press, 1978)

Andre Chouraqui, **Between East and West,** (Philadelphia: Jewish Publication Society, 1968)

Judith Laikin Elkin, "Thinking Latin," **Forum,** 42/43, pp.33-45

Gideon Shimoni, "Zionism in South Africa: An Historical Perspective," **Forum,** 37 (Spring 1980) pp.71-91

Dan Jacobson and Ronald Segal, "Apartheid and South African Jewry," **Commentary,** 24 (November 1957) pp.424-31

Peter Medding (ed.), **Jews in Australian Society** (Melbourne: Macmillan, 1973)

Additional Reading:

Maurice Freedman (ed.), A Minority in Britain, (London: Valentine, Mitchell, 1955)

S.A. and V.D.Lipman (eds.), Jewish Life in Britain, (London: K.G.Saur, 1980)

Elie Wiesel, The Jews of Silence, (New York: Holt, Rinehart and Winston, 1966)

Ronald Rubin, The Unredeemed, (Chicago: Quadrangle, 1968)

Norman Stillman, Jews of Arab Lands, (Philadelphia: Jewish Publication Society, 1979)

Shlomo Deshen and Walter Zenner (eds.), Jewish Society in the Middle East, (Washington: University Press of America, 1982)

Michael Pollak, Mandarins, Jews and Missionaries, (Philadelphia: Jewish Publication Society, 1979)

Moshe Yegar, "Jewish Communities in the Far East", Forum 38 (1980) pp.141-54

Robert Weisbrot, The Jews of Argentina, (Philadelphia: Jewish Publication Society, 1979)

Judith Laikin Elkin, The Jews of the Latin American Republics, (Chapel Hill: University of North Carolina, 1980)

Haim Avni, The History of Jewish Immigration to Argentina, 1810-1950, (Magnes: Jerusalem, 1982) [Hebrew]

Robert Soler, From Pale to Pampa, (Ann Arbor, Mich: U.M.I., 1977)

Gideon Shimoni, Jews and Zionism: the South African Experience, (Cape Town: Oxford University Press, 1980)

Daniel Elazar and Peter Medding, Jewish Communities in Frontier Societies, (New York: Holmes and Meier, 1983)

Peter Medding, From Assimilation to Group Survival, (Melbourne: Hart, 1968)

Dan Jacobson, "The Jews of South Africa", Commentary 23 (January 1957), pp.39-45

6. Ethical Issues in Jewish Life

Feminism versus Judaism and the problem of tradition in the modern world. Feminism has offered probably the most threatening challenge to Jewish social values in the past decade. Efforts to reconcile Judaism with the demand of women's equality and the influence of women's changing social position upon Jewish religious life provide the core of the first cluster of ethical issues discussed. The meaning of Israel the nation and its relation to traditional Jewish concepts of chosenness, exile, redemption, and moral responsibility of Jews for each other is the focus of the second cluster of ethical issues. Discussion drawn from the experience gained in class and through readings is expected to illuminate the complexity of the problems raised. No simple solutions are suggested or sought.

Required Reading:

Blu Greenberg, **On Women and Judaism,** (Philadelphia: Jewish Publication Society, 1981)

Elie Wiesel, **A Jew Today,** (New York: Vintage, 1979)

Additional Reading:

Charlotte Baum, Paula Hyman and Sonya Michel, **The Jewish Woman in America,** (New York: Dial, 1976)

Elizabeth Koltun (ed.), **The Jewish Woman,** (New York: Schocken, 1976)

Susannah Heschel (ed.), **On Being a Jewish Feminist,** (New York: Schocken, 1983)

Leslie Hazelton, **Israeli Women,** (New York: Simon & Schuster, 1977)

Evelyn Torton Beck (ed.), **Nice Jewish Girls,** (Watertown, Mass.: Persephone, 1982)

Elie Wiesel, **One Generation After,** (New York: Random House, 1976)

Anne Roiphe, **Generation Without Memory,** (New York: Linden/Simon & Schuster, 1981)

Paul Cowan, **An Orphan in History,** (New York: Doubleday, 1982)

Bernard Henri-Levy, **The Last Testament of God,** (New York: Harper and Row, 1981)

Arthur Waskow, **Godwrestling,** (New York: Schocken, 1978)

In addition to the required readings, the course benefits from guest lectures and films, e.g.: a slide presentation on Jewish life in Iran based upon an anthropologist's fieldwork there; a lecture on Australian Jewry by a visiting Australian sociologist; the film "Ranana," looking at Jewish life in a utopian summer colony now facing the problem of generational change; a documentary on Ethiopian Jews; and a guest lecture on Israel and the Islamic Arab world.

Requirements of the Course for Grading:

Students are expected to do the required reading and attend classes. Participation in class discussion is encouraged but not required due to the large class size of 30 to 35 students. In addition, there are six short papers of three typed pages each in response to the reading. The first paper discusses either Arendt or Berkovits, with the choice up to the student. The second paper discusses either Elon or Oz depending upon the student's choice. The third paper must deal with Cohen; the fourth paper can look at any other Diaspora community. The fifth and sixth papers must discuss the issues raised by Greenberg and Wiesel, respectively. All papers must be handed in prior to the first day of class discussion on the topic. No late papers are accepted. There are no examinations.

IV. CONCEPTUAL FRAMEWORK OF THE COURSE

The conceptual framework of the course is related to the needs leading to its creation, especially the demand for a second but different introductory course to the study of Judaism and the desire to address relevant ethical issues confronting contemporary Jews. (A course in ethical issues is offered regularly by the department of religion, but this course does not have room for treatment of specifically Jewish issues. There is also a survey course introducing students to the study of Jewish religion which approaches the subject historically.) The approach to the study of contemporary Jewry necessarily reflects these concerns: in fact, the choice of subject matter was dictated by this overall rationale. Contemporary Jewry provides an ideal subject, limited in historical time and space yet confronting central dilemmas that have challenged Jews in many periods of their history.

The course is implicitly interdisciplinary, drawing largely on history, sociology and religion, and secondarily on anthropology, political science and philosophy. History provides the contextual framework introducing each of the major subjects of the course: the post-Holocaust world, Israel, American Jews, Diaspora communities, and current Jewish dilemmas. Sociology provides much of the substantive material allowing for comparison of the various groups through thematic treatment of such problems as acculturation, community, identity, and demographic characteristics (including migration). Finally, religion supplies the tools to analyze such critical topics as exile, chosenness, the meaning of nationhood and the burden of responsibility, in addition to dealing with the tensions surrounding the relationship of tradition to the modern world. The other disciplinary methods usually appear in the films and guest lectures and in several of the works read. (For example, in discussing Arendt it is necessary to refer to her political theories on the origins of totalitarianism and to her philosophy of thought.) Because the course is designed to engage the student rather than accumulate a fixed body of knowledge, stress is placed on reading, writing and class discussion. Examinations are not needed because students are compelled to keep up with the assignments.

I. THE COURSE

COMPARATIVE JEWISH COMMUNITIES

Harriet Freidenreich

Temple University, USA; Department of History
One Semester of 14 weeks, 4 hours per week, totalling 56 hours
There are no prerequisites for students taking the course

II. ACADEMIC CONTEXT OF THE COURSE

This course has been offered at the advanced undergraduate level at Temple University, which is a state-supported public institution located in Philadelphia with a significant, but gradually diminishing, Jewish student population. Since History Department offerings have virtually no prerequisites, this course was open to all undergraduates. Most, but not all, of the students were Jewish. Most, but not all, were in Liberal Arts. A few were graduate students in Religion or History. The level of background knowledge varied greatly, from nil to that of rabbinical students (RRC). The course qualified as fulfilling a modern requirement for a certificate in Jewish Studies, but in all cases was an elective.

This course was given several times at Temple in the late 1970s, with enrollments ranging from 8 to 15, but has not been taught since due to its fairly specialized nature, a changing student population and declining enrollments in both history and in Jewish Studies. The reading list which follows is as given at the time, without updating.

III. OUTLINE OF THE COURSE*

1. Introduction

    Suggested Reading:

    S. Baron, **The Jewish Community** Vols. 1 and 2

2. The Traditional **Kehilla**: Eastern Europe

    Required Reading:

    J. Katz, **Tradition and Crisis**, Parts 1 & 2, pp. 3-209

    Suggested Reading:

    B. Weinryb, **Texts and Studies in the Communal History of Polish Jewry**

    I. Levitats, **The Jewish Community in Russia, 1772-1844**

    I. Cohen, **Vilna**

    W. Glicksman, **A Kehillah in Poland During the Inter-War Years**

3. The Modern **Kehilla**: Central Europe

    Required Reading:

    K. Wilhelm, "The Jewish Community in the Post-Emancipation Period," **Leo Baeck Institute Yearbook** 2 (1957), pp. 47-75

    S. Baron, "Freedom and Constraint in the Jewish Community," in **Essays and Studies in Memory of Linda R. Miller,** pp. 9-23

    Suggested Reading:
    A. Kober, **Cologne**

    M. Grunwald, **Vienna**

    G. Fleischman, "The Religious Congregation, 1918-1938," in **The Jews of Czechoslovakia**, 1, pp. 267-325

* Much of the bibliography for this course is available in xeroxed form in a Handbook which students may purchase.

H. Freidenreich, **Belgrade, Zagreb, Zagreb, Sarajevo: A Study of Jewish Communities in Yugoslavia before World War II** [unpublished dissertation]

H. Freidenreich, **The Jewish Community of Yugoslavia** (Center for Jewish Community Studies, Temple University)

4. The Consistorial System: Western Europe

Required Reading:

M. Marrus, "The Ties of Community" in his **The Politics of Assimilation**, Chaps. 3 & 4, pp. 28-83

J. Gutworth, "Antwerp Jewry Today," **Jewish Journal of Sociology** Vol. 10 No. 1 (June 1968), pp. 121-137

Suggested Reading:

P. Albert, "Le Role des consistoires israelites vers le milieu de XIXe siecle," **Revue des Etudes Juives** Vol. 130, Nos. 2, 3 & 4 (April-December 1971), pp. 231-254

P. Hyman, **The Jews in Post-Dreyfus France, 1906-1939** [unpublished dissertation] (Columbia University, 1975)

M. Salzberg, **The Jewish Community of France** (Center for Jewish Community Studies, Temple University)

A. Weiss, **The Jewish Community of Belgium** (Center for Jewish Community Studies, Temple University)

5. The Voluntary Community: British Model

Required Reading:

J. Parkes, "The History of the Anglo-Jewish Community," in M. Freedman (ed.), **A Minority in Britain**, pp. 3-51

V. Lipman, "Synagogal Organization in Anglo-Jewry," **Jewish Journal of Sociology** Vol. 1 No. 1 (1959), pp. 80-93

Suggested Reading:

M. Freedman (ed.), **A Minority in Britain**

S. J. Gould and S. Esh (eds.), **Jewish Life in Modern Britain**

V. Lipman, **Social History of the Jews in England, 1850-1950**

L. Gartner, **The Jewish Immigrant in England**

6. The Early American Community

   Required Reading:

   J. Marcus, "Religio-Communal Organization" and "Culture and Philanthropy" in **Early American Jewry**, pp. 429-493

   Suggested Reading:

   J. Marcus, **The Colonial American Jew, 1492-1776** [3 vols.]

   H. Grinstein, **The Rise of the Jewish Community of New York**

   E. Wolf and M. Whiteman, **The History of the Jews of Philadelphia**

   I. Fein, **The Making of an American Jewish Community: The History of Baltimore Jewry, 1773-1920**

   B. Korn, **The Early Jews of New Orleans**

7. The Immigrant Community

   Required Reading:

   M. Rischin, **The Promised City**

   Suggested Reading:

   A. Rothkoff, "The Orthodox Immigrant Community" in **Bernard Revel: Builder of American Jewish Orthodoxy**, pp. 3-26

   A. Goren, **New York Jews in Quest of Community**

   L. Wirth, **The Ghetto**

8. The Twentieth Century Community

   Required Reading:

   M. Sklare, **Conservative Judaism**, pp. 19-158 & 246-282

H. Gans, "The Origin of a Jewish Community in the Suburbs" in M. Sklare (ed.), **The Jewish Community in America**, pp. 19-41

Suggested Reading:

S. Rosenberg, **The Jewish Community in Rochester, 1843-1925**

S. Adler and T. Connolly, **From Ararat to Suburbia: The History of the Jewish Community of Buffalo**

L. Swichkow and L. Gartner, **The History of the Jews of Milwaukee**

M. Vorspan and L. Gartner, **A History of the Jews of Los Angeles**

M. Elovitz, **A Century of Jewish Life in Dixie: The Birmingham Experiment**

9. Communal Leadership and Institutions

Required Reading:

D. Elazar, "Decision-Making in the American Jewish Community," in M. Sklare (ed.), **The Jewish Community in America**, pp. 69-110

Suggested Reading:

I. Schorsch, **Jewish Reactions to German Anti-Semitism**

C. Roth, **History of the Great Synagogue**

A. Barnett, **The Western Synagogue through Two Centuries**

V. Lipman, **A Century of Social Service**

N. Cohen, **Not Free to Desist**

American Jewish Yearbook [bibliographies and articles]

Center for Jewish Community Studies [bibliographies and articles]

10. The Rabbinate

Required Reading:

M. Gruenewald, "The Modern Rabbi," **Leo Baeck Institute Yearbook** 2 (1957), pp. 85-97

M. Goulston, "The Status of the Anglo-Jewish Rabbinate," **Jewish Journal of Sociology** 10 (1968), pp. 55-82

B. Bamberger, "The American Rabbi - His Changing Role," **Judaism** 3 (1954), pp. 488-497

M. Sklare, **Conservative Judaism**, pp. 159-198

Suggested Reading:

A. Altmann, "The New Style of Preaching in Nineteenth-Century German Jewry," in **Studies in Nineteenth-Century Jewish Intellectual History**, pp. 65-116

I. Eisner, "Reminiscences of the Berlin Rabbinical Seminary," **Leo Baeck Institute Yearbook** 12 (1967), pp. 32-52

C. Liebman, "The Training of American Rabbis," **American Jewish Yearbook** (1968), pp. 3-112

C. Roth, "The Chief Rabbinate of England" in **Essays Presented to J. H. Hertz, Chief Rabbi**, pp. 371-384

11. Sub-Communities: The Orthodox and the Hasidim

Required Reading:

S. Poll, **The Hasidic Community of Williamsburg** Part 1, pp. 3-82

C. Liebman, "Orthodoxy in American Jewish Life," in M. Sklare (ed.), **The Jewish Community in America**, pp. 131-174

Suggested Reading:

G. Kranzler, **Williamsburg: A Jewish Community in Transition**

G. Klapperman, **The Story of Yeshiva University**

12. Rural Jews

Required Reading:

L. Levinger, "The Disappearing Small-Town Jew," **Commentary** Vol. 14 No. 2 (1952), pp. 157-163

Suggested Reading:

W. Cahnman, "The Village Jew," **Leo Baeck Institute Yearbook 14** (1974), pp. 107-130

J. Brandes, **Immigrants to Freedom: Jewish Communities in Rural New Jersey**

13. Other Countries

Required Reading:

I. Horowitz, "The Jewish Community of Buenos Aires," **Jewish Social Studies** Vol. 24 No. 4 (1962), pp. 195-222

G. Saron, "The Organization of South African Jewry and Its Problems," **Jewish Journal of Sociology** Vol. 5 No. 1 (1963), pp. 35-46

Suggested Reading:

S. Aschheim, **The Communal Organization of South African Jewry** (Centre for Jewish Community Studies [CJCS], Temple University)

Canadian Jewish Community Reports: Calgary, Edmonton, Hamilton, London, Montreal, Ottawa, Toronto, Vancouver, Windsor & Winnipeg (CJCS, Temple University)

P. Medding, **From Assimilation to Group Survival** [Australia]

D. Elazar, **The Jewish Community of Iran** (CJCS, Temple University)

Andre Chouraqui, **Between East and West** [North Africa]

14. Comparative Communities: Evaluation

Required Reading:

D. Elazar, "The Reconstitution of Jewish Communities in the Post-War Period," **Jewish Journal of Sociology** Vol. 11 No. 2 (1969), pp. 187-226

M. Davis, "Centers of Jewry in the Western Hemisphere: A Comparative Approach," **Jewish Journal of Sociology** Vol. 5 No. 1 (1963), pp. 4-26

L. Gartner, "The History of North American Jewish Communities: A Field for the Jewish Historian," **Jewish Journal of Sociology** Vol. 8 No. 1 (1965), pp. 22-29

Requirements of the Course for Grading:

1)   Class participation

2)   Mid-term and final examinations

3)   An 8 to 10 page research paper on a comparative topic, chosen from a list of suggested topics or designed by the student and approved by the instructor

Note: On at least one occasion the mid-term examination was replaced by an essay on "What the Jewish community is and/or ought to be," which had interesting pedagogical results when quotations from the students' essays were used as a basis for class discussion.

IV. CONCEPTUAL FRAMEWORK OF THE COURSE

This course, taught by a historian within a history department, is primarily historical in its approach, but also employs the perspectives of sociology, religion and political science where appropriate. Its organization is primarily geographical and topical, rather than strictly chronological.

Introduction. Discussion of comparative approach to studying Jewish communities. Present Baron and Elazar models for classification. Traditional vs. modern communities. Trend from compulsory to voluntary membership.

The Traditional "Kehilla:" Eastern Europe. Similarities and differences among medieval Jewish communities in Christian and Islamic worlds. Role of centralized institutions. Legal status and functions of local communities to 18th century, with focus on Poland.

The Modern "Kehilla:" Central Europe. Transition from traditional to modern communities. Role of state in weakening communal authority. Effects of emancipation. Development of Reform movement and Neo-Orthodoxy. **Klal Yisrael** vs. Secession. Changes in Jewish education. Demographic trends from small towns to large cities. **Centralverein** vs. Zionists. Problem of **Ostjuden.** Attempts at unification.

The Consistorial System: Western Europe. Why and how French Jewish community differs from that of Germany. Development of consistorial system from Napoleon to 20th century. Role of Rothschilds. Conflict between natives and immigrants. Post-World War II developments, e.g., **Fonds Socials.**

The Voluntary Community: British Model. Sephardim and Ashkenazim. Development of Chief Rabbinate. Role of United Synagogue. Immigrants, Orthodoxy and the Federation of Synagogues. British Reform and Liberal Judaism. British Board of Guardians: changes in Jewish philanthropy. British Board of Deputies: dealing with the outside world. Anglo-Jewry and British society.

Early American Community. Is America Different? Why do Jews affiliate? Synagogue as focus of Jewish life. Sephardic rite to **Minhag America.** Comparison of American Reform and German Reform. Development of secular communal institutions. Geographic shifts.

The Immigrant Community. Impact of Eastern European Jews on American Jewish community. Comparison of immigrant experience in New York with London, Paris and Vienna.

Twentieth Century Community. Americanization of immigrants in second generation and after. Population movement and areas of settlement. Conservative Judaism. Growth of federations. Voluntary organizations. Involvement of Jews in politics. Comparison of "native" communities in America and in Europe.

Communal Leadership/Rabbinate. Who leads the community? Lay and profesional leadership (Elazar model). Comparison of voluntary communal leadership in America and Europe. Increase in "professional Jews." Changing role of modern rabbinate: Germany, France, England and America.

Sub-communities. Revival of Orthodoxy; modern Orthodox vs. sectarian Orthodox. Hassidic Jews; Sephardim; Black Jews. How the broader Jewish community relates to its sub-communities and vice versa. Changing role of women in the Jewish community.

Rural and Small-town Jews. Comparison of Jewish communal life in small towns vs. big cities. Attempts to form Jewish agricultural colonies (e.g., South Jersey). Southern Jewry. Problems of Jewish survival in relative isolation: assimilation and intermarriage. Relations of Jews with neighbors.

Other Countries. Variations on above themes. Adaptations to different environments: Argentina, South Africa, Australia and Canada. Similarities and differences: origins, institutions, Jewish life.

Evaluation. Do the models work? Is the comparative approach useful? Compare Elazar, Davis and Gartner articles. How have Jewish communities changed in the past 200 years? Are there common trends? What are the major changes pre- and post-World War II? Impact of Israel on Diaspora communities.

I. THE COURSE

THE HISTORICAL BACKGROUND TO CONTEMPORARY ISSUES

Jonathan D. Sarna

Hebrew Union College-Jewish Institute of Religion, Cincinnati; Department of History

One semester of 15 weeks duration, twice a week, totalling 40 hours

II. ACADEMIC CONTEXT OF THE COURSE

This course is an elective open to rabbinic and graduate students, all of whom are beyond the B.A. level. Many of the students see the course as an introduction to issues they are likely to face as future rabbis and Jewish communal leaders. Most of the students have some Jewish background, but the course has proved popular with auditors from the local community, so no background is assumed. The course is heavily weighted toward contemporary issues likely to be encountered by specifically American rabbis.

III. OUTLINE OF THE COURSE

General Background:

Daniel Elazar, **Community and Polity** (Philadelphia, 1976)

Chaim Waxman, **America's Jews in Transition** (Philadelphia, 1983)

A. Issues of Personal Status

1. Jewish Identity - Who is a Jew?

Required Reading:

Salo Baron, "The Problem of Jewish Identity from an Historical Perspective," **Proceedings of the American Academy of Jewish Research** 46-47 (1980), pp. 33-67

Harold Himmelfarb, "Research on American Jewish Identity and Identification: Progress, Pitfalls, and Prospects," in Marshall Sklare (ed.) **Understanding American Jewry** (New Brunswick, N.J., 1982), pp. 56-95

Suggested Reading:

Philip Gleason, "Identifying Identity: A Semantic History," **Journal of American History** 69 (March 1983), pp. 910-931

2. Intermarriage

Required Reading:

Moshe Davis, "Mixed Marriage in Western Jewry," **Jewish Journal of Sociology** X (1968), pp. 177-220

Gerald Bubis, "Intermarriage, the Rabbi and the Jewish Communal Worker," **Journal of Jewish Communal Service** 50 (1973), pp. 85-97

Suggested Reading:

J.D. Sarna "Coping with Intermarriage," **The Jewish Spectator** 47 (Sept. 1982)

Bernard Lazerwitz, "Intermarriage and Conversion: A Guide for Future Research," **Jewish Journal of Sociology** 13 (1971), pp. 41-63

3. Proselytization

Required Reading:

"Proselytes," **Encyclopedia Judaica**, XIII, col. 1182-92

Alexander M. Schindler, "Presidential Address" (UAHC, 1978)

Suggested Reading:

J.R. Rosenbloom, **Conversion to Judaism** (Cincinnati, 1978)

4. Get Legislation

Required Reading:

J. David Bleich, "Jewish Divorce," **Ct. Law Review** 16:2 (Winter 1984)

Sh'ma 14/262 (November 25, 1983)

B. Issues of Church and State

5. The General Problem

Required Reading:

Henry J. Abraham, **Freedom and the Court** (New York, 1982), pp. 220-306

Eugene Lipman, "The Conference Considers Relations Between Religion and State," **Retrospect and Prospect**, B.W. Korn (ed.), (New York, 1965), pp. 114-128

Suggested Reading:

Philip B. Kurland, **Church and State** (Chicago, 1975)

A.P. Stokes & L. Pfeffer, **Church and State in the United States** (New York, 1964)

B. Meislin, **Jewish Law in American Tribunals** (New York, 1976)

6. Prayer in the Public Schools

Required Reading:

L.P. Gartner, "Temples of Liberty Unpolluted: American Jews and the Public Schools," in B.W. Korn, **A Bicentennial Festschrift for Jacob R. Marcus** (New York, 1976), pp. 157-189

F. Michael Perko, "The Building Up of Zion: Religion and Education in 19th Century Cincinnati," **Cincinnati Historical Society Bulletin** 38 (1980), pp. 97-114

N.W. Cohen, "School, Religion and Government--Recent American Jewish Opinions," in **Michael** 3 (1975), pp. 340-392

7. The Public Observance of Christmas

Required Reading:

Milton Matz, "The Meaning of Christmas to the American Jew," **Jewish Journal of Sociology** 3 (1961), pp. 129-137

Lynch et al. v. Donnelly et al. Supreme Court (82-1256) (The Pawtucket Creche Case)

C. Issues of Jewish Legitimacy

8. Anti-Semitism and Jewish Responses

Required Reading:

John Higham, **Send These to Me** (New York, 1975), pp. 116-195

J.D. Sarna, "Anti-Semitism and American History," **Commentary** 71 (March 1981), pp. 42-47

9. Christian Missions to the Jews and Responses to Them

Required Reading:

M. Sklare "The Conversion of the Jews," **Commentary** 56 (September 1973)

J.D. Sarna, "The American Jewish Response to 19th Century Christian Missions," **Journal of American History** 68 (June 1981), pp. 35-51

J.D. Sarna, "The Impact of Christian Missions on American Jews" (handout)

10. Accusations of Dual Loyalty

Required Reading:

O. Handlin, "Israel and the Mission of America," **Race and Nationality in American Life** (Boston, 1957), pp. 193-200

Monna Harrington, "Loyalties: Dual and Divided" **Harvard Encyclopedia of American Ethnic Groups** (Cambridge, Mass., 1980), pp. 676-686

D. Issues of Jewish Political Concern

11. Liberalism and Neo-Conservatism

Required Reading:

Arthur Liebman, **Jews and the Left** (New York, 1979), pp. 3-37

Ben Halpern, "The Roots of American Jewish Liberalism," **American Jewish History** 66 (Dec. 1976), pp. 190-214

Irving Kristol, "The Political Dilemma of American Jews," **Commentary** 78 (July 1984), pp. 23-29

12. Israel and the Diaspora

Charles Liebman, "Diaspora Influence on Israel: The Ben Gurion-Blaustein 'Exchange' and its Aftermath," **Jewish Social Studies** 36: 3-4 (1974), pp. 271-280

J.N. Porter, **The Sociology of American Jews** (Washington, D.C., 1980), pp. 256-272

Ruth Wisse, "The Delegitimation of Israel," **Commentary** 74 (July 1982)

Suggested Reading:

Ben Halpern, "Zion in the Mind of American Jews," in David Sidorsky (ed.) **The Future of the Jewish Community in America** (Philadelphia, 1973), pp. 22-45

Moshe Davis, **World Jewry and the State of Israel** (New York, 1977)

13. Feminism and the Jewish Community

Required Reading:

Ellen Umansky, "Women in Judaism," in R. Reuther & E. McLaughlin (eds.), **Women of Spirit** (New York, 1979), pp. 333-354

Present Tense 11 (Spring 1984), pp. 4-24

Susannah Heschel, **On Being a Jewish Feminist** (New York, 1983), pp. xiii-xxxiii; 120-151

Suggested Reading:

Blu Greenberg, **On Women and Judaism** (Phil., 1981)

14. Student reports

15. Conclusion

Requirements of the Course for Grading:

1) Readings

2) Class presentations

3) Research papers: an analysis of some historical event or issue with contemporary significance (to be decided in consultation with the instructor)

4) Final examination

IV. CONCEPTUAL FRAMEWORK OF THE COURSE

This course explores the following:

Jewish Identity. What do we mean by the term "identity"? How have Jews been defined historically? How are they defined today?

Intermarriage. What are the varieties of intermarriage and what are their implications? What are the causes of intermarriage, how have they changed, and why has the rate of intermarriage varied over time and place? Why is intermarriage a dilemma for modern Jews? What strategies have Jews used in attempting to prevent intermarriages from taking place?

Proselytization. What is involved in making a convert to Judaism? How does Judaism view the convert? Why have attitudes toward proselytization and proselytization rates varied over time? Why is there new interest in reaching out to non-Jews? What is the Schindler proposal, is it new, and what are its implications?

Get Legislation. What are the **halakhic** issues involved in divorce? What attempts have been made to solve the problem of the **agunah**? How have American courts viewed Jewish marriage and divorce law? What is the New York **get** law and why is it controversial?

Church and State: The General Problem. What is the tension between church and state? How did it arise? How has it been treated in American law? How have American Jews viewed the problem?

Prayer in the Public Schools. What is the history of religion and the public schools? How did public schools accommodate Jewish children before the Supreme Court ruling? What did the Supreme Court say, and what were the implications of the decision? Why are American Jews now divided on the issue?

Christmas. Why is Christmas a unique problem for Jews in terms of American law? What does the holiday reveal about American "civil religion?" How have Jews historically responded to the "Christmas problem"--and why? What did the Supreme Court say in the Pawtucket Creche case, and what are the case's implications?

Anti-Semitism. What is the history of American anti-Semitism? Has American anti-Semitism been different from European anti-Semitism? How have American Jews responded to anti-Semitism? What factors affect variations in the rate of American anti-Semitism? How have American Jews understood anti-Semitism?

Christian Missions. Why do Christians missionize Jews and what does this reveal about their attitudes toward them? What is the history of missionary activities in America: when do they rise and when do they fall? How have Jews responded to Christian missions? What impact have missionary activities had on the Jewish community and on Jewish-Christian relations?

Dual Loyalty. What does loyalty mean in the American context? What is disloyalty, what is dissent? When have loyalty issues arisen in America? Why? When have loyalty issues been raised against American Jews and how have they responded?

Liberalism and Neo-Conservatism. What has been the relationship of Jews to the American polity? Have Jews always been liberals? How has Jewish liberalism been explained? Why has liberalism declined? What is

Jewish neo-conservatism? What is the outlook for Jews in American politics?

Israel and the Diaspora. How did Zionism view diaspora Jewry? How did diaspora Jewry view Zionism? How does the State of Israel view diaspora Jewry? Is American Jewry viewed differently? How have American Jews understood their relationship to Israel? How has the relationship changed over time?

Jewish Feminism. What is the place of women in Judaism and American Judaism, and how has it changed over time? What is Jewish feminism, what are its varieties, and why did it arise when it did? What has been the response to Jewish feminism? What are the implications of feminism for the American Jewish community and for American Jewish religious movements?

Student reports. Have students succeeded in viewing contemporary events in historical context, and historical events with an eye toward their contemporary significance?

Conclusion. The value of viewing contemporary issues in historical context; the relationship between historical (diachronic) analysis and sociological (synchronic) analysis; course evaluations.

I. THE COURSE

OUTLINES OF CONTEMPORARY JEWRY

Gideon Shimoni

Hebrew University of Jerusalem, Institute of Contemporary Jewry

Three trimesters, 2 hours weekly, totalling 54 hours.

There are no prerequisites for students taking the course; however, some prior knowledge of Jewish history is assumed due to Israeli high school background.

II. ACADEMIC CONTEXT OF THE COURSE

Offered in Hebrew by the Institute of Contemporary Jewry, it is the core course of a four-course offering open to B.A. students majoring in any of the departments of the Faculty of Humanities and of the Social Sciences at the Hebrew University. (The Institute itself only offers post graduate courses.) Such four-course options are known as **"chativot"** [divisions] and are intended as ancillary courses aimed at broadening the student's knowledge in areas beyond his major course of choice. As such, "Outlines of Contemporary Jewry" is intended to provide a broad survey and at the same time to introduce the student to the multi-disciplinary composition of the Institute of Contemporary Jewry. This core course of the **"chativah"** is supplemented by three more specialized courses of equivalent duration-- one on the Holocaust, another on a particular region of the Contemporary Jewish Diaspora (the region varying from year to year) and yet another (of shorter duration and in the form of an exercise) alternating between aspects of the sociology of the Jews and of the history of Zionism. These aspects are therefore not emphasized in the core course itself.

This is also a recommended course for graduate students in the Hebrew University's Melton Center for Jewish Education in the Diaspora as well as for M.A. students accepted by the department of Contemporary Jewry but requiring preliminary supplementation courses.

An average of 30 students opt for this course. Most are Israeli high school graduates although, invariably, some students educated in Diaspora countries join the course. They are expected to purchase a mimeographed reader volume which contains all of the source readings used as a basis for discussion in the course as well as much of the required bibliography. A major consideration in selecting the bibliography is availability of items in Hebrew. These are sometimes chosen despite the existence of superior items available only in English.*

The lecture sessions are planned to interweave with the bibliography and sources provided by the reader volume. Some additional updated bibliographical references requiring library work are also prescribed.

III. OUTLINE OF THE COURSE
  A. Autumn Trimester – IDEOLOGICAL BASES OF CONTEMPORARY
                         JEWISH IDENTITY

    1. Defining "Contemporary Jewry," various approaches and problems.

       Marshall Sklare, "The Sociology of Contemporary Jewish Studies" in **The Jews in American Society**, Sklare, M. (ed.), (New York: 1974), pp. 2-30.

*In the bibliographical references which follow, books or articles available in English as well as Hebrew are cited in the English version first.

Yehuda Bauer, "Contemporary History – Some Methodological Problems," **History** vol. 61, No. 203, Oct. 1976, pp. 333-343.

Allan Bullock, "Is it Possible to Write Contemporary History?" in A. Bullock, **On the Track of Tyranny**, (London: 1960).

2. The diversification of Jewish identity in the context of the process of Jewish emancipation. (As introduction to a typology of contemporary Jewish identity.)

Salo Baron, "The Modern Age" in Schwartz, L. (ed.), **Great Ages and Ideas of the Jewish People**, (New York: 1956), pp. 315-485.

Ira Eisenstein, "Challenges of Modern Times" in Millgram, A.E., (ed.), **Great Jewish Ideas**, (B'nai B'rith, New York: 1964), pp. 265-280.

3. Secularized Models of Jewish Identity: (a) cosmopolitan in contrast to nationalist;   (b) Zionist compared to non-Zionist; (c) within Zionism – Ahad Haam's normative mode of Jewish identity and alternative non-normative modes (e.g., Brenner, Berdichevski, Klatzkin);   (d) The problematica of secularized Jewish identity in Israel today; (e) Stages in the development of secularized Jewish identity in the United States and its problematica today.

Eliezer Whartman, "Jewish Secularism in America – At the End of the Road?" **In the Dispersion**, no. 7, 1967, pp. 89-103. [Hebrew version in **Bitfutzot Hagolah**, 2/3 (37-38) Summer-Autumn, 1967, pp. 14-25].

Ben Halpern, **The American Jew: A Zionist Analysis**, (New York: 1956), pp. 77-88.

Eliezer Schweid, **Hayahadut Ve'Hatarbut Hachilonit**, (Tel Aviv: 1971), [Hebrew].

Source Reading:

Isaac Deutscher, "The Non-Jewish Jew" in Deutscher, I., **The Non-Jewish Jew and Other Essays,** (London: 1968).

George Steiner, "A Kind of Survivor," **Commentary,** Feb. 1965, pp. 32-38, and George Steiner, "The Wandering Jew" in **P'tachim,** vol. 1, 6, Tishre, 1969, pp. 18-23. [Hebrew].

Ahad Haam, "On Nationalism and Religion" in Hertzberg, A. (ed.), **The Zionist Idea,** pp. 261-262. [Hebrew].

Ahad Haam, "Al Shtei Hase'ipim" and "Hamusar Haleumi" in **The Collected Works of Ahad Haam,** (Jerusalem: 1957). [Hebrew].

Joseph Hayim Brenner, "Bachayim U'basifrut" in **Collected Works,** vol. 3 (Am Oved, Tel Aviv: 1951) pp. 39-54. [Hebrew]

Simon Dubnow, **Michtavim al Hayahadut Hayeshana Ve'hachadasha,** (Tel Aviv: 1937), pp. 16-21, 56-59. [Hebrew]

Israel Knox, "Secularism Today and Tomorrow" in **Point of View,** vol. 1, no. 1, Spring 1961.

Joseph O. Landis, "Secular Jewishness: The Fourth Dimension of Jewish Life," **Journal of Jewish Communal Service,** XXXIX, Fall 1962, pp. 84-88.

Saul L. Goodman, "Jewish Secularism in America: Permanence and Change," **Judaism,** vol. 9, no. 4, Fall 1960, pp. 319, 328-330.

4. Religious Modes of Jewish Identity: Halachically-bound modes (ultra-orthodox and modern orthodox); rational-religious modes (Reconstructionism); post-rational religious modes (e.g., Heschel).

Simon Noveck (ed.), **Great Jewish Thinkers of the Twentieth Century,** (B'nai B'rith, New York: 1963), chapters 1, 7, 9, 10.

David Hartman, "The Breakdown of Tradition and the Quest for
Renewal: Reflections on Three Jewish Responses to Modernity."
Part I.   J.D. Soloveitchik, **Forum,** Spring 1980,
no. 37, pp. 9-24;
Part II. Mordecai Kaplan, **Forum,** Summer 1980, no.
38, pp 43-64;
Part III. Abraham T. Heschel, **Forum,** Fall 1980, no.
39, pp. 61-76.

Eugene B. Borowitz, **Choices in Modern Jewish Thought,**
(New York: 1983), Chapters 4, 5, 7, 8.

Source Reading:

Mordecai M. Kaplan, "Aims of Reconstructionism," in **The
Reconstructionist,** vol. 28, no. 9, June 1962, pp. 23-26.
And Mordecai M. Kaplan, A selection of extracts from Noveck,
S. (ed.), **Contemporary Jewish Thought: A Reader,** (B'nai
B'rith, New York: 1963), pp. 333-350.

Abraham J. Heschel "Between God and Man: An Interpretation of
Judaism," (New York: 1965) pp. 72-79. And **God in Search of
Man: A Philosophy of Judaism,** (New York: 1955) pp. 118-120.

Arthur A. Cohen, "Why I Choose to be a Jew," in Glatzer, N.
(ed.), **The Dynamics of Emancipation,** (Boston: 1965),
pp. 240-251.

Will Herberg, **Judaism and Modern Man,** (Philadelphia:
1951), pp. 262-265.

Joseph Dov Soloveitchik, "The Lonely Man of Faith" in
Glatzer, N. (ed.), **Modern Jewish Thought: A Source Reader**
(New York: 1977), pp. 198-202.

5.   The relationship between the typology of modes of Jewish
     Identity formulated in the class and the Orthodox, Conserva-
     tive and Reform (Progressive) trends of Judaism in the
     Diaspora.

Charles Liebman, "Orthodox Judaism Today," in **Midstream**, Aug.-Sept., 1979, pp. 19-26. [Hebrew version in **Tfutzot Israel**, Spring 1980].

Marshall Sklare, "Recent Developments in Conservative Judaism", **Midstream**, vol. 18, no. 1, January 1972, pp. 3-19. [Hebrew version in **Tfutzot Israel**, Sept.-Dec., 1974].

David Polish, "The New Reform and Authority," **Judaism**, Winter 1974. [Hebrew version in **Tfutzot Israel**, May-Aug., 1974).

Marshall Sklare (ed.), **The Jewish Community in America**, (New York: 1974), "Religious Movements," pp. 131-220.

Source Reading:

Moshe Davis, **The Emergence of Conservative Judaism**, (Philadelphia: 1963), pp. 11-14.

"Who and What are the Reform Jews," **Tfutzot Israel**, Year 4, no. 11, Dec. 1977, pp. 11-20. [Hebrew].

Mordecai Waxman, "The Conservatives," **Tfutzot Israel**, Year 1, no. 4, May 1977, pp. 1-7. [Hebrew]; and Tuvia Freedman, **Conservative Judaism: Questions and Answers**, (Jerusalem: 1973). [Hebrew].

B. Winter Trimester - THE JEW WITHIN MAJORITY SOCIETIES

1.   The significance of emancipation and a survey of types of Jewish emancipation in the 19th and 20th centuries: "single-stroke" emancipation (as in France), gradualist (as in Britain), autonomist (as in Poland), Communist (as in the Soviet Union), colonial (as in Algeria).

Salo Baron, "The Modern Age," in Schwartz, L. (ed.), **Great Ages and Ideas of the Jewish People**, (New York: 1956), pp. 315-485 (especially "The Dynamics of Emancipation," pp. 315-338).

2. The disparity between the theory and practice of emancipation. The historical phenomenon of Jew-hatred and the emergence of anti-Semitism.

Shmuel Ettinger, **Anti-Semitism in the Modern Period,** (Jerusalem: 1969), pp. 1-27, 207-222. [Hebrew. Partly translated into English in **Dispersion and Unity,** 9, 1969, pp. 17-37]. Also Shmuel Ettinger, "Anti-Semitism in Our Time," **The Jerusalem Quarterly,** No. 23, Spring 1982, pp. 95-113.

Jacob Katz, **From Prejudice to Destruction: Anti-Semitism, 1700-1933,** (Cambridge, Mass.: 1980), pp. 303-328.

3. Comparative analysis of the outcome of emancipation in various countries of the 'Old World': Poland, The Soviet Union, Germany, Britain, Algeria (emphasis on the period between the two World wars).

Ezra Mendelsohn, "Poland" in Tsur, J. (ed.), **The Diaspora: Eastern Europe,** (Keter, Jerusalem: 1976), pp. 171-211 [Hebrew].

Yitzchak Ro'i and Mordechai Altshuler, "The Soviet Union" in Tsur, J. (ed.), **The Diaspora: Eastern Europe,** (Keter, Jerusalem: 1976), pp. 5-82. [Hebrew].

Herbert Frieden, "Germany" in Tsur, J. (ed.), **The Diaspora: Western Europe,** (Keter, Jerusalem: 1976), pp. 51-78. [Hebrew].

Mordechai Altshuler and Ezra Mendelsohn, "The Jews of the Soviet Union and Poland Between the Wars: A Comparative Analysis" in Wigoder, G. (ed.), **Contemporary Jewry: Studies in Honor of Moshe Davis,** (Jerusalem: 1984), pp. 53-64. [Hebrew].

Erich Kahler, "The Jews and the Germans" in Kahler, E., **The Jews Among the Nations,** (New York: 1966), pp. 95-119.

Gershom Scholem, "Jews and Germans," in Scholem, G., **On Jews and Judaism in Crisis,** (New York: 1978), pp. 71-92. [Hebrew version in **Dvarim Bego,** vol. 1, (Tel Aviv: 1976), pp. 96-113].

Shmuel Ettinger, "Russia and the Jews: An Attempt at an Historical Summary" in Ettinger, S., **Anti-Semitism in the Modern Period,** (Jerusalem: 1979), pp. 169-189 [Hebrew]. Also Shmuel Ettinger, **The Jewish Reawakening in the Soviet Union,** (Institute of Contemporary Jewry, Shazar Library, Series 12, no. 5, Jerusalem: 1982). [Hebrew].

Michel Abitbol, "Emancipation and Jewish Communal Organiza-tion in North Africa at the Beginning of the Colonial Period," **Pe'amim,** no. 2, (Yad Ben Zvi, Jerusalem: 1979), pp. 32-39. [Hebrew].

Cecil Roth, "The Anglo-Jewish Community in the Context of World Jewry" in Gould, J. and Esh, S., **Jewish Life in Modern Britain,** (London: 1964), pp. 93-110. [Hebrew version, 1976].

4. Is the "New World" different? Comparative analysis of the reception of Jewish immigration and the evolving status of the Jews in various countries: (i) The United States.

Ben Halpern, "America is Different," in Sklare, M. (ed.), **The Jew in American Society,** (New York: 1974), pp. 67-92.

Lloyd P. Gartner, "Immigration and the Formation of American Jewry" in Sklare, M. (ed.), **The Jew in American Society,** (New York: 1974), pp. 31-50.

Marshall Sklare, **America's Jews,** (New York: 1971), chapter 1, pp. 3-36. [Hebrew version, Tel Aviv: 1972].

Daniel J. Elazar, **Community and Polity,** (Philadelphia: 1976), chapter 1, pp. 11-31.

Abraham Karp, "Ideology and Identity in Jewish Group Survival in America," **American Jewish Historical Quarterly** LXV, June 1976, pp. 310-384. [Hebrew version in **Tfutzot Israel,** July-Dec. 1976, pp. 187-220].

B. Sobel and L. Sobel, "Blacks and Jews: Clash Between Two Minority Groups in America" in Rose, P.I. (ed.), **The Ghetto and Beyond - Essays on Jewish Life in America,** (New York: 1969), pp. 384-408. [Hebrew version in **Bitfutzot Hagolah,** 2/3, 37/38, Summer-Autumn, 1967, pp. 46-59].

"What Worries the Jews of America Today?" **Tfutzot Israel,** Jan.-March 1979, pp. 33-52, 65-80. [Hebrew].

Source Reading:

Oscar Janowsky, "The Image of the American Jewish Community" in Janowsky, O. (ed.), **The American Jew: A Reappraisal,** (Philadelphia: 1964), pp. 391-393.

Bezalel Sherman, **The Jews of the United States,** (Tel Aviv 1966), pp. 176-177. [Hebrew version, Tel Aviv: 1966].

Milton Gordon, **Assimilation in American Life,** (New York: 1964), pp. 56, 98, 120, 128, 142.

Charles Y. Gluck and Rodney Stark, **Christian Beliefs and Anti-Semitism,** (New York: 1966), pp. 207-212.

Getrude T. Selznick and Stephen Steinberg, **The Tenacity of Prejudice: Anti-Semitism in Contemporary America,** (New York: 1969), pp. 184-188, 191-193.

Charles Herbert Stember et al, **Jews in the Mind of America,** (New York: 1966), pp. 208, 211-217.

Marshall Sklare, Joseph Greenblum and Benajmin Ringer, **Not Quite at Home - How an American Jewish Community Lives With Itself and its Neighbors: The Lakeville Studies,** (New York: 1969). [Hebrew version in **Tfutzot Israel,** Sept.-Oct., 1969].

Group Life in America: A Task Force Report, (New York, The American Jewish Committee: 1972), pp. 4-6, 20-23, 51-53, 83-87.

5. Continuation of comparative analysis of the reception of Jewish immigration and the evolving status of the Jews in various countries: (ii) Canada, South Africa and Argentina.

Moshe Davis, "Centers of Jewry in the Western Hemisphere: A Comparative Approach," **The Jewish Journal of Sociology** V, no. 1, June 1963, pp. 4-26.

Gideon Shimoni, **Jews and Zionism: The South African Experience, 1910-1967**, (Cape Town: 1980), pp. 1-12, 272-304

Gideon Shimoni, **The Jewish Community in the Apartheid Society of South Africa**, (Institute of Contemporary Jewry, Shazar Library, Series 6, Jerusalem: 1973). [Hebrew]. Also **Jewish National Identification in the Diaspora Today: South African Jewry**, (Institute of Contemporary Jewry, Shazar Library, Series 12, no. 2, Jerusalem: 1982). [Hebrew].

Gideon Shimoni, "Canadian Jewry in Comparative Perspective," **Gesher**, Spring-Summer 1980, pp. 82-87. [Hebrew].

Morton Weinfeld, William Shaffir and Irwin Cotler, **The Canadian Jewish Mosaic**, (Toronto: 1981), pp. 415-439.

Haim Avni, **Latin American Jewry in an Age of Change**, (Institute of Contemporary Jewry, Shazar Library, Series 5, no. 6, Jerusalem: 1972). [Hebrew].

Haim Avni, **Zionism and its Message in Latin America**, (Institute of Contemporary Jewry, Shazar Library, Series 8, no. 3, Jerusalem: 1977). [Hebrew].

Daniel Elazar with Peter Medding, **Jewish Communities in Frontier Societies**, (New York: 1983), Part Two: "Argentina," pp. 61-136.

Source Reading:

Claude Ryan, "A French-Canadian Looks at the Jews," **Viewpoints: Canadian Jewish Quarterly**, No. 3, 1969. [Hebrew version in **Tfutzot Israel**, Jan.-Feb., 1971, pp. 59-66].

Report of the Royal Commission on Bilingualism and Bicultu-
ralism, (Ottawa: 1969), Book IV, pp. 3-12.

Reports to South African Jewry: (South African Jewish
Board of Deputies) July 1965 to Nov. 1967, pp. 5-6;
June 1970 May 1972, p. 6; 1978-1980, pp. 9-12.

Prof. Jorge Graciarena, "Pluralism and Integration – Can
Separate Groups Survive," Proceedings of the Experts
Conference on Latin America and the Future of its Jewish
Communities, (New York: 1972), pp. 104-198.

C. Summer Trimester – PATTERNS OF JEWISH IDENTIFICATION AND
ASSIMILATION

1. Demographic processes affecting world Jewry.

Uziel O. Schmelz, World Jewish Population – Regional Estimates and Projections, (Institute of Contemporary Jewry,
Jerusalem: 1981). [Hebrew version in Tfutzot Israel, year
18, no. 4, Winter 1980, pp. 147-166].

2. The phenomenon of mixed marriage and its impact upon Contemporary Jewry.

Arnold Schwarz, "Intermarriage in the United States," in
Sklare, M. (ed.), The Jew in American Society, (New York:
1974), pp. 303-334.

"Explorations in Intermarriage," American Jewish Yearbook
1973, pp. 292-299.

Sergio Della Pergola, "Mixed Marriages in Demographic
Perspective," Tfutzot Israel, Year 18, no. 4, Winter
1980, pp. 127-146. [Hebrew].

Marshall Sklare, America's Jews, (New York: 1971),
chapter 6: "The Interaction of Jew and Gentile: The Case of
Intermarriage," pp. 203-209.

3. Processes of acculturation and assimilation contrasted with processes of affiliation and identification (with special reference to American Jewry).

    Charles Liebman, "American Jewry: Identity and Affiliation," in Sidorsky, D. (ed.), **The Future of the Jewish Community in America,** (New York: 1973) pp. 127-154.

    Daniel J. Elazar, **Community and Polity,** (Philadelphia: 1976), Chapter 3: "The Community and its Environment," pp. 70-98 and Chapter 4: "The American Environment and Jewish Religious Life," pp. 99-128.

    Marshall Sklare, **America's Jews,** (New York: 1971), Chapter 3: "Family and Identity," pp. 73-102; Chapter 4: "Community."

    Chaim I. Waxman, **America's Jews in Transition,** (Philadelphia: 1983), Chapters 3, 4, 5, 6, 10.

    Steven M. Cohen, **American Modernity and Jewish Identity,** (New York: 1983), "Epilogue: In the Aftermath of Modernity: Diverse Consequences for Jewish Identity," pp. 171-179.

    Simon N. Herman, **Jewish Identity: A Social-Psychological Perspective,** (California: 1977), pp. 17-83.

4. The nature and significance of the Israel-Diaspora Relationship; ideological issues and sociological realities.

    Nathan Rotenstreich, **The State of Israel and the Jewish Golah Today,** (Institute of Contemporary Jewry, Shazar Library, Series 7, no. 2, Jerusalem: 1975). [Hebrew]. Similar article available also in Nathan Rotenstreich, **Essays on Zionism and the Contemporary Jewish Condition,** (New York: 1980), pp. 48-57.

    Jacob Neusner, "A Zionism of Jewish Peoplehood" in Neusner, J., **Stranger at Home: The Holocaust, Zionism and American Judaism,** (Chicago: 1981), pp. 135-145.

    Charles S. Liebman, **The Ambivalent American Jew,** (Philadelphia: 1973), Chapter 4: "American Jews and Israel," pp. 88-108.

Steven M. Cohen, **American Modernity and Jewish Identity,** (New York: 1983), Chapter 8: "Pro-Israelism as the Politics of Ethnic Survival," pp. 154-170.

Moshe Davis (ed.), **World Jewry and the State of Israel,** (New York: 1977), Part III.

Moshe Davis (ed.), **Zionism in Transition,** (New York: 1980), Part IV.

Requirements of the Course for Grading:

A short mid-term paper and a final 3 hour examination questionnaire.

IV. CONCEPTUAL FRAMEWORK OF THE COURSE

This course aims to provide a broad and multi-disciplinary survey of major aspects in the study of Contemporary Jewry. It falls into three sections, coinciding with three trimesters of study, each informed by an organizing conceptual framework as follows:

After a brief introduction to various possibilities of defining the term "contemporary" and to the major research approaches to this area of study, the course begins the exploration of the first of its three sections:

1. Ideological Bases of Contemporary Jewish Identity.

The main disciplinary emphasis is the history of Jewish thought and the central question posed is what is the contemporary ideational content of being Jewish? In answer to this question a ramified typology is charted by the class and finally summed up in a diagram indicating the interrelationships between the various modes of Jewish identity, religious and secularized, characterizing contemporary Jewry. First, the historical background of Jewish emancipation is examined in order to explain the diversification of modes of Jewish identity. Thereafter, the difference between transcendental (religious) and immanent (secularized) understandings

of Jewish identity is considered. Cosmopolitan modes are contrasted
with nationalist modes and within the national category Zionist and
non-Zionist approaches are compared. More detailed analysis is then
undertaken of the cultural dimensions of Zionist ideology arising
from Ahad Haam's seminal thought. The development of a secularized
Zionist identity and its current dilemmas are compared and
contrasted with past autonomist trends in Eastern Europe and with
patterns of development in the United States. Finally, the
relationship between the typology of modes of Jewish identity
formulated in the class and the Orthodox, Conservative and Reform
trends of Judaism, is discussed.

In the course of this treatment of the subject, some attention is
given to the political and social significance of modern Jewish
political movements, especially Zionism (in its major ideological
variations) and the Bund. However, the main emphasis throughout is
on the significance of these developments for Jewish identity. (Some
of the participants in the course take a parallel exercise on the
general history of Zionism.)

2. The Jews within Majority Societies
The main disciplinary emphases in this section are historical and
sociological. The conceptual framework is a comparative examination
of the character of emancipation and its outcome in various regions
of the Diaspora. This involves an analysis of the majority society's
ethnic homogeneity or heterogeneity, its national consciousness, the
relation between state and religion, and specific economic and
political developments. After thus examining some models from the
"Old World" (Poland, the Soviet Union, Germany, Britain and
Algeria, all with emphasis on the period between the two World
Wars), the analysis moves on to a comparison with the evolving

status of the Jews in societies of the New World, major attention being devoted to the United States. The underlying question posed is "Is the 'New World' - and more particularly the United States - different?" The status of the Jews in the society of the United States is compared and contrasted to that in Canada, South Africa and Argentina as examples of smaller "New World" communities. In the course of this analysis the phenomenon of anti-Semitism is examined, consideration being given both to its historical origins and to its current manifestations. (While the Holocaust is constantly kept in mind and frequent reference is made to its significance, it is not given a central place in this course since the participants take a parallel course entirely devoted to this subject.)

3. Patterns of Jewish Identification and Assimilation

The primary emphasis of the third section of the course is sociological. The major conceptual framework is the application of Daniel Elazar's "concentric circles of Jewish identification" (as discussed in his **Community and Polity**). Critical use is also made of Milton Gordon's analysis of assimilation (in his **Assimilation in American Society**). In this context special attention is paid to demographic processes and to the phenomenon of mixed marriage and its impact upon Jewish life today. Also the study of Jewish ethnic identity as developed by Simon Herman is discussed. Whilst most emphasis is placed upon Jewry in the United States, comparisons are drawn with some other countries in the Diaspora and also with Jewish identity in Israel. Finally, attention is turned to the nature and significance of the Israel-Diaspora relationship. This is considered both as an ideological issue and in the light of research into the evolving actualities of that relationship.

I. THE COURSE

JEWISH IDENTITY IN THE MODERN WORLD

Stuart Schoenfeld

Glendon College, York University; cross-listed as Sociology and Social Science

September to April (26 weeks), 3 hours per week, totalling 78 hours

There are no prerequisites for students taking the course

II. ACADEMIC CONTEXT OF THE COURSE

Glendon College is a bilingual (English-French) liberal arts college of about 2,000 students; about 10% are Jewish. Most Glendon students are full-time; some are middle-aged, part time students. The College is 60% female.

Glendon is affiliated with York University; the Glendon campus is a half-hour drive from the rest of the York campus. York University has several thousand Jewish students, offers Jewish studies courses in a range of disciplines, and offers a Jewish Studies major. Students from Glendon may take Jewish Studies courses in other faculties, but almost none do so. Jewish Studies in the Glendon curriculum are limited to this course and one on the Bible.

"Jewish Identity in the Modern World" is taught at the third-year level for either sociology or social science credit. The class usually has about 15 students. There is no assumption that students entering the course have any previous background in Jewish studies.

III. OUTLINE OF THE COURSE

The course consists of six units, each of which has many subtopics. While some attention is paid to each unit, the emphasis on different units, and the sub-topics considered under each, varies from year to year. This outline describes the course as it was taught in the academic year 1983-84.

The course combines lectures, class discussions, field trips and seminars. The readings listed below are assigned to all students and are the basis for lectures. An additional "Selected Bibliography," which considerably extends the topics and references under each major heading, provides a guide to topics and references for seminars. About one-third of class time is spent in seminars.

A. Modernization and Jewish Identity

1. Modernization and Consciousness

Peter Berger, Bridgette Berger & Hansfried Kellner, "The Pluralization of Social Life Worlds," chap. 3 in **The Homeless Mind** (New York: Random House, 1973)

2. Jewish Identity

Stuart Schoenfeld, "Elements of Jewish Identity" (handout: attached to syllabus. See below p. 81)

B. Emancipation, Assimilation and Cultural Contact

1. Jews and Revolutionary Socialism: Jewish Identity in the U.S.S.R

Aleksander Voronel, "The Social Preconditions of the National Awakening of the Jews in the U.S.S.R," in M. Decter (ed.), **I Am a Jew: Essays on Jewish Identity in the Soviet Union** (New York: Anti-Defamation League, 1972)

2. Intermarriage and Cultural Change

Thomas Luckmann, **The Invisible Religion** (London: Macmillan, 1967), concluding chapter

Eric Rosenthal, "Intermarriage and Jewry," in Bernard Martin (ed.) **Movements and Issues in American Judaism** (Westport, Conn.: Greenwood Press, 1978), pp. 260-283

C. Tradition and Loss: European Jews, Anti-Semitism and the Holocaust

   1. Jewish Identity and Modern Anti-Semitism

      Saul Friedlander, "Some Aspects of the Historical Significance of the Holocaust," **Jerusalem Quarterly** 1, Fall 1976, pp. 36-59.

      Richard Rubenstein, **The Cunning of History** (1978)

      Simon Herman, "In the Shadow of the Holocaust," Ch. 6 in **Jewish Identity (1977).**

      Robert Alter, "Deformations of the Holocaust," Commentary 21 (1981), 2 (February), pp. 48-54

D. Jewish Nationalism and the Jewish State

   1. Varieties of Zionism

      Arthur Hertzberg, "Ideological Evolution," **Zionism** (Jerusalem; Keter, 1973) (reprinted from **Encyclopedia Judaica**), chapter 4, pp. 20-62.

   2. Israeli Politics and the Politics of the Middle East

   3. Ashkenazim and Sephardim

      Norman Berdichevsky, "The Persistence of the Yemini Quarter in an Israeli Town," in Ernest Krausz (ed.), **Studies of Israeli Society, Volume 1: Migration, Ethnicity and Community** (1980)

      Shlomo Deshen and Moshe Shokeid, **The Predicament of Homecoming** (Ithaca: Cornell University Press, 1974)

   4. The Religious Issue

E. Change and Controversy in Judaism

   1. Pluralistic Judaism in the United States

      Nathan Glazer **American Judaism,** 2nd edition (Chicago: University of Chicago Press, 1972)

F. Diaspora Community: Family Life, Education, Organization and Federations

IV. CONCEPTUAL FRAMEWORK OF THE COURSE

As the course evolved through several years of teaching, the conceptual and pedagogical framework developed in response to three central problems: 1) how to communicate to students, who are unlikely to take any other university course on a Jewish topic, the breadth and depth of Jewish self-consciousness as it has been expressed over four thousand years under widely varying social conditions; 2) how to relate the contemporary fragmentation of ways of being Jewish to the distinctive social and cultural trends associated with modernization; and 3) given the richness of the material covered in the course, how to avoid overwhelming students and give them the opportunity to pursue the personal questions which often have motivated them to take the course.

To deal with these problems the course combines 1) a detailed, conceptually organized, outline of topics and subtopics relevant to the study of Jewish identity in a period of social and cultural change; 2) lectures based on common readings; and 3) seminars chosen from a list of subtopics, which allow students to pursue what is particularly interesting to them. By following this approach, it is hoped that students will acquire some basic information about the topics discussed understand them in a social-historical context, explore a subtopic that, is of personal interest, and leave with more questions than they came in with. (The last is a particularly important objective. The course gives students a conceptual framework for asking many more questions than can be covered in class and a bibliography which indicates how they may pursue their interest farther.)

The course begins with an introductory unit titled "Modernization and Jewish Identity." This unit covers: 1) a brief overview of Jewish history, with particular attention to its social and cultural dimensions; 2) the concept of "modernization;" 3) the relationship of the social and cultural changes summarized in the concept of "modernization" to "consciousness," i.e., the way people experience their participation in society; 4) the "handout," statement entitled "Elements of Jewish Identity" (see appendix to this syllabus on p. 81) which states the approach to Jewish identity elaborated in the course's various units. This statement contrasts a premodern multi-dimensional consciousness of Jewish identity with the modern segmentation of the various dimensions of Jewish identity. Visually, traditional Jewish identity is presented on the blackboard as five superimposed circles, contrasting with five overlapping circles representing the variety of uni-dimensional and multi-dimensional options of modern Jewish identity; 5) students are given a copy of the "Selected Bibliography," which is organized according to the units of the course. (Each subsequent unit of the course examines a different dimension of modern Jewish identity; each unit in the bibliography organizes topics and subtopics related to that dimension and indicates appropriate readings.)

The remaining units of the course correspond to the elements of Jewish identity, but they do not follow the same order as the "handout" statement. The units and the dimensions identified on the outline correspond as follows:

"Emancipation, Assimilation and Cultural Contact"--Universalism

"Tradition and Loss"--Outsiders

"Jewish Nationalism and the Jewish State"--Nationhood

"Change and Controversy in Judaism"--Religion

"Diaspora Community"--Community.

Most units include topics which indicate how the element of Jewish identity highlighted in that unit may combine with another element, e.g., religious Zionism as a combination of religion and nationhood. In each of these units there are lectures and some common readings, but much of class time is used for seminars based on topics and references which students choose from the "Selected Bibliography." Therefore, the precise schedule and the amount of the course spent on each unit depends upon the choices the students make. The mid-term examination is usually designed to test whether students can relate the contents of the common readings to the framework used in the "Selected Bibliography." The final examination is usually a "take-home" which asks questions requiring integration.

Unit B as an Example

The unit examining universalism as a type of Jewish identity-- "Emancipation, Assimilation and Cultural Contact"--may be taken as an example of how the course works.

The introductory lecture for this unit discusses this type of Jewish identity in general terms. As a "proto-modern" form of consciousness--cosmopolitan, rationalistic, skeptical, individualistic yet morally engaged with the welfare of humanity--this type of Jewish identity illustrates most dramatically the process of redefining Jewish identity to fit "progressive" cultural ideals. It is related to the considerable over-representation of Jews among revolutionaries, psychoanalysts and scholars. Associated with such phrases as "the non-Jewish Jew," "the heretical tradition," and "Jewishness as memory," this approach to Jewish identity is often derived from the experience of marginality, linking it to some extent with the "outsider" theme in modern Jewish identity.

Remaining lectures and common readings cover two topics: first, how this understanding of Jewish identity is connected to changes in the general cultural understanding of marriage and to intermarriage; and second, what happened to Jewish identity in the U.S.S.R. where, with the assistance of Jewish revolutionaries, this understanding of Jewish identity was authoritatively imposed and others were suppressed.

The other topics and references in the bibliography may be used by students for seminar presentations.

Bibliography for Unit B: Emancipation, Assimilation and Cultural Contact

I.   General Treatments

Howard Sachar, "Emancipation in the West," in **The Course of Modern Jewish History** (New York: Dell, 1977), ch. 3, pp. 53-71.

Jacob Katz, **Out of the Ghetto** (Cambridge, Mass.: Harvard University Press, 1973).

Paul R. Mendes-Flohr and Jehuda Reinharz (eds.), **The Jew in the Modern World** (New York: Oxford University Press, 1980), section III, "Emancipation."

II. The Rejection of Jewish Identity

(Subtopics: Jewish Identity as Anarchronistic; Christian Missionaries to the Jews; Jewish Conversion to Christianity)

Karl Marx, **On the Jewish Question,** Isaac Deutscher, **The Non-Jewish Jew** (New York: Oxford University Press, 1968).

Lucy Dawidowicz (ed.), **The Golden Tradition** (New York: Holt, Rinehart and Winston, 1967), section VIII, "Marginals."

Mendes-Flohr and Reinharz (eds.), **The Jew in the Modern World,** section VI, "Jewish Identity Challenged and Redefined," esp. sections #4, 5, 6, 8, 9, 11, 14; section VII, "Political and Racial Anti-Semitism," esp. sections #9 (Bauer) and #10 (Marx).

Michael Meyer, **The Origins of the Modern Jew** (Detroit: Wayne State University Press, 1967), ch. 4, "Rationalism and Romanticism: Two Roads to Conversion."

III. Jewish Culture and Western Culture: Intellectual Encounters

(Subtopics: Outsiders or Aliens; Freud; The Ideal of Social Justice)

Howard Sachar, "The Impact of Jews on Western Culture," in his **The Course of Jewish History** (New York: Delta, 1977), ch. 19.

John M. Cuddihy, **The Ordeal of Civility** (New York: Basic Books, 1974).

Peter Gay, **Freud, Jews and Other Germans** (New York: Oxford University Press, 1978).

Samuel Sandmel, "After the Ghetto: Jews in Western Culture, Art, and Intellect," in A. Leland Jamison (ed.), **Tradition and Change in Jewish Experience** (1977), pp. 198-210.

Maurice Samuel, **The Gentleman and the Jew** (New York: A.A. Knopf, 1952).

Raphael Patai, **The Jewish Mind** (New York: Charles Scribner's Sons, 1977).

Peter S. Rose, ed., **The Ghetto and Beyond** (New York: Random House, 1969), the five selections in the section "Outsiders Within."

Milton Gordon, "A Qualification of the Marginal Man Theory" and "Marginality and the Jewish Intellectual" in **Human Nature, Class, and Ethnicity** (New York: Oxford University Press, 1978).

Bernard Henri-Levi, **The Testament of God** (New York: Harper and Row, 1981).

Cuddihy, **op. cit.**, part I, "Freud."

Peter Gay, **op. cit.**, ch. 1.

Marthe Robert, **From Oedipus to Moses: Freud's Jewish Identity** (Garden City, N.Y.: Anchor Books, 1976).

Eric Fromm, **You Shall Be As Gods** (New York: Holt, Rinehart and Winston, 1966).

IV. Popular Culture and Jewish Identity

(Subtopics: Comedians; the movies; television; stage; writers; Jewish themes in children's literature)

Irving Howe, "Journeys Outward," in **World of Our Fathers** (New York: Harcourt, Brace, Jovanovitch, 1976), ch. 17.

Peter Rose, ed., **The Ghetto and Beyond**, the five readings in the section "Outsiders Within."

V.   Intermarriage and the "Invisible Religion"

Thomas Luckmann, **The Invisible Religion** (London: Macmillan, 1967).

Eric Rosenthal, "Intermarriage and Jewry: A Function of Acculturation, Community Organization and Family Structure," in Bernard Martin (ed.), **Movements and Issues in American Judaism** (Westport, Conn.: Greenwood Press, 1978), pp. 260-283.

Morton Weinfeld, "Intermarriage: Agony and Adaptation," in M. Weinfeld, W. Shaffir and I. Cotler, eds., **The Canadian Jewish Mosaic** (Toronto: John Wiley and Sons, 1981), pp. 365-382.

VI.   The Politics of Assimilation

(Subtopics: Jews and Liberalism; Jews and Labor; Jews and Revolutionary Socialism)

Charles Liebman, "Jewish Liberalism," in **The Ambivalent American Jew** (Philadelphia: Jewish Publication Society, 1973), ch. 7.

Liberalism and the Jews: A Symposium; a special issue of **Commentary** vol. 69, #1 (January, 1980).

Stephen D. Isaacs, **Jews and American Politics** (Garden City, N.Y.: Doubleday, 1974).

Lucy Dawidowicz and Leon G. Goldstein, "The American Jewish Liberal Tradition," in M. Sklare (ed.), **The Jewish Community in America** (New York: Behrman House, 1974), pp. 285-300.

Lucy Dawidowicz, "The Jewishness of the American Labor Movement," in **The Jewish Presence**, pp. 116-130.

Irving Howe, "Jewish Labor, Jewish Socialism" and "Breakup of the Left," in **World of Our Fathers**, chs. 9 and 10.

H.M. Sachar, "The Growth of Jewish Socialism," in **The Course of Modern Jewish History**, ch. 14.

Robert Brym, **The Jewish Intelligentsia and Russian Marxism** (London: Macmillan, 1978).

Lucy Dawidowicz, "In the Revolutionary Movements," in **The Golden Tradition**, section X.

Arthur Liebman, **Jews and the Left** (New York: John Wiley, 1979).

Daniel Aaron, "Some Reflections on Communism and the Jewish Writer," in Peter Rose (ed.), **The Ghetto and Beyond**, pp. 253-269.

VII. The Russian Revolution and the Jews

(Subtopics: The Jews in the Czarist Russian Empire; Russian Jews in Communist Ideology: the Legacy of Marx, Lenin and Stalin; the suppression and marginal toleration of Judaism; the supression of Zionism; the **Yevsekzia**; Biro-Bidzhan; Jews in Stalin's era, in Khruschev's era, in Brezhnev's era; Soviet anti-Semitism; Soviet Jewish emigration; Prisoners of Zion)

Lionel Kochan, ed., **The Jews in Soviet Russia Since 1917, 3rd ed.** (London: Oxford University Press, 1978).

Martin Gilbert, **The Jews of Russia,** (London: National Council for Soviet Jewry, 1976).

The **American Jewish Yearbook** annually updates, with bibliography, conditions in the U.S.S.R.

Aleksander Voronel, "The Social Preconditions of the National Awakening of the Jews in the U.S.S.R.," in M. Decter, ed., I Am A Jew: **Essays on Jewish Identity in the Soviet Union** (New York: Anti-Defamation League, 1972).

Present Tense vol. 8, #1 (Autumn, 1980) contains a collection of articles on Soviet Jews.

William Korey, "The Future of Soviet Jewry, Emigration or Assimilation," **Foreign Affairs,** vol. 58 #1 (Fall, 1979): pp. 67-81.

Appendix: Text of "Handout" entitled Elements of Jewish Identity

Jewish identity means different things to different people. The following list identifies different themes in the modern understanding of what it means to be Jewish. It is a sociologically-derived list based on what modern Jews have said about their identity. It is presented, however, as a **d'var Torah,** an explication of a biblical text, because the themes of modern Jewish consciousness are historically-derived, although in modified form, from Jewish self-understanding as presented in Jewish sacred books. In pre-modern times, the different elements of Jewish identity were superimposed upon each other and are mutually-reinforcing. Only under conditions of modern life have these elements separated into many ways of being Jewish.

The text: "The Lord said to Abram, 'Go forth from your nation and from your father's house to the land that I will show you. I will make of you a great nation, and I will bless you; I will make your name great, and you shall be a blessing. I will bless those who bless you and curse him that curses you; And all the families of the earth shall bless themselves by you.'" (**Genesis** 12:1-4)

Elements of Jewish Identity

A. Elements based directly on the text:

1. **Religion:** Jews believe in a supernatural being, God, the creator and ruler of the universe, who has revealed himself at different times to the Jews and who has a Covenant with them.

2. **Nationhood:** The Jews are a distinct people among the peoples of the earth.

3. **Universalism:** The Jews are part of humanity; their Covenant explicitly includes extending the blessings of God to "all the families of the earth".

B. Elements added historically, consistent with the text:

4. **Community:** When Jews have lacked a territorial base to express their nationhood, they have created social boundaries--familial ritualistic and organizational--which set them apart from others. This experience of community life has a dynamic of its own separate from the reasons for it, and may be valued for its own sake.

5. Outsiders: This is the obverse of #4. Every "we" implies a "they." Because Jews have set themselves apart, they have related to their host societies as outsiders. But there is always something more. Historically, Jews have been suspected, viewed with contempt, degraded, persecuted and murdered. Consequently, self-conscious awareness of this has become an element of Jewish identity.

Under the conditions of modern life, individual Jews may experience and explain their Jewish identity in terms of only one of these elements, or they may identify with more than one.

Syllabi in University Teaching of Contemporary Jewish Civilization

B. Modern-Contemporary Jewish History Courses

I. THE COURSE

INTRODUCTION TO MODERN JEWISH HISTORY

David Bankier
Hebrew University, Jerusalem; Rothberg School for Overseas Students
One semester, comprising 24 hours
There are no prerequisites for students taking the course

II. ACADEMIC CONTEXT OF THE COURSE

The course is conducted in Spanish within the framework of the "four-year program" of the School for Overseas Students. Participants come from various countries, both with and without previous knowledge in Judaica. Because of the heterogeneity of the students, an attempt is made in class sessions to bridge the differences and gaps in knowledge.

The course attempts to offer an introduction to major trends in modern Jewish history until contemporary times, focusing on the main developments in the legal and social status of European Jewry, the challenges of emancipation and the responses of Jews to the process of modernization. Jewish nationalism, Zionism and Israel are only treated marginally since all students are required to take another course on this subject in addition to the course on Jewish history.

One major problem in giving the course is the lack of an adequate bibliography in Spanish. Consequently, the course is to some extent formulated in adaptation to the reading material available in Spanish.

III. OUTLINE OF THE COURSE

1. Demographic changes, migration and urbanization, and economic activities of the Jews as a minority group.

   Reading:

   S. Ettinger, "El desarrollo Socio-Económico del pueblo judío en la edad moderna," in D. Bankier (ed.), **Introducción a la historia del pueblo judío**, Vol. 1 (Jerusalem: 1978), pp. 159-167

   S. Kusnetz, "Estructura económica y vida de los judíos," in Bankier, **ibid.**, pp. 168-194

   I. Leschinsky, "Cenit y ocaso de la moderna historia judía," **Arajim** 3-4 (1950), pp. 193-212

2. The waning influence of autonomous institutions in Western and Eastern Europe.

   Reading:

   S. Ettinger, "Las tendencias fundamentales de la historia de Israel en los tiempos modernos," in Bankier, **op cit.**, pp. 1-4

   J. Katz, "El ascenso de la sociedad neutral," in Bankier, **ibid.**, pp. 31-35

   S. Stern, "El judío en la transición del ghetto a la emancipación," in D. Bankier (ed.), **La emancipación judía**, (Jerusalem: 1983), pp. 60-78

3. European society and the Jews in the 17th and 18th centuries, the Enlightenment, and the French Revolution.

   Reading:

   S. Ettinger, "Los comienzos del cambio de actitud de la sociedad europea hacia los judíos," in Bankier, **La emancipación judía**, pp. 27-59

   S. Baron, "Nuevos enfoques acerca de la emancipación judía," in Bankier, **ibid.**, pp. 238-267

   S. Stern, "El judío de corte," in Bankier, **Introducción**, pp. 19-30

4. The emancipation process.

Reading:

B. Dinur, "Emancipación," in Bankier, **Introducción**, pp. 111-125

E. Tcherikower, "La Revolución Francesa y los judíos," in Bankier, **ibid.**, pp. 71-93

J. Katz, "El término 'Emancipación Judía', su origen y su impacto histórico," in Bankier, **La emancipación judía**, pp. 107-137

5. Jewish enlightenment: a comparative approach.

Reading:

J. Katz, "La visión iluminista del futuro," in Bankier, **Introducción**, pp. 36-40

Y. Slutzky and A. Schohat, "Haskalá," in Bankier, **ibid.**, pp. 60-70

I. Halpern, "El iluminismo en Europa Oriental," **Bases** 20 (1964), pp. 134-142

J. Agus, "La edad de la razón," in Bankier, **Introducción**, pp. 71-93

6. Cultural and religious changes in the 19th century.

Reading:

J. Katz, La emancipacíon y los estudios judaicos," in Bankier, **Introducción**, pp. 132-138

J. Petuchowsky, "Judaísmo reformista," in Bankier, **ibid.**, pp. 138-140

7. Ideological and social roots of modern antisemitism.

Reading:

S. Ettinger, "Las raíces del antisemitismo contemporáneo," in Bankier, **Introducción**, pp. 141-152

A. Bein, "La cuestión judía en la literatura antisemita moderna," in D. Bankier (ed.), **El tercer Reich y la cuestion Judía**, (Jerusalem: 1979), pp. 32-47

8. Jewish nationalism: the Zionist idea.

    Reading:

    S. Baron, "El impacto de la revolución de 1848 sobre la emancipación judía," in Bankier, **La emancipación judía**, pp. 138-201

    J. Katz, "El movimiento nacional judío," **Dispersión y Unidad** 9 (1970), pp. 26-39

    A. Hertzberg, **La idea sionista** (CEJ, Buenos Aires: 1976)

9. Social radicalism, the Bund, European Socialism and Jewish nationality.

    Reading:

    M. Mishkinsky, "Bund," in Bankier, **Introducción**, pp. 209-212

    J. Talmon, **Los judíos y la revolución**

    R. Wistrich, "El marxismo y el nacionalismo judío," in Bankier, **Introducción**, pp. 153-158.

10. The Jews as a national minority: the Latin American case.

    Reading:

    S.M. Lipset, **Estudio de las comunidades judías en un contexto comparativo**, (CEJ, Buenos Aires: 1980)

    N. Lerner, "Los nacionalismos latinoamericanos y las minorías," **Dispersión y Unidad** 17 (1976), pp. 155-167

    I. Horowitz, "La etnia judía y el nacionalismo latinoamericano," **Dispersión y Unidad** 12 (1973), pp. 158-166

11. The Jews as a national minority: the case of the Soviet Union.

    Reading:

    M. Altschuler, "El partido comunista soviético y la existencia nacional judía (1918-1932)," **Bases** 33/34 (1968), pp. 21-33

    S. Ettinger, "Las raíces del antisemitismo soviético y la lucha de los judíos," **Dispersion y Unidad** 10 (1967), pp. 193-207

    Z. Katz, "El Kremlin y los judíos," **Dispersión y Unidad** 10 (1971), pp. 208-216.

12. The Holocaust.

Reading:

J. Talmon, **El significado universal del antisemitismo moderno**

E. Nolte, **El Fascismo en su época** (Madrid, 1967), pp. 47-80, 428-437, 459-484

S. Friedlander, "La significación histórica del Holocausto," in Bankier, **El Tercer Reich**, pp. 96-106

Requirements of the Course for Grading:

A paper (6-10 pages), usually an analysis of a primary source, and a final examination.

IV. CONCEPTUAL FRAMEWORK OF THE COURSE

The course covers a wide range of issues in Jewish history since the Haskala, concentrating both on internal community dynamics and on Jewish responses to developments in the wider society.

The course begins by looking at the decline of Jewish population over the last century with reference to the debate over demographic projections between American and Israeli analysts. With this picture of the contemporary community in mind, the course goes on to examine Jewish life in the Pale of Settlement and the immigration centers in Europe and America. The tensions between traditionalists and their critics within these communities are discussed, together with the various Jewish responses to modernity and emancipation: religious reform, revolution, the science of Judaism and Jewish nationalism in both its Zionist and non-Zionist forms.

The development of European public opinion about Jews and Judaism is traced from the beginning of the modern era, with particular concentration on the ambivalent attitudes towards the Jews displayed by the absolutist monarchs and the champions of emancipation. The terms of emancipation are examined, as well as the question of whether or not these terms were fulfilled by the Jews.

The course goes on to examine the ending of the emancipation controversy with the attendant secularization of traditional anti-Jewish hatred and formation of political antisemitism. Two examples are dealt with in detail: the Nazis - steps towards the Final Solution and the uniqueness of Nazi antisemitism; the Soviet Union - Jewish nationality in the USSR, the anti-Zionist campaign and other manifestations of Soviet antisemitism.

To conclude this survey of the impact of the modern state on Jewish life, there follows a comparative study between Jewish demands for minority rights in the multi-national empires and Jewish self-perceptions and demands in Latin America. The course concludes with the post-Holocaust decades, focusing on the consolidation of Jewish centers throughout the world and the development of new cultural and organizational patterns.

I.   THE COURSE

MODERN JEWISH HISTORY   1780-1948

Vicki Caron
University of Washington, Seattle, History Department
One Quarter of 10 weeks, 5 hours per week, totalling 50 hours
Knowledge assumed: General background in Modern European History

II. ACADEMIC CONTEXT OF THE COURSE

This course is offered as an upper-level undergraduate history course. It is also open to graduate students. Since the University of Washington is a state institution, the students come from a wide variety of backgrounds. For many, this course will constitute their first exposure to Jewish History.

The main focus of this course is on the History of Jews in Europe, with an emphasis on Western and Central Europe. Major themes in East European Jewish History and, to a lesser extent, American Jewish History are touched on as well.

III. OUTLINE OF THE COURSE

I.   Introduction

1. 16th-18th Century Background

II.   Enlightenment and Emancipation

2. European Expectations and the Jewish Enlightenment

Jacob Katz, **Out of the Ghetto** (Cambridge, Mass.: 1973) chs. 4-5, pp. 42-79; or Michael Meyer, **The Origins of the Modern Jew** (Detroit: 1979), chs. 1-2, pp. 11-56.

Moses Mendelssohn, **Jerusalem**, trans. A. Arkush (Hanover & London: 1983) pp. 77-139.

Recommended:

Arthur Hertzberg, **The French Enlightenment and the Jews** (New York: 1970), pp. 268-313.

3. The French Revolution and Napoleon

Arthur Hertzberg, **The French Enlightenment and the Jews**, pp. 314-368.

Diogene Tama, **Transactions of the Parisian Sanhedrin** (Trans. F.D. Kirwan, Cincinnati, Hebrew Union College: 1956) pp. 1-12, 22-24, 30-36, 53-57, 69-83, 88-95.

Simeon Maslin, **Selected Documents of Napoleonic Jewry** (Cincinnati, Hebrew Union College: 1957), pp. 5-12, 20-23, 35-39, 56-60, 74-80, 108-109.

4. The German Path Towards Emancipation

Herbert Strauss, "Pre-Emancipation Prussian Policies Towards the Jews, 1815-1847," **Leo Baeck Institute Yearbook (LBIYB)**, XI (1966), pp. 107-136.

H.D. Schmidt, "The Terms of Emancipation, 1781-1812," **LBIYB**, I (1956), pp. 28-47.

R. Rürup, "Jewish Emancipation and Bourgeois Society," **LBIYB**, 14 (1969), pp. 67-91.

III. Jewish Responses to Emancipation

5. Social and Ideological Assimilation

Michael Meyer, **The Origins of the Modern Jew**, chs. 3-4, pp. 57-114.

Jacob Katz, **Out of the Ghetto**, pp. 104-123, 176-190.

Recommended:

Solomon Maimon, **Solomon Maimon, An Autobiography** (New York: 1947).

6. Reform Judaism

David Philipson, **The Reform Movement in Judaism**, 2nd ed., (New York: 1931) chs. 1-2, 4, 6-7a.

W. Gunther Plaut, **The Rise of Reform Judaism** (New York: 1963) pp. 27-41, 185-195.

Recommended:

Michael Marrus, The Politics of Assimilation (Oxford: 1971), pp. 85-121.

Jacob Katz, **Out of the Ghetto**, ch. 8, pp. 124-131.

Michael Meyer, **The Origins of the Modern Jew**, ch. 5, pp. 115-143.

7. The Science of Judaism and Neo-Orthodoxy

Michael Meyer, **The Origins of the Modern Jew**, ch. 6, pp. 144-182.

Immanuel Wolf, "On the Concept of a Science of Judaism," **LBIYB**, II (1957), pp. 194-204.

Max Wiener, **Abraham Geiger and Liberal Judaism** (Cincinnati: 1981) pp. 149-215.

Heinreich Graetz, **The Structure of Jewish History and Other Essays**, trans. Ismar Schorsch (New York: 1975), pp. 63-74, 133-139.

Samson Raphael Hirsch, **The Nineteen Letters of Ben Uziel** (New York: 1969), letters 1, 7, 9, 10, 13-18.

Graetz, **The Structure of Jewish History**, pp. 1-62.

Max Wiener, **Abraham Geiger and Liberal Judaism**, pp. 3-80.

IV. Anti-Semitism and Jewish Responses

8. The Rise of Radical Anti-Semitism

Paul Massing, **Rehearsal for Destruction** (New York: 1949), including documents 2, 3, 4, 5, 6, or

George Mosse, **The Crisis of German Ideology** (New York: 1964) parts 1 & 2.

Recommended:

Carl Schorske, **Fin-de-Siècle Vienna** (New York: 1980), pp. 116-180.

9. Assimilationist Responses to Anti-Semitism

Ismar Schorsch, **Organized Jewish Reactions to German Anti-Semitism, 1870-1914** (New York: 1972) pp. 23-148.

or

Michael Marrus, **The Politics of Assimilation**, pp. 122-242.

10. The Zionist Solution

Arthur Hertzberg (ed.), **The Zionist Idea** (New York: 1982), pp. 199-230.

Walter Laqueur, **A History of Zionism** (New York: 1972), pp. 84-135.

Recommended:

Sachar, **The Course of Modern Jewish History** (New York: 1958), ch. 8.

V. Eastern European Jewry: The Failure of Emancipation

11. East European Jews Encounter Modernity

Lucy Dawidowicz, **The Golden Tradition** (New York: 1967), pp. 5-89 or Sachar, **The Course of Modern Jewish History**, chs. 9-10.

Lucy Dawidowicz, **The Golden Tradition**, pp. 113-129, 137-142, 148-153, 160-168.

12. The Search for Alternatives: Socialism and Zionism

Lucy Dawidowicz, **The Golden Tradition**, pp. 405-448.

Arthur Hertzberg, **The Zionist Idea** (New York: 1981), pp. 247-277, 329-387.

Recommended:

Sachar, **The Course of Modern Jewish History**, ch. 14.

Ezra Mendelsohn, **Class Struggle in the Pale** (Cambridge: 1970).

VI. The Impact of East European Immigration

13. The Native-Immigrant Encounter

Lloyd Gartner, **The Jewish Immigrant in England** (London: 1960) pp. 100-141, 187-240.

or

Paula Hyman, **From Dreyfus to Vichy** (New York: 1979), pp. 89-152.

Recommended:

Sachar, **The Course of Modern Jewish History**, chs. 15-16.

14. The Cultural Repercussions

Samuel Hugo Bergmann, **Faith and Reason** (New York: 1961), chs. 2, 3, 4.

Recommended:

Martin Buber, **On Judaism** (New York: 1967), pp. 11-94, 108-148.

Nahum Glatzer, ed., **Franz Rosenzweig: His Life and Thought** (New York: 1953) pp. ix-xxxviii, 1-85, 214-250.

15. Jewish Politics in World War I: The Balfour Declaration and National Minority Rights

Isaiah Friedman, **The Question of Palestine, 1914-1918** (New York: 1973), pp. 25-64, 227-332.

Simon Dubnow, **Nationalism and History** (New York: 1970), pp. 131-142.

Recommended:

Oscar Janowsky, **The Jews and Minority Rights** (London: 1933) pp. 264-369.

Isaiah Friedman, **Germany, Turkey and Zionism 1897-1918** (Oxford: 1977).

VII. Jews in European Culture

16. Jews and Weimar Culture

Peter Gay, **Freud, Jews and Other Germans** (Oxford: 1978) pp. 3-28, 93-188.

Recommended:

Isaac Deutscher, **The Non-Jewish Jew** (Oxford: 1968), pp. 25-60.

17. Jews as Radical Intellectuals: The Case of Freud

John M. Cuddihy, **The Ordeal of Civility** (New York: 1974) pp. 17-103.

Recommended:

Peter Gay, **Freud, Jews and Other Germans**, pp. 29-92.

Carl Schorske, **Fin-de-Siècle Vienna**, pp. 181-207.

Freud, **Moses and Monotheism** (New York: 1939).

VIII. The Nazi Seizure of Power

18. Hitler's Rise to Power

Karl Schleunes, **The Twisted Road to Auschwitz** (Urbana, Ill.: 1970), pp. 62-262 or Lucy Dawidowicz, **The War Against the Jews** (New York: 1975), pp. 3-28, 63-264.

19. Jewish Responses to Nazism

LBIYB I (1956), pp. 57-104.

Frances Henry, **Victims and Neighbors** (South Hadley, Mass.: 1984).

Recommended:

John K. Dickinson, **German and Jew** (Chicago: 1967).

20. The Refugee Crisis and the Struggle for Palestine

Henry Feingold, **The Politics of Rescue** (New Brunswick, N.J.: 1970) p.p. 3-68, 126-166, 295-307.

Walter Laqueur, **The Israel-Arab Reader**, 2nd ed. (New York: 1968), pp. 46-84.

Recommended:

A.J. Sherman, **Island Refuge: Britain and Refugees from the Third Reich** (Berkeley: 1973).

Requirements of the Course for Grading:

Reading: All books and articles are kept on reserve in the undergraduate library. Students are required to come to class prepared to discuss the readings for that day. A recommended text for additional background reading is: Howard Morley Sachar, **The Course of Modern Jewish History.**

Examinations: A take-home at mid-term and take-home final. These examinations are based on the lectures, discussions and reading.

IV. CONCEPTUAL FRAMEWORK OF THE COURSE

Introduction: The 16th–18th Century Background. Survey of historical events—both those internal to the Jewish community as well as those transpiring in the general society—which helped pave the way for emancipation during the 16th–18th centuries. Consideration of whether emancipation marks a continuation of earlier trends in Jewish history or whether it marks a radical break with the past. With regard to external changes, factors discussed include: the rise of capitalism; the emergence of the absolutist state; and the development of new political and religious ideologies favorable to toleration. Internal factors include: the modernizing role of Marranos; Sabbatianism as a modernizing force; the rise of the Court Jews; and acculturation in the pre-emancipation period. Discussion of those elements of modernity still absent in the 18th century which make it legitimate to speak of emancipation as a new phenomenon.

European Expectations and the Jewish Enlightenment. Discussion of the ambivalent nature of enlightenment thought regarding Jews and Judaism, with particular reference to Arthur Hertzberg's **The French Enlightenment and the Jews.** Consideration of the extent to which proponents of Jewish emancipation shared the assumptions of those who opposed emancipation. What changes in Jewish behavior did pro-emancipation spokesmen anticipate following the change in Jewish legal status? And, to what extent were Jews willing to meet these expectations? Discussion of the Haskalah movement and Moses Mendelssohn's **Jerusalem.**

The French Revolution and Napoleon. The French Revolution as a case study for examining 1) the debate over Jewish emancipation; 2) the extent to which the actual socioeconomic conditions of Jews in Alsace-Lorraine, which gave rise to a popular anti-semitic movement during the Revolution, imposed limits on the ideology of emancipation. Comparison of the responses of different sectors of French Jewry to emancipation, with particular reference to Salo Baron's theory regarding the relation of emancipation to the rise of the modern nation-state. Consideration of whether Napoleon's Jewish legislation represents an extension of the goals of emancipation or whether it marks a reversal of those ideals. Discussion of the Sanhedrin and whether or not it "sold out."

The German Path towards Emancipation. Historical survey of the struggle for emancipation in Prussia and the particular pressures the Prussian solution, in contrast to the French one, imposed upon Prussian Jewry. Comparative analysis of the various proposals put forth by representatives of the political right, left and center for solving the so-called "Jewish Question" during the decades prior to formal emancipation. Discussion of the way in which the emancipation debate in Prussia highlights certain aspects of German society in general (the weakness of German liberalism, the absence of a notion of cultural pluralism, the strength of the notion of the Christian state, etc.).

Social and Ideological Assimilation. Discussion of the meaning of assimilation in socioeconomic terms (urbanization, social mobility, fertility, etc.), and cultural terms (education, conversion and intermarriage rates). Examination of the extent to which these changes conformed to enlightenment expectations regarding Jewish behavior in the post-emancipation era. Discussion of the cultural significance of conversion as the most radical type of assimilation, focusing on a number of case studies (David Friedlander; the Salon Jewesses; Heine; Mendelssohn's descendants; the Ratisbonnes; Karl Marx's father, etc.). Consideration of conversion as one logical outcome of Mendelssohn's definition of Judaism.

Reform Judaism. Discussion of the various stages in the development of the Reform movement in Germany and the essential elements of the Reform definition of Judaism. Examination of the goals of the Reformers at various stages of the movement's development. Discussion of the ideology of Franco-Judaism as the French counterpart to Reform.

The Science of Judaism and Neo-Orthodoxy. Aspirations and goals of **Wissenschaft** Scholarship, with particular reference to the way this scholarship was related to the struggle for emancipation. Discussion of the success of **Wissenschaft** scholarship in providing a solution to the problem of Jewish identity. Discussion of Samson Raphael Hirsch and neo-Orthodoxy as an alternative to the Reform definition of Judaism, and a comparison of these two movements.

The Rise of Radical Anti-Semitism. Discussion of whether there was in fact a "new" anti-semitism which arose at the end of the 19th century. Attempt to situate anti-semitism within the context of the emerging "New Right" – the impact of the crisis of capitalism, and the ensuing dislocation of the lower middle classes; the crisis of nationalism and the rise of the Volkish ideology; the politicization of anti-semitism in France, Germany and Austria. Consideration of the impact of anti-semitism upon other major political parties.

Assimilationist Responses to Anti-Semitism. Discussion of the types of strategies Western and Central European Jews developed to fight anti-semitism and consideration of the extent to which these strategies bear out Hannah Arendt's charge that assimilated Jews were politically naive. Discussion of the **Centralverein** and the way in which this organization modified formerly-held notions regarding the legitimacy of collective Jewish political action in the post-emancipation era. Impact of the **Centralverein** on German politics and on Jewish identity. Analysis of French Jewish responses to the Dreyfus Affair and comparison to the German scene.

The Zionist Solution. Analysis of Zionism as a post-emancipation phenomenon. Consideration of whether Zionism signifies a complete break with emancipation or whether it shares certain assumptions with

19th-century assimilationist ideologies. Examination of major 19th-century Zionist theorists, with emphasis on the thought and political activities of Theodor Herzl. Attempt to situate Herzl on the European political spectrum, i.e., does he represent the last gasp of a dying European Liberalism or is he a representative of the New Right, as Carl Schorske has recently maintained? To what extent does Zionism mark a new departure in the political behavior of post-Emancipation Jewry?

Eastern European Jews Encounter Modernity. Political Background on the situation of Eastern European Jewry since the late 18th century. Analysis of contradictory nature of Czarist programs towards Jews throughout the 19th century. Impact of the Era of Great Reforms on Russian Jewish life. Internal developments within the Jewish community, including the rise of East European Haskalah, and the revival of secular Yiddish and Hebrew Culture at the end of the 19th century.

The Search for Alternatives: Socialism and Zionism. Jewish Socialism and Zionism in Eastern Europe as responses to the failure of Emancipation and the deteriorating political and economic conditions of Jewish life at the end of the 19th century. Comparison of Zionism in Eastern Europe to Herzl's political Zionism. Analysis of the socioeconomic conditions in the Pale and the factors contributing to the emergence of a distinctly Jewish labor movement. Cultural, political and psychological impact of these movements.

The Native-Immigrant Encounter. Immigration to the West as an alternative solution to the problem of East European Jewry. Cultural, political and social impact of East European Jewish immigration in various Western countries.   Cultural and economic tensions between immigrants and natives. Examination of the emergence of a Jewish labor movement in Western Europe and the United States.   Institutional impact of immigration.

The Cultural Repercussions: The 20th-century Jewish Renaissance Movement.   Analysis of the historical factors which account for the rise of the Renaissance movement on the eve of World War I (generational revolt; the rise of anti-semitism; the encounter with East European Jews; the emergence of Zionism and disillusionment with assimilation).   Discussion of the ways in which the Jewish Renaissance movement delineates a new direction in Jewish History (new definitions of Jewish identity; a new view of the role of Jews in European society and culture; new sources of leadership within the Jewish community). Case studies of individuals involved in the movement (Hermann Cohen, Edmond Fleg, Franz Kafka, Leo Baeck, Martin Buber, Franz Rosenzweig), with particular emphasis upon Buber and Rosenzweig and their writings. The institutionalization of the ideology in the **Freies Juedisches Lehrhaus.**

Jewish Politics in World War I: the Balfour Declaration and National Minority Rights.   Jewish political behavior in World War I as a test case of Hannah Arendt's thesis regarding the political naivete of modern Jewry.   Examination of the lobbying efforts of Jews in the United States and in Europe for National Minority Rights and for the Balfour Declaration. Analysis of the political factors involved in the success of these efforts.   World War I as: 1) an opportunity to forge new bonds between Eastern and Western European Jews; and 2) a sign of the growing political strength of East European Jewish spokesmen in the West.

Jews and Weimar Culture. Consideration of the widely-held perception that Jews dominated certain sectors of European culture and society. Analysis of the significance of the role of Jews in 20th-century European society and culture, and consideration of whether their disproportionate numbers in certain spheres of cultural and economic activity was in any way conditioned by their Jewish background. Discussion of the role of Jews as radical, often left-wing, intellectuals, with reference to the theories of Peter Gay, Carl Schorske, Istvan Deak, Martin Jay, George Mosse, Donald Niewyk, John M. Cuddihy, Isaac Deutscher, and Jacob Talmon. Examination of the impact of the myth of Jewish domination upon Jewish self-conceptions, e.g., Jewish self-hatred, disdain for East European Jews, etc.

Jews as Radical Intellectuals: The Case of Freud. Consideration of whether Freud's Jewish background exercised any influence upon his development of psychoanalytic theory, with particular attention to the arguments of Peter Gay, Carl Schorske, and John M. Cuddihy.

Hitler's Rise to Power. Examination of Hitler's anti-Jewish policies and the Jewish response, with particular focus on why so many Jews remained in Germany after 1933. Consideration of whether Jews themselves could have done more to stop Hitler's rise to power. Examination of the defense efforts of the **Centralverein** during the 1920s. Analysis of: 1) the role of anti-semitism in the Nazi rise to power, i.e., was anti-semitism the decisive factor in winning popular support for the Nazis?; and 2) the fluctuations in Nazi anti-Jewish policies during the 30's, in order better to understand why German Jews read the situation as they did.

Jewish Responses to Nazism. Further examination of why so many Jews remained in Germany after 1933 by focusing upon the individual level of response (to what extent did Nazi anti-semitism influence the interaction of Jews and non-Jews on a day-to-day basis?; to what extent could the continuation of personal relations with non-Jews offer glimmers of hope?); and upon the communal level of response, as represented by the **Reichsvertretung.** Analysis of objective impediments to emigration (the Depression and foreign currency controls; the age structure of German Jewry; the reluctance of Western nations to open their doors; etc.) and subjective obstacles (psychological resistance; the fact that daily life often remained tolerable, etc.). Survey of the rise of anti-semitism elsewhere in Europe and in the United States and Jewish responses on a national and international level. Comparison of effectiveness of Jewish politics in the 1930s to the World War I period.

The Refugee Crisis and the Struggle for Palestine. Analysis of the factors accounting for the reluctance of the Western democracies to accept refugees (Depression, appeasement, public opinion, anti-Jewish sentiment, etc.). Response of international and national Jewish organizations to the refugee crisis and the growing stress upon a Palestinian rather than a domestic solution to the problem. Analysis of British immigration policy in Palestine since the Balfour Declaration. Brief discussion of the creation of the State of Israel.

I. THE COURSE

MODERN JEWISH HISTORY – 1700 TO CONTEMPORARY TIMES

David Cesarani
University of Leeds, England; School of History
One year course, comprising 20 one-hour lectures with approximately 12 one-hour tutorials, totalling 32 hours
There are no prerequisites for students taking the course

II. ACADEMIC CONTEXT OF THE COURSE

Only three universities in England have anything approaching integrated departments of modern Jewish studies. Consequently, modern Jewish history has to be inserted into departments of history or departments specializing in Hebrew language studies, Jewish religion and so forth. This course is fashioned in order to allow its integration into a general history department, with an inter-disciplinary appeal to students in other fields. These students are mainly non-Jewish, which is another consideration. The course here attempts to supply an introduction to the subject to students with little or no background knowledge, in circumstances that are not wholly supportive of any kind of modern Jewish studies.

The course may be the only exposure to such a subject which is available to both Jewish and non-Jewish students. For this reason, it tries to comprehend questions of historiography, religion and culture. The burden on such a framework is enormous and there is a danger of the course becoming too elliptical or diffuse. There is additional pressure in this direction from the circumstances and application of the course. It has to meet the requirements of a number of departments: sociology, politics, theology as well as history. This necessitates a conceptual approach and detracts from a purely chronological procedure. Also, it has to be designed and legitimized partly according to the criteria drawn from the general milieu. This is not only an ideological statement about modern Jewish history (which would, in any case, only be relevant in an informed context), but a practical imperative to ensure the acceptability and accessibility of the course.

For these reasons, the course may be applicable to teachers operating under similar conditions where the local Jewish community is relatively small, the number of Jewish students limited, and the general outlook of the university or department one that is only developing towards pluralism in practice.

III. OUTLINE OF THE COURSE
1. Traditional Jewish society in Eastern and Western Europe. Forces for Change: economic and social.
2. Forces for Change: ideological and political.
3. Emancipation and its effects: 'modernization'?
4. Responses to emancipation: 'adaptation'?
5. The 'modernization' of East European Jewry.
6. The emergence of modern anti-Jewish movements.
7. The crisis of 1880 in Russian Jewry: migration, immigrant Jewry and its impact on western Jewry.
8. Explanations of Jewish social structure and economic activity
9. Socialism and the Jews.
10. The Jews and 'modernist' culture.
11. American Jewry.
12. Jewish nationalism: theory – Hess to Borochov.
13. Jewish nationalism: practice – BILU to the Balfour Declaration.

14. The impact of World War I and the Russian Revolution: Jewish society between the wars.

15. Germany, anti-semitism and the rise of Hitler. The Final Solution, 1939-45.

16. Palestine, the 'Yishuv' and the foundations of modern Israel. Israeli society from Independence to the Six-Day War.

17. Post-war Jewish society in the Americas, Europe and South Africa.

Reading: readings are directed primarily towards essay writing.

They are collected under broad topic headings.*

1. The Jews and 'Modernity'.

Salo W. Baron, " The Modern Age" in ed. Leo Schwartz, **Great Ages and Ideas of the Jewish People**, (1956).

Ben Zion Dinur, **Israel and the Diaspora**, (1961).

Michael Meyer, **The Origins of the Modern Jew**, (1967).

Jacob Katz, **Tradition and Crisis**, (1961).

Todd Endelman, "The Checquered Career of 'Jew' King. A Study in Anglo-Jewish Social History," **American Jewish Studies Review** 7-8, (1982-83).

Shmuel Ettinger, "The Modern Period," in H. Ben Sasson (ed.), **History of the Jewish People**, (1976).

2. Models and Theories of Emancipation.

Salo W. Baron, "Newer Approaches to Emancipation," **Diogenes** 29 (Spring 1960).

Arthur Hertzberg, **The French Enlightenment and the Jews**, (1968).

Jacob Katz, **Out of the Ghetto**, (1973).

* Date is of most recent or paperback edition.

Reinhard Rürup, "Jewish Emancipation and Bourgeois Society," **Leo Baeck Institute Yearbook**, 14 (1969).

Abraham Gilam, **The Emancipation of the Jews in England, 1830-1860**, (1983).

3. Jewish 'Adaptation' in the Nineteenth Century.

Michael Meyer, **The Origins of the Modern Jew**, (1967).

David Rudavsky, **Modern Jewish Religious Movements**, (1979)

Stephen Sharot, **Judaism. A Sociology**, (1976).

Sol Liptzin, **Germany's Stepchildren**, (1944).

Hannah Arendt, **Rachel Vanhagen**, (1957).

Michael Marrus, **The Politics of Assimilation**, (1971).

Todd Endelman, **The Jews of Georgian England, 1716-1830**, (1979).

4. The 'Modernization' of Jewish Communities in the Nineteenth Century.

Phyllis Albert, **The Modernization of French Jewry**, (1977)

Jehuda Reinharz, **Fatherland or Promised Land**, (1975).

V.D. Lipman, "The Age of Emancipation 1815-1880," in V.D. Lipman (ed.), **Three Centuries of Anglo-Jewish History**, (1961).

5. East European Jewry under the Tsars.

Louis Greenberg, **The Jews of Russia**, (1965).

Salo W. Baron, **The Russian Jews under Tsars and Soviets**, (1976).

Michael Stanislawski, **The Jews Under Tsar Nicholas I, 1825-1855**, (1983).

Ezra Mendelsohn, **Class Struggle in the Pale**, (1970).

Simon Dubnow, **History of the Jews in Russia and Poland,** (1916).

Steve Zipperstein, "Jewish Enlightenment in Odessa," **Jewish Social Studies** 44, (1982).

6. Anti-Semitism: Theories and Interpolations.

Koppel Pinson (ed.), **Essays on Anti-Semitism,** (1946).

Hannah Arendt, **The Origins of Totalitarianism,** (1958).

Jean-Paul Sartre, **Anti-Semite and Jew,** (1974).

Arthur Hertzberg, **The French Enlightenment and the Jews,** (1968).

Uriel Tal, **Christians and Jews in Germany,** (1975).

George Mosse, **The Crisis of German Ideology,** (1964).

Colin Holmes, **Anti-Semitism in British Society, 1876-1939,** (1979).

P.G.J. Pulzer, **The Rise of Political Anti-Semitism in Germany and Austria,** (1964).

Jacob Katz, **From Prejudice to Destruction, Antisemitism 1700-1933,** (1980).

7. 1881 and its Impact: The Crisis of Russian Jewry and the Mass Migration.

Jonathan Frankel, "The Crisis of 1881-82 as a Turning Point in Modern Jewish History," in D. Berger (ed.), **The Legacy of Jewish Immigration: 1881 and its Impact,** (1983).

Zosa Szajkowski, "The European Attitude to Eastern European Jewish Immigration 1881-1893," **Publications of the American Jewish Historical Society** 41, (1951-52).

Lloyd P. Gartner, **The Jewish Immigrant in England 1870-1914,** (1960).

Israel Finestein, "Jewish Immigration in British Party Politics in the 1890s," in **Migration and Settlement,** Proceedings of the Anglo-American Jewish Historical Conference, (1970).

Paula Hyman, **From Dreyfus to Vichy: The Remaking of French Jewry, 1906-1939,** (1979).

Lloyd P. Gartner, "Immigration and the Formation of American Jewry, 1840-1925," in Marshall Sklare (ed.), **American Jews: A Reader,** (1983).

Steven Aschheim, **Brothers and Strangers: The East European Jew in Germany and German Jewish Consciousness, 1800-1923,** (1982).

8. Jewish Social Structure and Economic Activity.

Louis Wirth, **The Ghetto,** (1975).

Bill Williams, **The Making of Manchester Jewry,** (1976).

Steven Hertzberg, **Stranger Within the Gates: The Jews of Atlanta,** (1978).

Harold Pollins, **Economic History of the Jews in England,** (1983).

Joe Buchman, **Immigrants and the Class Struggle,** (1983).

Werner Sombart, **The Jews and Modern Capitalism,** (1951).

R.H. Tawney, **Religion and the Rise of Capitalism,** (1966).

9. Socialism and the Jews.

Karl Marx, **On the Jewish Question,** (1964).

Abraham Leon, **The Jewish Question: A Marxist Interpretation,** (1970).

Robert Wistrich, **Revolutionary Jews,** (1976).

Robert Wistrich, **Socialism and the Jews,** (1982).

Edmund Silbener, "British Socialism and the Jews," **Historia Judaica,** 14:1, (1952).

Ezra Mendelsohn, **Class Struggle in the Pale** (1970).

Jonathan Frankel, **Prophecy and Politics: Socialism, Nationalism and the Russian Jews, 1862-1917,** (1981).

Henry Tobias, **The Bund,** (1972).

Zvi Y. Gitelman, **Jewish Nationality and Soviet Politics,** (1972).

10. The Jews and 'Modernist' Culture.

Peter Gay, **Freud, Jews and Other Germans,** (1978).

John Cuddihy, **The Ordeal of Civility,** (1974).

Carl Schorske, **Fin de Siècle Vienna,** (1981).

Frederich Grunfeld, **Prophets Without Honor,** (1979).

11. American Jewry.

H. Feingold, **Zion in America,** (1974).

John Higham, **Strangers in the Land,** (1975).

Irving Howe, **World of Our Fathers,** (1976).

Arthur Goren, **New York Jews and the Quest for Community: The New York Kehilla Experiment,** (1970).

Joel Blau, **Judaism in America,** (1976).

12. Zionism.

Walter Laqueur, **A History of Zionism,** (1976).

David Vital, **The Origins of Zionism,** (1975).

David Vital, **Zionism: The Formative Years,** (1982).

Arthur Hertzberg, **The Zionist Idea,** (1969).

Amos Elon, **Herzl,** (1975).

Leon Simon, **Ahad Ha'am,** (1960).

Stephen Poppel, **Zionism in Germany,** (1977).

Gideon Shimoni, **Jews and Zionism: The South African Experience, 1910-1967,** (1980).

Melvin Urofsky, **American Zionism from Herzl to the Holocaust,** (1975).

Stuart Cohen, **English Zionists and British Jews,** (1982).

Ezra Mendelsohn, **Zionism in Poland, 1915-1926,** (1982).

13.   Inter-war Jewry.

Celia Heller, **On the Edge of Destruction: Jews of Poland Between the Two World Wars,** (1977).

Bella Vago, George Mosse (eds.), **Jews and Non-Jews in Eastern Europe 1918-1945,** (1974).

David Weinberg, **A Community on Trial: The Jews of Paris in the 1930s,** (1974).

Paula Hyman, **From Dreyfus to Vichy,** (1979).

Donald Neiwyk, **The Jews of Weimar Germany,** (1980).

Harold Pollins, **Economic History of the Jews in England,** (1983).

D.D. Moore, **At Home in America: Second Generation Jews in New York,** (1980).

Bernard Johnpoll, **The Politics of Futility: The General Jewish Workers Bund of Poland 1917-1943,** (1967).

Lionel Kochan (ed.), **The Jews in the Soviet Union Since 1917,** (1978).

14.   Germany, Hitler, the Final Solution.

Lucy Dawidowicz, **The Holocaust and the Historians,** (1981).

Lucy Dawidowicz, **The War Against the Jews,** (1975).

Geoff Eley, "Holocaust History," **London Review of Books,** 5:4.

Paul Massing, **Rehearsal for Destruction,** (1967).

Richard Levy, **The Downfall of the Anti-Semitic Parties in Imperial Germany,** (1979).

Karl Dietrich Bracher, **The German Dictatorship,** (1970).

William S. Allen, **The Nazi Seizure of Power,** (1965).

Jeremy Nouhes, **The Nazi Party in Lower Saxony,** (1971).

Karl Schleunes, **The Twisted Road to Auschwitz,** (1970).

Gerald Reitlinger, **The Final Solution,** (1968).

Raul Hilberg, **The Destruction of the German Jews,** (1967).

Isaiah Trunk, **Jewish Responses to Nazi Persecution,** (1979).

Yehuda Bauer, **A History of the Holocaust,** (1982).

Yehuda Bauer, **The Holocaust in Historical Perspective,** (1978).

A.D. Mosse, **While Six Million Died,** (1968).

Bernard Wasserstein, **Britain and the Jews of Europe 1939-45,** (1979).

Michael Marrus and Robert O. Paxton, **Vichy France and the Jews,** (1981).

15. The Foundations and Development of Modern Israel.

Leonard Stein, **The Balfour Declaration,** (1961).

Isaiah Friedman, **The Question of Palestine 1914-1918: British-Jewish-Arab Relations,** (1973).

Edward Said, **The Question of Palestine,** (1979).

Christopher Sykes, **Crossroads to Israel**, (1965).

Neville Mandel, **The Arabs and Zionism Before World War One**, (1976).

Yehoshuah Porath, **The Emergence of the Palestinian Arab National Movement 1918-1929**, (1976).

George Antonius, **The Arab Awakening**, (1938).

Shai Lochman, "Arab Rebellion and Terrorism in Palestine 1929-1939," in Elie Kedourie (ed.), **Zionism and Arabism in Palestine**, (1982).

Michael J. Cohen, **Retreat from the Mandate**, (1979).

Yehuda Bauer, **From Diplomacy to Resistance**, (1970).

J.C. Hurwitz, **The Struggle for Palestine**, (1976).

Noah Lucas, **The Modern History of Israel**, (1974).

Yoram Peri, **Between Battles and Ballots**, (1983).

16. Post-War Jewish Society.

Lionel Kochan (ed.), **The Jews in the Soviet Union Since 1917**, (1978).

Gideon Shimoni, **Jews and Zionism: The South African Experience**, (1980).

Chaim Waxman, **America's Jews in Transition**, (1983).

J. Laikin Elkin, **The Jews of the Latin American Republics**, (1980).

Hannah Arendt, **Eichmann in Jerusalem**, (1961).

André Chouraqui, **Between East and West**, (1968).

Maurice Freedman (ed.), **A Minority in Britain**, (1955).

IV.   CONCEPTUAL FRAMEWORK OF THE COURSE

The course is intended as an introduction to modern Jewish history since ca. 1700. It is designed to complement the studies of undergraduates in other departments and to have the widest possible appeal.

The course unfolds chronologically, but focuses on historio-graphical debates and conceptual problems. It begins with an examination of 'traditional' Jewish society in Europe in the eighteenth century, and the internal and external forces acting to change it. The process of transformation in the nineteenth century is approached via questions such as 'modernization' and 'adaptation.' These are associated with debates concerning the nature of 'emancipation.' The course examines Jewish responses to change in the nineteenth century --acculturation, assimilation, integration--in particular, those affecting Jewish religious belief and practice. The characteristics of 'post-emancipation' communities are analyzed in terms of political behavior (the emancipation struggles, Jews in the 1848 revolutions, socialism and the Jews, Jewish nationalism); economic behavior (migration, immigrant societies, 'Jewish' industries, 'Jewish' trade unionism, social mobility); and cultural productivity. The course looks at differing explanations of these phenomena which accentuate either Jewish uniqueness or specific contextual determinants. The course also tackles varying accounts of the origin of anti-semitism and its functions in late nineteenth-century politics. The last sections deal with the Holocaust and Zionism, surveying interpretations which stress the singularity of the Jewish experience and those which locate it within a universal constellation of economic, social and political forces.

I. THE COURSE

MODERN JEWISH HISTORY: 1780-1980

Evyatar Friesel

Hebrew University of Jerusalem, School for Overseas Students: One-Year Program, English-Speaking Section

One Semester - 25 meetings, 2 hours each, twice a week, totalling 50 hours; plus 15 tutorials in groups

II. ACADEMIC CONTEXT OF THE COURSE

The English-speaking section of the One-Year Program receives students for one year of studies in Jerusalem. Its aim is the combination of academic studies with the opportunity of living in Jerusalem and in Israel, and of becoming familiar with the country. The program is well-established, having been in existence nearly twenty years. The English-speaking section receives about 400 students per year. They are mainly, but not only, from the United States and Canada and most are Jewish. The section offers a wide range of courses in various fields, mainly in the humanities, with an emphasis on Jewish-related and Israel-related themes. For those students with an adequate knowledge of Hebrew, the courses in all the regular faculties of the Hebrew University are open.

Candidates are screened prior to acceptance. Most will already have completed one or two years of studies in their respective universities and may receive credit for the courses they complete in Jerusalem. The number of students participating ranges from 40 to 60.

115

III. OUTLINE OF THE COURSE

Basic Books:

Ettinger, S. "The Modern Period," in: Ben Sasson, H.H., (ed.), A History of the Jewish People, (London: 1976), Part III – Ettinger.

Sachar, H.M. The Course of Modern Jewish History, (New York: 1958) – Sachar.

Mendes-Flohr, P.R., Reinharz, J. (eds.), The Jew in the Modern World – A Documentary History, (Oxford: 1980) – J.M.W.

Carta's Atlas of the Jewish People in Modern Times, (Jerusalem, 1983) (in Hebrew) – Atlas.

1. The Demographic Development of the Jews During the Modern Age: Jewish Migrations (2 meetings)

   Reading:

   Ettinger, pp. 733-740, 750, 790-799, 859-865.

   Atlas, pp. 11-15, 41, 84-85, 144-145.

2. The Legal and Social Situation of the Jews During the 18th and 19th Centuries: West Europe; East Europe; Moslem Countries (2 meetings)

   Reading:

   Ettinger, pp. 755-763, 800-812, 864-869.

   J.M.W., pp. 103-195 (France), pp. 127-128 (Prussia), pp. 138-139 (Prussia), pp. 303-306 (Russia 1827), pp. 309 (Russia 1882).

   Atlas, pp. 26, 30-31.

3. Economic Activities of the Jews During the 18th-20th Centuries (1 meeting)

Reading:

Ettinger, pp. 734-740, 790-799, 864-869.

Atlas, pp. 90-92.

4. New Definitions of Jewishness and New Religious Trends During the 19th and 20th Centuries: New Jewish Self-Definitions - Hassidism; Religious Reform (3 meetings)

Reading:

Ettinger, pp. 768-776, 787-789, 825-833, 834-839.

Meyer, M.A. "Abraham Geiger's Historical Judaism," in Petuchowski, Jacob, (ed.), **New Perspectives on Abraham Geiger**, (New York: 1975), pp. 3-16.

Wiener, M., (ed.) **Abraham Geiger and Liberal Judaism**, (Philadelphia: 1962), pp. 83-84, 149-169.

J.M.W., pp. 230-231 (Deutscher), pp. 239-240 (Hess), pp. 243-245 (Koestler).

Atlas, p. 49 (Hassidism), p. 61 (Jewish newspapers), pp. 54-57 (religious trends).

5. Modern Anti-Semitism: Sources, Ideology, Organization (2 meetings)

Reading:

Ettinger, pp. 870-890.

Sachar, Chap. XI.

Ettinger, S. "The Origins of Modern Anti-Semitism" in **Dispersion & Unity**, vol. 9, 1969, pp. 17-37.

J.M.W., pp. 262-265 (Bauer), pp. 271-273 (Marr), pp. 273-274 (Duehring), pp. 276-278 (Drumont), pp. 280-284 (Treitschke), pp. 288-292 (Chamberlain), pp. 2870-288 (Fritsch), pp. 284-287 (Mommsen), pp. 484-487, 495 (Hitler).

Atlas, p. 44.

6. New Ideological Trends, from the End of the 19th Century: Jewish Nationalism; Jewish Socialism; New Forms of Inter-Jewish Activities; Zionism – the Idea; Zionism – the Beginnings of the Modern Jewish Settlement in Eretz Israel (3 meetings)

Reading:

Dubnow, S. **Nationalism and History**, (Philadelphia: 1958), pp. 40-65.

Ettinger, pp. 845-846, 891-907, 908-914, 915-926, 848-852, 939-942.

Sachar, pp. 284-304.

Sachar, H.M. A **History of Israel**, (Jerusalem: 1976), pp. 65-88.

J.M.W., pp. 339-342 (Bund), pp. 430-432 (Ahad Ha'Am).

Hertzberg, A. **The Zionist Idea**, (New York: 1971), pp. 191-198 (Pinsker), pp. 262-269 (Ahad Ha'Am).

Atlas, p. 66.

J.M.W., pp. 386-387 (American Jewish Committee).

7. The Rise of American Jewry (3 meetings)

Reading:

Gartner, L.P., "Immigration and the Formation of American Jewry, 1840-1925" in Ben-Sasson, Ettinger, (eds.), **Jewish Society Through the Ages**, (London: 1971), pp. 297-312.

Sachar, pp. 160-180, 305-322, 520-554.

Halpern, B. "America is Different" in Halpern, B. **The American Jew**, (New York: 1956), pp. 11-33.

Higham, J. "Social Discrimination Against Jews in America, 1830-1930," in **Proceedings of the American Jewish Historical Society**, Vol. 47, 1957.

Howe, I. **The World of Our Fathers**, (New York: 1976), Chap. 18 (At Ease in America?).

Rischin, M. **The Promised City**, (New York: 1970), pp. 95–111 (Germans vs. Russians).

Atlas, pp. 108–110, 126–129.

8. Jewish Centers in the Twentieth Century: Eastern Europe – Poland, Soviet Union, etc.; the Jewish Communities in Asia and Africa; the Jewish Communities on the American Continent; German Jewry – the Rise of Nazism (3 meetings)

   Reading:

   Ettinger, pp. 949–963, 964–978, 1017–1022.

   Sachar, pp. 348–368.

   J.M.W., pp. 492 (Nazi laws against the Jews).

   Cohen, Hayyim J., **The Jews of the Middle East**, (Jerusalem: 1973), pp. 14–67.

   Chouraqui, André N., **Between East and West – A History of the Jews of North Africa**, (Philadelphia: 1968), pp. 141–183, 263–284.

   Atlas, pp. 94–99, 104, 134–137, 170.

9. The Development of the Jewish National Home, 1917–1939 (2 meetings)

   Reading:

   Ettinger, pp. 989–1016.

   Sachar, pp. 369–392.

   J.M.W., pp. 461 (Mandate), pp. 467–470 (1939 White Paper and Jewish Agency reaction).

10. The Forties: the Holocaust; the Creation of the Jewish State (2 meetings)

   Reading:

   Ettinger, pp. 1018-1039.

   Sachar, pp. 460-488.

   J.M.W., pp. 470 (Biltmore Program), pp. 476-477 (United Nations Resolution), pp. 504-507 (Wannsee Conference), pp. 479-481 (Law of Return), pp. 414-417 (Ben Gurion - Blaustein).

   Atlas, pp. 114-117, 138-141.

11. The Jewish People During the Second Part of the Twentieth Century: Israel and the Diaspora; Sociological Problems of Modern Jewry - Assimilation, Intermarriage, Low Fertility; Anti-Semitism in Our Day; the Jewish People in the 1980s (2 meetings)

   Reading:

   Bokser, B.Z., "Israel and the American Synagogue," in **Road to Jewish Survival**, M. Berger, et al., (eds.), (New York: 1967), pp. 295-298.

   Kaplan, H.M., "A Proposed Platform for the Greater Zionism," in **A New Zionism**, (New York: 1959), pp. 187-189.

   Atlas, pp. 18-21, 144-145.

IV. CONCEPTUAL FRAMEWORK OF THE COURSE

   The major issue of the course is the question of how Jewish society copes with "modernization." The Jewish historical experience in the modern period (as well as in earlier periods) is perceived as a perennial effort to find a mid-way between the influences of the surrounding society and the sustaining of Jewish individuality.   The delicate interplay between centrifugal and centripetal tendencies is traced and analyzed in the context of the conditions which prevailed and the ideologies which developed, from the 17th to the 20th centuries.

Four different models of Jewish historical development emerge: a) East European; b) West European; c) Moslem; d) American. Treatment of the American model dwells mainly on Jews in the United States, but reference is made also to the other countries on the American continent, as well as South Africa and Australia. The main difference between the four models lies in the diverse ideological, social and political values and conditions influencing the relationship between Jews and non-Jews in each place. These differences result in diverse solutions to the general historical problem upon which the course is focused, that of Jewish adaptation to the environment while seeking to maintain Jewish specificity.

The stimulus to the evolving relationship between Jews and non-Jews emanates from the general society. Jewish society reacts to the ideas and values which are generated by the general society in which it exists. Seen from a Jewish perspective, the influences emanating from the outside society have two main tendencies: a) a positive one - the very possibility of the integration of the Jews into the environing society (although, as stated, the character of that integration is different in each of the models mentioned); b) a negative one - in the form of anti-semitism, which is explained as a historical factor manifest throughout the centuries, which continues in modern times with new rationales, adopting variegated forms from mild social discrimination to virulent racial hatred.

This conceptual formulation encompasses most of the manifestations of modern Jewish history. It provides a key for the historical analysis of the different ideologies and movements active in Jewish life: Haskalah, Hassidism, Reform, Orthodoxy, Jewish Socialism, Jewish Nationalism, Zionism and so on, each considered according to its "message" from the point of view of the encounter of "internal" and "external" trends in Jewish history. It also allows for an integrated perception of the phenomenon of anti-semitism in Jewish history. Anti-semitism is analyzed as the negative facet of a relationship between Jews and non-Jews which was not without many positive aspects. It opens a way for a historical understanding of the Holocaust: the most extreme negative expression of that same many-faceted relationship between Jews and non-Jews. It explains also the continuation of anti-semitism today, although under new circumstances and in new forms.

The above-mentioned models of Jewish historical development and life are shown to be quite fluid, considered from the point of view of the relative strength of their two components--the influence of surrounding society and the weight of Jewish individuality. A synoptic view of modern Jewish history seems to justify the conclusion that throughout the modern era there is a gradual change in the relationship between these two components, in favor of Jewish individuality. That tendency is recognizable in Western Jewries, the turning-point being the last decade of the 19th century and first decade of the 20th century.

Regarding Zionism, a distinction is made in the course between Zionism and Jewish life in Israel. Zionism is analyzed as a movement belonging to the trends and movements which developed in the context of the Diaspora and of the relations between Jews and non-Jews. A new explanation is offered regarding the meaning of Zionism in modern Jewish history. The classical idea of Zionism aiming towards the "normalization" of Jewish life and society is reconsidered. Following the general line of analysis so far presented, Zionism is perceived as a movement manifesting two radical positions: one, a strong emphasis on Jewish individuality, rather than integration into the surrounding society; and two, a thrust towards the <u>modernization</u> (rather than <u>normalization</u>) of Jewish society. Zionism is presented as the most radical form of Jewish group adaptation to the conditions and ideologies of modern Western society: it aims at Jewish individuality in its most complete form and is in ideological accord with the forms of modern Western society, i.e., Jewish statehood.

The presentation of Israel and Jewish society in Israel also fits into the historical analysis presented in the course. Yet, although Israeli society continues established historical trends in Jewish life, it also changes them. As in the Diaspora, so in Israel too, one may discern the interaction of "internal" and "external" factors. But while in the Diaspora the stimulant is from the outside inwards (i.e., Jewish society reacting to the influences of the surrounding society), in Israel the dynamics of that relationship have changed. Jewish society in Israel generates trends and ideas of its own in a larger measure than does the Diaspora. In other words, the absorption of values and ideologies from the surrounding world (Western and, up to a point, Middle Eastern) are filtered through those generated within Israeli society. This change in the balance between internal and external influences introduces a new reality into modern Jewish life. The contours of this reality are only now emerging and it is still too early to comprehend all its implications.

THE COURSE

JEWISH RESPONSES TO MODERNITY

Alexander Orbach
University of Pittsburgh; Department of Religious Studies
One semester of 14 weeks, 3 sessions per week, totalling 42 sessions
There are no prerequisites for students taking the course

II. ACADEMIC CONTEXT OF THE COURSE

This course is offered through the Jewish Studies Program at the University of Pittsburgh in Pittsburgh, Pennsylvania. The university is a public, state-related institution with an enrollment of approximately 15,000 undergraduate students and just under 10,000 graduate students. While this course is intended for undergraduates just beginning their studies, an occasional graduate student from the departments of history, sociology and religious studies has enrolled in the course over the years.

Approximately half of the undergraduates at the university are themselves first generation college students within their respective families. These students are hard-working and especially eager to please their instructors as they seek to advance in their studies as quickly as possible. Yet, as students, they are rather passive and particularly oriented to the goal of acquiring those skills which they believe will aid them in the job market upon completion of their studies. The fact that so many of the students live within the county and commute to school from the family home adds to their already busy schedules and has a decided impact on their ability to devote full attention to their studies.

This course is one of a number of courses that students can take in order to satisfy the college history requirement for graduation. Within the Jewish Studies program, it is viewed as an introductory course to the overall study of the modern Jewish experience. Students are encouraged to take it before studying Soviet Jewry, American Jewish History, Modern Israel, the Holocaust and Contemporary Jewry. However, since very few students do take more than one other course in modern Jewry, this course serves not only as an introduction to the field, but also as their only exposure to the material. Hence every effort is made to cover the salient themes in each of the above-mentioned topics.

III. OUTLINE OF THE COURSE

1. Students are required to purchase the following books:

Jacob Katz, **Out of the Ghetto** (Schocken Books: 1973).

Paul Mendes-Flohr and Judah Reinharz (eds.), **The Jew in the Modern World** (Oxford University Press: 1980).

Michael Meyer, **The Origins of the Modern Jew** (Wayne State University Press: 1967).

2. In addition, readings from the following works, placed on reserve in the university library, are assigned over the course of the semester.

W. Ackerman (ed.), **Out of Our People's Past** (United Synagogue: 1977).

L. Dawidowicz (ed.), **The Golden Tradition** (Beacon Press: 1967).

L. Dawidowicz (ed.), **Holocaust Reader** (Behrman House: 1976).

A. Hertzberg, **The French Enlightenment and the Jews** (Columbia University Press: 1968).

A. Hertzberg (ed.), **The Zionist Idea** (Atheneum: 1970).

J. Katz, **Exclusiveness and Tolerance** (Schocken Books: 1961).

J. Katz, **Tradition and Crisis** (Schocken Books: 1961).

J. Parkes, **Antisemitism** (Quadrangle, [Chicago]: 1963).

P. Pulzer, **The Rise of Political Antisemitism in Germany and Austria** (Wiley: 1964)

D. Rudavsky, **Modern Jewish Religious Movements: Emancipation and Adjustment** (Behrman House: 1979).

3. Organization of the assigned readings

    1) Ghetto life in the pre-modern era.

        Katz, **Out of the Ghetto**, pp. 9-28.
        Rudavsky, **Modern Jewish Religious Movements**, pp. 19-33.
        Ackerman, **Out of Our People's Past**, pp. 104-117, 129-131.

    2) The New Era--the traditional world undermined

        Katz, **Out of the Ghetto**, pp. 28-57.
        Katz, **Tradition and Crisis**, pp. 260-274.

    3) The Enlightenment and the Jews

        Katz, **Out of the Ghetto**, pp. 57-80.
        Mendes-Flohr and Reinharz, **The Jew in the Modern World**, pp. 12-16, 27-34, 44-46, 61-67, 79-80, 95-100.
        Rudavsky, **Modern Jewish Religious Movements**, pp. 35-49.

    4) Moses Mendelssohn

        Meyer, **The Origins of the Modern Jew**, pp. 11-56.
        Katz, **Exclusiveness and Tolerance**, pp. 169-181.
        Mendes-Flohr and Reinharz, JMW, pp. 38-44, 77-79, 86-88.

    5) The Emancipation of European Jewry

        Katz, **Out of the Ghetto**, pp. 80-104, 161-175.
        Katz, **Exclusiveness and Tolerance**, pp. 182-196.
        Hertzberg, **The French Enlightenment and the Jews**, pp. 179-187.

Mendes-Flohr and Reinharz, **JMW**, pp. 103-107, 116-121, 127-128, 132-136, 137-139.

Recommended: J. Blau, **Modern Varieties of Judaism**, pp. 1-27.

6) Jewish life at the beginning of the 19th century

a. the abandonment of Judaism

Katz, **Out of the Ghetto**, pp. 104-123.
Meyer, **Origins of the Modern Jew**, pp. 85-113.
Mendes-Flohr and Reinharz, **JMW**, pp. 220-226.

b. the reform of Judaism

Katz, **Out of the Ghetto**, pp. 124-160.
Meyer, **Origins of the Modern Jew**, pp. 115-143.
Mendes-Flohr and Reinharz, **JMW**, pp. 140-149, 159-168, 153-156.
Ackerman, **Out of Our People's Past**, pp. 280-283, 289-293.

Recommended: J. Blau, **Modern Varieties of Judaism**, pp. 28-88.

c. Jewish science

Meyer, **The Origins of the Modern Jew**, pp. 144-182.
Mendes-Flohr and Reinharz, **JMW**, pp. 194-195, 190-193, 188-189.
Rudavsky, **Modern Jewish Religious Movements**, pp. 186-218.

7) A profile of emancipated Jewry

Katz, **Out of the Ghetto**, pp. 176-222.
Mendes-Flohr and Reinharz, **JMW**, pp. 215-218.

8) East European Jewry

Ackerman, **Out of Our People's Past**, pp. 366-372, 377-384.
Mendes-Flohr and Reinharz, **JMW**, pp. 303-309, 310-313.

9) Modern antisemitism

Parkes, **Antisemitism**, chapters III, V.
Mendes-Flohr and Reinharz, **JMW**, pp. 271-284, 287-291.
Ackerman, **Out of Our People's Past**, pp. 430-432, 437-439.

Recommended: Pulzer, **The Rise of Political Antisemitism**, pp. 75-188.

10) Jewish responses to antisemitism

a. flight

Mendes-Flohr and Reinharz, **JMW**, pp. 374-377, 529.
Ackerman, **Out of Our People's Past**, pp. 612-626.
Parkes, **Antisemitism**, chapter VI.

b. Jewish nationalism--Zionism

Hertzberg, **The Zionist Idea**, pp. 211-231, 262-277, 368-387.
Ackerman, **Out of Our People's Past**, pp. 455-456, 458-460.

c. revolution

Dawidowicz, **The Golden Tradition**, pp. 405-410, 411-422, 426-434, 435-441.
Ackerman, **Out of Our People's Past**, pp. 593-609.

11) The 20th century

a. America's Jews

Mendes-Flohr and Reinharz, **JMW**, pp. 380-384, 387-404, 530.
Ackerman, **Out of Our People's Past**, pp. 649-671.

b. From the Russian Revolution (1917) to the Second World War in Russia and Poland

Mendes-Flohr and Reinharz, **JMW**, pp. 344-353.
Ackerman, **Out of Our People's Past**, pp. 542-553.

c. The Holocaust

Mendes-Flohr and Reinharz, **JMW**, pp. 484-487, 490-496, 504-508, 513-520.
Dawidowicz, **Holocaust Reader**, pp. 334-337, 359, 381.

d. Jewish statehood--Israel 1948

Mendes-Flohr and Reinharz, **JMW**, pp. 476-481, 541-542.

Requirements of the Course for Grading:

Students are required to submit three written exercises over the course of the term. These take the following forms: a take-home mid-term examination due in the sixth week of the semester; a review of a book selected from a list to be distributed later in the term and due in the twelfth week of the term; and, a take-home final exam due one week after the completion of the term. Questions for both the mid-term examination and the final are distributed to students in class in the week before the due date. The mid-term essay contributes 30% to the final course grade; the book review also is 30%, and the final essay counts for 40% of the course grade.

IV. CONCEPTUAL FRAMEWORK OF THE COURSE

As is evident from the course outline and its academic context, this is essentially a course on modern Jewish history spanning the period 1750-1950. Thus, at the very least, students are introduced to and become familiar with the varied experiences of the world Jewish community in that era as they unfolded in Europe, the Near East and North America. In the presentation of the material, the challenge-and-response model is employed by emphasizing the manner in which social, political and especially cultural developments in the general society undermined the basis of traditional Jewish community life and Jewish identity. Thus, the course is able to focus on the manner in which modern Jews responded to those confrontations in order to establish new communal forms as well as to delineate for themselves new identities as Jews and as citizens of the polities in which they found themselves. Thereafter, attention is turned to the emergence of modern antisemitism in the last quarter of the nineteenth century and the threat it posed to those new identities and to the status of emancipated Jewry.

The reactions of the Jewish communities to these new forms of antisemitism in both emancipated and unemancipated countries is reviewed especially carefully. It is at this juncture that the emergence of modern Jewish ideologies is also discussed: Jewish nationalism in its various formulations, and Jewish socialism, too. Finally, as part of the treatment of the reactions to antisemitism, the focus moves to the pattern of Jewish migrations and settlement in the late nineteenth century and the first decades of the twentieth century. This facilitates tracing the development of modern Jewry from its initial European setting to locations in North America as well as the Near East.

Finally, the course treats the experiences of modern Jews in the twentieth century. Specifically, an attempt is made to show the impact of Soviet communism, American democracy and freedom, the Nazi assault, and the creation of the modern state of Israel on contemporary Jewry and its ability to shape and organize its own environment. These topics are treated least rigorously of all as they are presented in a general way in order to introduce students to the problems they posed to Jewish life as it developed, and in order to encourage students to study them more seriously and at greater depth in the specific courses offered by the program at the University.

In general then, through this course, students gain an exposure to the experiences of modern Jewry and a familiarity with the contemporary issues facing the Jewish community. At the same time, students, especially the non-Jewish students in the class (estimated at 30%), are able to see how the powerful forces of modernization affected a distinct ethnic-religious community which had managed over the centuries to retain its unique identity and communal structure. Through their study, students can see how the demands of modernity led to estrangement from traditional values and folkways; to a shift of interest from the ethnic group to the general, national community; and to a consequential reformulation of identity, community, and even religion.

In sum, the course seeks to fulfill the integrative function of the study of history through a close study of a particular group and its experience. This facilitates exploration of a wide range of topics and issues which affect not only Jews but all groups and communities.

I. THE COURSE

THE HISTORY OF SOUTH AFRICAN JEWRY –
1800 TO CONTEMPORARY TIMES*

Milton Shain
University of Cape Town, Cape Town, South Africa, Department of History
Single semester option (14 weeks, three lectures per week, fortnightly
    tutorials, totalling 49 sessions)

The proposed course is a second or third year undergraduate semester
elective. Students will have completed a one-year survey of western
civilization (c. 476-1939) but would probably not have read Jewish
history. As students do not necessarily have a knowledge of Hebrew or
of a European language, readings are limited to English.

II. ACADEMIC CONTEXT OF THE COURSE

The University of Cape Town is a large urban university. Of its
approximately 12,000 students, about 2,000 are Jewish. "The History of
South African Jewry c. 1800 – Present" will be given in the Department
of History to about twenty second and/or third year students. The
course is specifically designed to survey and examine themes in South
African Jewish history and, to encourage and stimulate graduate
research in the field. To facilitate and enhance the quality of such
research, South African Jewry is analyzed within the context of modern
Jewish history.** This serves to:

*This is a proposed course which may be implemented in 1986.

**Of course, general South African history forms a necessary back-
ground to the Jewish experience. The best introductory survey is:
T.R.H. Davenport, **South Africa: A History,** (1980).

(1)   contextualize the South African Jewish experience within the frame-
       work of modern Jewish history
(2)   explain the origins of the present-day community
(3)   provide a comparative framework and research methodology.

III. OUTLINE OF THE COURSE

(a)   THE NATURE OF MODERN JEWISH HISTORY

Students are introduced to the problems of periodization in modern
Jewish history and to trends and issues in modern Jewish
historiography.   The emphasis is upon providing a comparative
framework for the teaching of South African Jewry.

Recommended Reading:

R.   Alter,   "Emancipation,   Enlightenment   and   All   That"   in
Commentary, February, 1972.

S. Baron, "Newer Approaches to Jewish Emancipation" in **Diogenes**
29, Spring, 1960.

P. Hyman, "The History of European Jewry: Recent Trends in the
Literature," in **The Journal of Modern History,** Vol.   54, 2,
June, 1982.

M. Marrus, "European Jewry and the Politics of Assimilation:
Assessment and Reassessment," in **The Journal of Modern History,**
Vol. 49, I, March, 1977.

M.A. Meyer, "Where does the Modern Period of Jewish History
Begin?" in **Judaism** 24, No. 3, Summer, 1975.

L. Schoffer, "The History of European Jewry: Search for a Method,"
in **Leo Baeck Institute Yearbook** 24, 1979

Additional Reading:

J. Katz, Out of the Ghetto: The Social Background of Jewish Emancipation, (1973).

L. Kochan, The Jew and His History, (1977).

M.A. Meyer (ed.), Ideas of Jewish History, (1974).

R. Rürup, "Jewish Emancipation and Bourgeois Society," in Leo Baeck Institute Yearbook 14, 1969.

(b)   SOUTH AFRICAN JEWRY TO c. 1870

The Jewish frontier experience is examined. This includes the role of the Jewish pioneer, the emergence and nature of Jewish communal organizations and institutions and the interaction between Jew and non-Jew.

Recommended Reading:

I. Abrahams, Birth of a Community. A History of Western Province Jewry from Earliest Times to the End of the South African War, 1902, (1955).

S.A. Aronstam, A Historical and Socio-Cultural Survey of the Bloemfontein Jewish Community with Special Reference to the Conceptions of Jewish Welfare Work," unpublished Ph.D. dissertation, University of Orange Free State, 1974.

S.G. Cohen, "A History of the Jews of Durban 1825-1918," unpublished M.A. thesis, University of Natal, 1977.

D.J. Elazar and P. Medding, Jewish Communities in Frontier Societies: Argentina, Australia, and South Africa, (1983).

D. Fleischer and A. Caccia, Merchant Pioneers: The House of Mosenthal, (1983).

M.P. Grossman, "A Study in the Trends and Tendencies of Hebrew and Yiddish Writings in South Africa since their Beginning in the Early Nineties of the Last Century to 1930," 2 volumes, unpublished Ph.D. dissertation, University of Witwatersrand, 1973.

L. Herrman, **History of the Jews in South Africa,** (1935); **The Cape Town Hebrew Congregation: A Centenary History 1841-1941,** (1941).

M. Katz, "The History of Jewish Education in South Africa 1841-1980," 2 volumes, unpublished Ph.D. dissertation, University of Cape Town, 1980.

M. Kropman, "The Contribution of Pioneer Traders to the Ciskei," unpublished M. Soc. Sc. thesis, University of Cape Town, 1977.

G. Saron and L. Hotz (eds.), **The Jews in South Africa. A History,** (1955).

M. Shain, **Jewry and Cape Society. The Origins and Activities of the Jewish Board of Deputies for the Cape Colony,** (1983).

M. Sonnenberg, **The Way I Saw It,** (1957).

Additional Reading:

T. Endelman, **The Jews of Georgian England 1714 – 1830,** (1979).

T. Endelman, "The Checquered Career of 'Jew' King. A Study in Anglo Social History," in **A.J.S. Review,** Vol. 78, 1982-83.

T. Endelman, "Liberalism, Laissez-Faire and Anglo-Jewry, 1700 – 1905," in **Contemporary Jewry,** Fall- Winter, Vol. 5, No. 2, 1980.

V.D. Lipman, "The Age of Emancipation 1815 – 1880," in V.D. Lipman (ed.), **Three Centuries of Anglo-Jewish History,** (1961).

(c)   IMMIGRATION, ADAPTATION AND REACTION 1870 – 1913

The impact of Eastern European immigration from 1870 until the first Union debate on immigration in 1913 is examined. This includes the formation of the Zionist Federation (1898), the Tvl/Natal Board of Deputies (1903) and the Cape Board of Deputies (1904). Anti-alienism and anti-alien legislation are examined in comparative context.

Recommended Reading:

E. Alexander, Morris Alexander. A Biography (1953).

S.M. Aronstam, op. cit.

L. Cohen, Reminiscences of Johannesburg and London, (1924).

S.G. Cohen, op. cit.

M. Gitlin,The Vision Amazing. The Story of South African Zionism, (1950).

M. Katz, op. cit.

R. Krut, "Building a Home and a Community. Jews in Johannesburg 1886 - 1914," unpublished Ph.D. dissertation, University of London (forthcoming).

G. Saron and L. Hotz (eds.), op. cit.

M. Shain, Jewry and Cape Society, op. cit.

M. Shain, "Diamonds, Pogroms and Undesirables: anti-alienism and legislation in the Cape Colony" in South African Historical Journal, No. 12, November, 1980.

M. Shain, "The Jewish Population and Politics in the Cape Colony 1898 - 1910," unpublished M.A. thesis, University of South Africa, 1978.

M. Shain, "From Pariah to Parvenu: the anti-Jewish stereotype in South Africa to 1910," Jewish Journal of Sociology Vol. XXVI, No. 2, Dec. 1984, pp. 111-127.

G. Simonovitz, "The Background to Jewish Immigration to South Africa and the Development of the Jewish Community in the South African Republic between 1890 and 1902," unpublished B.A. Hons. thesis, University of Witwatersrand, 1960.

C. Van Onselen, "Randlords and Rotgut, 1886 – 1903," in **Studies in the Social and Economic History of the Witwatersrand 1886 – 1914, Vol. I, New Babylon,** (1982).

Additional Reading:

S. Aschheim, **Brothers and Strangers: The East European Jew in Germany and German-Jewish Consciousness, 1800 – 1923,** (1982).

S. Baron, **The Russian Jews under Tsars and Soviets,** (1976).

J. Buckman, **Immigrants and the Class Struggle. The Jewish Immigrant in Leeds, 1880 – 1914,** (1983).

J. Frankel, **Prophecy and Politics: Socialism, Nationalism and the Russian Jews 1862 – 1917,** (1981).

B. Gainer, **The Alien Invasion. The Origins of the Alien Act,** (1972).

J. Garrard, **The English and Immigration,** (1971).

L.P. Gartner, **The Jewish Immigrant in England, 1870 – 1914,** (1960).

L. P. Gartner, "Immigration and the Formation of American Jewry 1840 – 1925," in H.H. Ben Sasson and S. Ettinger (eds.), **Jewish Society Through the Ages,** (1971).

C. Holmes, **Anti-Semitism in British Society 1879 – 1939,** (1979).

K. Lunn (ed.), **Hosts, Immigrants and Minorities,** (1981).

M. Marrus, **The Politics of Assimilation. A Study of the French Jewish Community at the Time of the Dreyfus Affair,** (1971).

S. Poppel, "New Views on Jewish Integration in Germany" in **Central European History 9, March, 1976.**

I. Schorsch, **Jewish Reactions to German Anti-Semitism 1870 - 1914,** (1972).

S. Sharot, "Native Jewry and the Anglicization of Immigrants in London, 1870 - 1905," in **The Jewish Journal of Sociology** 16, 1, 1974.

U. Tal, **Christians and Jews in Imperial Germany,** (1975).

J. White, **Rothschild Buildings,** (1980).

(d)   THE "JEWISH QUESTION" 1913 - 1948

The so-called "Jewish Question" in South Africa is examined. Attempts to restrict Jewish immigration are traced.   South African responses, both Jewish and non-Jewish, are examined.

Recommended Reading:

E. Alexander, **op. cit.**

E. Bradlow, "Immigration into the Union 1910 - 1948: Policies and Attitudes," 2 volumes, upublished Ph.D. dissertation, University of Cape Town, 1978.

M. Cohen, "Anti-Jewish Manifestations in the Union of South Africa during the Nineteen Thirties," unpublished B.A. Hons. thesis, University of Cape Town, 1968.

S.L. Friedman, "Jews, Germans and Afrikaners: Nationalist Press Reactions to the Final Solution," unpublished B.A. Hons. thesis, University of Cape Town, 1982.

G. Shimoni, **Jews and Zionism.   The South African Experience 1910 - 1967,** (1980).

South African Board of Deputies, **South African Jews in World War Two,** (1950).

Additional Reading:

M. Gilbert, **Auschwitz and Allies**, (1981).

J. Katz, **From Prejudice to Destruction: Anti-Semitism 1700 - 1933, (1981).**

R. **Rubinstein, After Auschwitz,** (1966).

B. Wasserstein, **Britain and the Jews of Europe,** (1979).

S. Wilson, **Ideology and Experience: Antisemitism in France at the Time of the Dreyfus Affair,** (1982).

(e)   THE JEWISH POLITY AND POLITICAL BEHAVIOR 1912 - 1948

The evolution and role of representative institutions are examined until the advent of National Party rule in 1948 together with Jews in politics and the political behavior of the Jewish community.

Recommended Reading:

T. Adler, "Lithuania's Diaspora: The Johannesburg Jewish Workers Club, 1928 - 1948," in **Journal of Southern African Studies,** Vol. 6, No. 1, October, 1979.

E. Alexander, **op. cit.**

S.G. Cohen, "A History of the Jews of Durban 1919 - 1961," unpublished Ph.D. dissertation, University of Natal, (1982).

D.J. Elazar and P. Medding, **op. cit.**

M. Gitlin, **op. cit.**

M. Katz, **op. cit.**

M. Kentridge, **I Recall. Memoirs of Morris Kentridge,** (1959).

E. Mantzaris, "The Promise of the Impossible Revolution: The Cape Town Industrial Socialist League, 1918 – 1921," Saunders et. al. (eds.), **Studies in the History of Cape Town**, Vol. 4, 1981.

G. Saron and L. Hotz, **op. cit.**

G. Shimoni, **op. cit.**

H. Sonnabend, **Statistical Survey of Johannesburg Jewish Population**, (1935).

Additional Reading:

S. Cohen, **English Zionists and British Jews. The Communal Politics of Anglo Jewry 1895 – 1920**, (1982).

P. Hyman, **From Dreyfus to Vichy. The Remaking of French Jewry**, (1979).

W. Laqueur, **A History of Zionism**, (1962).

(f)   SOUTH AFRICAN JEWRY SINCE 1948

The relationship between South African Jewry and Israel; Jews in an Apartheid society; the sociology of South African Jewry and the present day community structures are analyzed.

Recommended Reading:

M. Adelberg, "The Future of the Jewish Community in South Africa," in **S.A. International**, Vol. 12, No. 3, January, 1982.

M. Arkin (ed.), **South African Jewry**, (1984).

S.G. Cohen, "A History of the Jews of Durban 1919 – 1961," **op. cit.**

A.A. Dubb, S. Della Pergola et. al., **South African Jewish Population Study**, (1978).

A.A. Dubb, **Jewish South Africans: A Sociological View of the Johannesburg Community,** (1978).

D.J. Elazar and P. Medding, **op. cit.**

H. Lever, **The South African Voter:** Some Aspects of Voting **Behavior,** (1972).

G. Kark, "The Jewish Day School Matriculant," unpublished M. Ed., University of Witwatersrand, 1972.

M. Katz, **op. cit.**

G. Shimoni, **op. cit.**

B. Steinberg, "Jewish Education in South Africa," in H. Himmelfarb and S. Della Pergola (eds.), **Jewish Education Worldwide,** (forthcoming).

S. Strelitz, "Jewish Identity in Cape Town with Special Reference to Out-Marriage," in **The Jewish Journal of Sociology,** Vol. 13, June, 1971.

Additional Reading:

G. Alderman, **The Jewish Community in British Politics,** (1983).

S.M. Cohen, **American Modernity and Jewish Identity,** (1983).

J. Gould, **Jewish Life in Modern Britain,** (1961).

S. Herman, **Jewish Identity,** (1977).

C. Liebman, **The Ambivalent American Jew,** (1973).

M. Sklare, **America's Jews,** (1971).

IV. CONCEPTUAL FRAMEWORK OF THE COURSE

The aim of the proposed course is to survey the history of South African Jewry and to stimulate and encourage students to proceed at graduate level with research into South African Jewry both in its historical and contemporary dimensions. The course therefore introduces students to issues and trends in modern and contemporary Jewish historiography as the broader context for evaluating the South African experience. It is for this reason that the additional reading goes beyond the literature on South Africa.

The program combines a thematic and survey approach beginning in the early nineteenth century with an examination of the Jew as pioneer, the emergence and nature of Jewish communal organizations and the interaction between Jew and non-Jew. The impact of Eastern European immigration after 1870 is analyzed within a comparative framework. The "Jewish Question," the role of representative Jewish organizations and the political behavior of South African Jewry are examined for the period 1912 - 1948. Thereafter, the relationship between South African Jewry and Israel, the sociology of South African Jewry, Jewry and Apartheid, and the contemporary Jewish polity are analyzed. Throughout the course possible subjects for research are considered and comparative issues and methodologies discussed.

I. THE COURSE

MODERN JEWISH HISTORY – 1880 TO CONTEMPORARY TIMES

David Weinberg
University of Michigan; Jewish Studies Program
One Semester (13 weeks) – 3 hours per week, totalling 39 hours
There are no prerequisites for students taking the course. However, students are urged to take the earlier survey, "Jewish History, 1700-1880," before enrolling in the course.

II. ACADEMIC CONTEXT OF THE COURSE

This course provides four academic credits. It is conducted in lecture format with periodic discussion sessions held on a voluntary basis. It is geared mainly to juniors and seniors.

The University of Michigan is a large American university situated in the upper Mid-West. Of its approximately 40,000 students, between four and six thousand are Jewish. Jewish students come from nearby urban centers such as Detroit and Chicago, as well as from the East Coast.

The Jewish Studies Program is an interdisciplinary program comprising courses in Hebrew, Yiddish and Jewish History. In addition, there are courses in Political Science and Sociology on Jewish themes taught occasionally by interested faculty. The Jewish history component includes two surveys and courses on the Holocaust and on the history of Israel. There are only a handful of Jewish Studies majors, for whom the present course is a requirement. The course generally attracts between 100 and 150 students per semester. Most of the students who enroll are seeking either to fulfill Humanities requirements or to enrich their own Jewish knowledge. Of the Jewish students, a few have Yeshiva or Day School experience, some have been to Israel, while most have attended a religious school in their local synagogues. In addition, there are a small number of non-Jewish students in attendance – history majors, Christian fundamentalists, and individuals curious about Jews and Judaism. In sum, the course has a self-selected audience which, though lacking Judaica background, is generally enthusiastic and eager to learn.

III. OUTLINE OF THE COURSE

1. The Nature of Modern Jewish History – a discussion of emancipation and its ramifications; the dilemma of the modern Jew seeking to maintain his own identity while at the same time attempting to integrate into the larger society; dispelling some myths about Jewish History––Jewish History divorced from general history, **Leidensgeschichte**, Jewish Studies as consciousness-raising.

2. The Great Wave: East European Migration and the Response of Western Jewry – a discussion of East European Jewish migration westward as a form of "auto-emancipation;" the cultural, social, and economic significance of the migration; the response of West European Jews to immigrants.

> Reading: Jacob Lestschinsky, "Jewish Migrations, 1840–1946," in **The Jews: Their History, Culture and Religion**, Volume 2 (JPS, 1949), pp. 1198–1237.

Zosa Szajkowski, "The European Attitude to East European Jewish Migration, 1881-1893," **Publications of the American Jewish Historical Society,** Volume XLI (December 1951), pp. 148-152.

3. Jewish Socialism - the second form of "auto-emancipation" in East Europe at the end of the nineteenth century; the roots of Jewish socialism in Russia; the rise of the Bund - the reasons for its intitial success and its ultimate failure; the dilemma of the secular Jew.

Reading: Moshe Mishkinsky, "The Jewish Labor Movement," in Ben-Sasson and Ettinger (eds.), **Jewish Society Through the Ages** (London, 1971) pp. 284-296.

Henry Tobias, "The Bund and Lenin until 1903," **Russian Review,** XX (October 1963), pp. 344-357; and XXXIV (1965), pp. 393-406.

4. Proto-Zionism and Herzl's Jewish State - the third form of "auto-emancipation;" origins of Zionism; Zionism as continuous with and a rejection of western emancipation; the early efforts at Palestine settlement; the impact of western liberal thought on Herzl's vision.

Reading: Arthur Hertzberg, **The Zionist Idea** (Atheneum, 1970), Parts 2-5.

5. The Response to Herzl: Cultural Zionism, Socialist Zionism, and Revisionism - a discussion of Zionist alternatives to Political Zionism; Ahad Ha-Am's critique of Herzl - what is Jewish about the Jewish State?; Practical Zionism and the Kibbutz movement; Jabotinsky and activist Zionism.

Reading: Hertzberg, Parts 6, 7, 10.

6. European Jewry in the Interwar Period: France and Germany – a discussion of the social, economic and cultural structure of West European Jewry in the 1920s and 1930s; the implications of a nationalist, pluralistic and voluntarist community upon Jewish thought and behavior; the relationship between assimilation and response to anti-Semitism.

> Reading: Donald Niewyck, **The Jews in Weimar Germany** (LSU Press, 1980), Chs. II, IV, V

> David Weinberg, A **Community on Trial** (Chicago, 1977), Chs. 5-7, 9

> OR Paula Hyman, **From Dreyfus to Vichy**, (Columbia, 1979), Chs. 1, 5, 8

> Michael Marrus, "European Jewry and the Politics of Assimilation: Assessment and Reassessment," **Journal of Modern History**, Vol. 49, 1 (March 1977), pp. 89-109.

7. European Jewry in the Interwar Period: Poland and Russia – the nature of autonomism in interwar Poland; Diaspora nationalism as an alternative to both western assimilationism and Zionism; the fate of Jewry under Soviet rule--individual integration at the expense of communal identity.

> Reading: Pawel Korzec, "Anti-Semitism in Poland as an Intellectual, Social and Political Movement," in Joshua Fishman (ed.) **Studies on Polish Jewry, 1919-1939**, (YIVO Institute, 1974), pp. 12-104.

> Leonard Schapiro, "The Role of the Jews in the Russian Revolutionary Movement," **Slavonic and East European Review**, XL (December 1961), pp. 148-167.

> Alfred Greenbaum, "Soviet Jewry during the Lenin-Stalin Period," **Soviet Studies**, XVI (April 1965), pp. 406-421; and XVII (July 1965).

8. The Rise of Modern Anti-Semitism: Nazi and Racial Ideology – a comparison of religious, cultural, and racial anti-Semitism; the relationship between forms of anti-Semitism and the status of Jews in society; racial anti-Semitism as an attempt to incorporate assimilated and non-assimilated Jews under one rubric.

Reading: Lucy Dawidowicz, **The War Against the Jews** (Bantam, 1976), I.

George Mosse (ed.), **Nazi Culture** (Schocken, 1981), Ch. 3.

9. The Holocaust: The Final Solution and the Jewish Response – the relationship between racial ideology and the perpetration of genocide; Nazism as an escape from freedom; the nature of physical and psychological dehumanization in the concentration camp; Jewish resistance – physical and psychological, individual and collective; the attempt to understand the Holocaust.

Reading: Dawidowicz, II.

Primo Levi, **Survival in Auschwitz** (Collier, 1961).

10. Jews Under Islam: The Struggle Between Islam and the West – a discussion of Jews in the Middle East and North Africa in the period of emancipation; similarities and dissimilarities with East European and West European Jews; the impact of European colonization on the status of oriental Jews; the fate of Jews under Islam in the wake of the establishment of the State of Israel.

Reading: Norman Stillman, **The Jews of Arab Lands** (JPS, 1979), pp. 95–110.

André Chouraqui, **Between East and West** (Atheneum, 1973), pp. 113–183.

11.   The Emergence of New Centers of Jewish Life: The American Experience – the impact of successive waves of Jewish migration on the structure and behavior of the community; how different is the American Jewish community?; the nature of American Jewish identity; religious denominationalism; the debate over the future of the American Jewish community.

Reading: Nathan Glazer, **American Judaism** (Chicago, 1972).

Sidney Goldstein, "American Jewry, 1970: A Demographic Profile," in Marshall Sklare (ed.), **The Jew in American Society,** (Behrman, 1974), pp. 93–162.

Charles S. Liebman, "The Religion of American Jews," in **The Jew in American Society,** pp. 223–252.

12.   The Emergence of New Centers of Jewish Life: The State of Israel – the events surrounding the creation of the State; Israel as a Jewish State – the ideal and the reality: Israel as a cultural center, relationships with the Arab population; the conflict between "Jew" and "Israeli;" the ethnic question in Israel.

Reading: J.C. Hurewitz, **The Struggle for Palestine** (Schocken, 1976), 5–12.

Walter Laqueur, **A History of Zionism** (Schocken, 1976), Ch. 5.

Shlomo Avineri, "Israel: Two Nations?" in Michael Curtis and Mordechai Chertoff (eds.), **Israel: Social Structure and Change** (Transaction, 1973), pp. 281–305.

13.   The Creative Tension: Jews and Non-Jews in the Modern Era; Israel and the Diaspora – the nature of the relations between Jews and non-Jews and its impact upon Jewish thought and behavior; the interchange between the Diaspora and Israel as a source of conflict and creativity in modern Jewish life; the challenge of aliyah and the need to justify continued Jewish life in the Diaspora.

Readings: Hillel Halkin, **Letters to an American Jewish Friend** (JPS, 1977).

Requirements of the Course for Grading:

1)   There are two examinations in the course given in the fourth and eighth weeks.   In addition, there is a comprehensive take-home final which is due during "Finals Week."   Examinations are primarily essays but identifications are occasionally included.

2)   There is a series of informal discussions at which attendance is voluntary.   Student participation in discussions is taken into account in cases of borderline final grades.

3)   In cases where students have substantial background, there is the possibility of writing a short research paper in lieu of an examination.

IV. CONCEPTUAL FRAMEWORK OF THE COURSE

As a survey, the purpose of the course is to introduce students to major events in modern Jewish history. The major theme is the impact of emancipation upon Jewish thought and behavior. In particular, students are asked to examine the relationship between differing forms of emancipation and the ideational and communal structure of three major centers of world Jewry in the late 19th and early 20th centuries: West Europe, East Europe, and the Islamic lands.

In the cases of the United States and Israel, students are asked to consider ideological and social structures in a community which did not need to struggle for emancipation and in a community which has attained political sovereignty.

The modern Jewish experience is defined in terms of two creative tensions: first, the need to maintain Jewish identity while at the same time participating in the larger society; and second, the inter-relationship between Diaspora and Israeli Jewry sharing a common identity yet differing in outlook on the future of Jews and Judaism.

As a survey, the course can only touch upon the subjects under discussion.   Consequently, a tendency toward generalization and also some blurring of nuances are unavoidable.   Furthermore, the course is limited by the language abilities of most students.   Despite the many English-language publications in modern Jewish history, there are a number of subjects for which there are no adequate readings, notably, East European Jewry and Jews under Islam.   Finally, despite the importance of maintaining ideological neutrality and academic integrity, one cannot ignore the fact that many students bring hidden agendas to the course, most notably the desire to raise their Jewish consciousness and commitment.   Such questions cannot be avoided but an attempt is generally made to reserve them for office and private discussions.

Syllabi in University Teaching of Contemporary Jewish Civilization

C. Thematic Courses in Contemporary Jewry

I.   THE COURSE

THE JEWS OF LATIN AMERICA: AN HISTORICAL AND CONTEMPORARY SURVEY

Haim Avni*

Brandeis University, USA: Department of Near Eastern and Judaic Studies
Three hours per week for one thirteen-week semester, totalling 39 hours

II.   ACADEMIC CONTEXT OF THE COURSE

This course was an elective for juniors, seniors and graduate students of the Department of Near Eastern and Judaic Studies. Students from other departments were also eligible for the course, among them a special group from the Benjamin S. Hornstein Program in Communal Service, which is a graduate studies program. Most participants had some background in modern Jewish history, but none in the specific area of Latin American Jewry.

The aim of the course is to acquaint the students with the history and realities of Jewish life in an area with which they have had almost no previous contact, while focusing on those aspects which are related to general problems in modern and contemporary Jewish studies and particularly those relevant to an understanding of Jewish communal life today.   The emphasis throughout is less on detailed information than on exposing the students to the broader issues involved.

*Prof. Avni is on the faculty of the Institute of Contemporary Jewry, the Hebrew University of Jerusalem. This course was offered by him as a guest lecturer at Brandeis University.

III. OUTLINE OF THE COURSE

1. Introduction: "Euro-America" and "Indo-America" - the diversity of general and Jewish experiences in Latin America.

Required Reading:

David Schers and Hadassa Singer, "The Jewish Communities of Latin America: External and Internal Factors in their Development," **Jewish Social Studies** Vol. 39 No. 3, (Summer 1977), pp. 241-258

Haim Avni, "Jewish Communities in Latin America," in Louis Henkin (ed.), **World Politics and the Jewish Condition** (New York: Quadrangle, 1972), pp. 238-274.

2. The illegitimate Jewish presence: Jews in Ibero-America before its independence.

Required Reading:

Boleslao Lewin, "The Struggle Against Jewish Immigration into Latin America in Colonial Times," **Yivo Annual of Jewish Social Science** Vol. 7, (New York, 1952), pp. 212-228

Judith Laikin Elkin, **Jews of the Latin American Republics** (Chapel Hill: University of North Carolina, 1980), pp. 3-23

Arnold Wiznitzer, "The Exodus from Brazil and Arrival in New Amsterdam of Jewish Pilgrim Fathers, 1654," in Martin A. Cohen (ed.), **The Jewish Experience in Latin America** (Philadelphia: American Jewish Historical Society, 1971 [2 vols.]), Vol. 2, pp. 313-330

3. The legalization of Jewish existence in Ibero-America and the policies of immigration followed by some of the new nations.

Required Reading:

Salo Baron, "Jewish Emancipation," **Encyclopaedia of the Social Sciences** (New York: Macmillan, 1937)

Richard Popkin, "Moses Mendelssohn and Francisco de Miranda," **Jewish Social Studies** Vol. 40 (1978), pp. 4-18

4. "Indian-Jews," "Portuguese" Jews and the establishment of Jewish communities in Ibero-America.

Required Reading:

Benno Weiser, "Ecuador: Eight Years on Ararat," **Commentary** 3 (June 1947), pp. 531-536

Seymour B. Liebman, "The Mestizo Jews of Mexico," **American Jewish Archives** 19 (November 1967), pp. 144-174

Dennis Sasso, "One Century of Jewish Life in Panama," **Reconstructionist** Vol. 42 No. 6 (September 1976/Elul 5736), pp. 18-24

Isidoro Aizenberg, "Efforts to Establish a Jewish Cemetery in Nineteenth Century Caracas," **American Jewish Historical Quarterly** Vol. 67 No. 3 (March 1978) pp. 224-232

5. Why not the Dominican Republic? Jewish economic activities in the undeveloped countries of "Indo-America."

Required Reading:

Isaac Goldenberg, **The Fragmented Life of Don Jacobo Lerner** (New York: Pocket Books, 1978) [selections]. Also in Roberta Kalechofsky (ed.), **Echad: An Anthology of Latin American Jewish Writings** (Micah, 1980), pp. 175-192

Mark Wishnitzer, "The Historical Background of the Settlement of Jewish Refugees in Santo Domingo," **Jewish Social Studies** Vol. 4, No. 1 (January 1942), pp. 45-58

Richard Symanski and Nancy Barlay, "The Jewish Colony of Sosua," **Annals of the Association of American Geographers** Vol. 63 No. 3 (September 1973), pp. 366-378

6. Jewish life and institutions in the land of the Aztecs: the case of Mexican Jewry.

Required Reading:

Maurice Beck Hexter, **The Jews in Mexico** (New York: New York City Emergency Committee on Jewish Refugees, 1926). Reprinted in

Jewish Social Service Quarterly 2 (March-June 1926), pp. 188-196, 274-286

Corinne A. Krause, "Mexico, Another Promised Land?" **American Jewish Historical Quarterly** Vol. 61 No. 4 (June 1972), pp. 325-341

7. Euro-America: agricultural settlement versus urban economic activities of the Jews.

Required Reading:

Eugene F. Sofer, **From Pale to Pampa: A Social History of the Jews of Buenos Aires** (Holmes and Meier: New York: 1982), pp. 91-123

Judith Laikin Elkin, "Goodnight, Sweet Gaucho: A Revisionist View of the Jewish Agricultural Experiment in Argentina," **American Jewish Historical Quarterly** 67 (March 1978), pp. 208-223

Alberto Gerschunoff, **Jewish Gauchos of the Pampas** (New York: Abelard-Schuman, 1955). [Partly reproduced in Kalechofsky, **op. cit.**, pp. 30-35]

8. Argentina: a Jewish community in a land of immigrants.

Required Reading:

Haim Avni, "Argentine Jewry: Its Socio-Political Status and Organizational Patterns," **Dispersion and Unity** 12 (1971), pp. 128-162; **Dispersion and Unity** 13/14 (1971/72), pp. 161-208

9. Euro-America: the interrupted development of Brazilian Jewry.

Required Reading:

"Brazil," **Encyclopaedia Judaica** (Jerusalem, 1971)

Robert Levine, "Brazil's Jews during the Vargas Era and After," **Luso-Brazilian Review** 5 (Summer 1968), pp. 45-58

Alfred Hirschberg, "The Economic Adjustment of Jewish Refugees in Sao Paulo," **Jewish Social Studies** 7 (January 1945), pp. 31-40

10. Education and patterns of Jewish identity in Latin America

Required Reading:

Victor Perera, "Growing Up Jewish in Guatemala," **Present Tense** Vol. 1 No. 2 (Winter 1974), pp. 55-59. Reprinted in Kalechofsky, **op. cit.**, pp. 71-80

Jacob Levitz, "Jewish Education in Mexico: Background and Educational Patterns," **Jewish Education** Vol. 26 No. 3 (Spring 1956), pp. 35-41

Haim Avni, "Argentine Jewry ...," **Dispersion and Unity** 15 (1972/73), pp. 158-215

11. Latin America and the State of Israel from Lake Success until today.

Required Reading:

Joel Barromi and Carlos Feldman, "Latin American Voting on Israeli Issues in the UN General Assembly 1947-1968," **Jewish Social Studies** Vol. 36 No. 2 (April 1974), pp. 142-165

Yoram Shapira, "Israeli International Cooperation Program with Latin America: The Political Angle," **Inter-American Economic Affairs** Vol. 30 No. 2, pp. 3-31

Irving Louis Horowitz, "Jewish Ethnicism and Latin American Nationalism," **Midstream** Vol. 18 No. 9 (November 1972), pp. 22-28

12. Antisemitism in Latin America - imported, local and official (the Timerman case).

Required Reading:

Jerry W. Knudson, "Antisemitism in Latin America," **Patterns of Prejudice** Vol. 6 No. 5 (Sep/Oct 1972), pp. 1-10; and **ibid.** Vol. 6 No. 6 (Nov/Dec 1972), pp. 22-30

Haim Avni, "Anti-Semitism in Latin America after the Yom Kippur War - a New Departure?" in M. Davis (ed.), **World Jewry and the State of Israel** (New York: Arno, 1977), pp. 53-82

Jacobo Timerman, **Prisoner Without a Name, Cell Without a Number** (New York: Knopf, 1981) [25 pages of student's choice]

13. Facing the future in "Indo-America" and "Euro-America:" emigration and continuity.

Required Reading:

Fernando Penelosa, "Pre-Migration Background and Assimilation of Latin American Immigrants in Israel," **Jewish Social Studies** Vol. 34 No. 2 (April 1972), pp. 122-139

Seymour Liebman, "The Cuban Jewish Community in South Florida," **American Jewish Year Book** 70 (1969), pp. 238-246

Optional Suggested Reading:

Martin Sable, **Latin American Jewry: A Research Guide** (Cincinnati: Hebrew Union College, 1978)

Harry Sandberg, "The Jews of Latin America," **American Jewish Yearbook** 19 (1917-18), pp. 35-105

Uziel O. Schmelz. "Critical Assessment of Jewish Population Estimates for Argentina and Latin America," in U. Schmelz **et al** (eds.), **Studies in Jewish Demography: Survey for 1969-1971** (Jerusalem: Hebrew University, 1975), pp. 25-52

Seymour Liebman, **The Jews in New Spain: Faith, Flame and the Inquisitions** (Coral Gables: University of Miami, 1970)

Francis Merriman Stranger, "Church and State in Peru during the First Century of Independence," **Hispanic American Historical Review** Vol. 2 No. 4 (November 1927), pp. 418-437, Reprinted in Frederick Pike (ed.), **The Conflict Between Church and State in Latin America** (New York: Alfred A. Knopf, 1964), pp. 143-153

Isaac Emmanuel and Suzanne Emmanuel, **A History of the Jews of the Netherlands Antilles** 2 Vols. (Assen: Royal Van Gorcum / Cincinnati: American Jewish Archives, 1970), pp. 1-50

Bernard Ansel, "European Adventurer in Tierra del Fuego: Julio Popper", **Hispanic American Historical Review** 50 (February 1970), pp. 89-110

Morton Winsberg, **Colonia Baron Hirsch: A Jewish Agricultural Colony in Argentina** (University of Florida, 1964)

Morton Winsberg, "Jewish Agricultural Colonization in Entre Rios," **American Journal of Economics and Sociology** 26 (July 1968), pp. 289-95; 27 (October 1968), pp. 423-8; 28 (April 1969), pp. 179-91

Latin America and the Future of Its Jewish Communities: Proceedings of the Experts Conference, New York 3-4 June 1972 (London/ New York: Institute of Jewish Affairs, 1972)

Edy Kaufman, Yoram Shapira & Joel Barromi, **Israel - Latin American Relations** (New Brunswick, New Jersey: Transaction, 1974)

Requirements of the Course for Grading:

Students are expected to read the required material and to be ready to discuss it according to previously indicated guiding questions. They must also complete two papers of 10 to 15 pages each, based not only on the material covered during the class work, but also on some of the optional suggested readings.

IV. CONCEPTUAL FRAMEWORK OF THE COURSE

Introduction. 'Latin America' and its ethnic-regional components: a) immigration countries; b) autochthonous countries; similarities and differences of Jewish life and institutions; demographic size and structure of the various communities.

The illegitimate Jewish presence. A continent kept officially "Judenrein;" the Dutch-Brazilian episode and the role of the Dutch and British Caribbeans during the colonial period.

The legalization of Jewish existence. Emancipation of the Latin American nations and emancipation of the Jews; the common philosophical background; trends in favor of and against the legal Jewish presence.

"Indian" Jews, "Portuguese" Jews and Jews in "Indo-America." The legend of autochtonic Jewish presence; earliest Jewish settlers in the 19th century; the first meetings between Jewish history and Indo-American history.

Why not Santo Domingo? The Jewish agricultural colony in the Dominican Republic as a characteristic instance of the problem of the economic integration of Jewish immigrants in undeveloped national economies.

The case of Mexican Jewry. The development of a large community in an "Indo-American" country; the impact of the proximity of the United States on the particular orientation of Mexican Jews; similarities and differences between Mexican Jewry and the communities in the southern cone of Latin America.

"Euro-America:" agricultural settlement vs. urban economic activity. The realities of rural economies in Argentina as compared with those of the Dominican Republic; Jews as farmers – an outline of the history of Baron de Hirsch's project; Jewish urban occupations and the problem of socio-economic mobility in the colonies and in the towns.

Argentina: a Jewish community in a land of immigrants. The phenomenon of geographic and economic concentration of non-Jewish and Jewish immigrants in Argentina; the problem of ethnic, cultural and religious pluralism; characteristics of Jewish institutional life: in accord with or contrary to the general trends of Argentinian society?

Euro-America: the interrupted development of Brazilian Jewry. Similarities and differences between Brazil and Argentina: rural settlement, urban occupations, cultural life; the decisive period of the 1930s – the anti-Jewish policies of the Vargas regime; demographic and cultural consequences.

Education and patterns of Jewish identity in Latin America. The needs of Jewish affirmation in Indo-America as compared with Euro-America; organized Jewish responses in both regions – the Jewish school systems in Mexico and in Argentina.

Latin America and the State of Israel. The legitimacy of adherence to Zionism in Latin America; Latin American voting in United Nations resolutions on Israel; the impact of relations between Latin America and the State of Israel upon the Jewish communities.

Antisemitism in Latin America. Legends and realities regarding hostility towards the Jews; cultural and ideological foundations of antisemitism in Argentina; the perils of Governmental antisemitism; the military regime in Argentina (1976-1984) and the Jews.

Facing the future. The case of Cuba: liquidation of a Jewish community as a result of basic structural changes in the host society; emigration to Israel and to other countries; political instability and its impact on the middle classes and on the Jewish communities; communal efforts to assure development and continuity.

I. THE COURSE

THE FINAL SOLUTION: PERSPECTIVES ON THE HOLOCAUST

Michael Brown

York University, Toronto; Division of Humanities (an interdisciplinary department housing historians, philosophers, and literary and religion specialists) and the Program in Religious Studies

Three meeting-hours a week for 24-26 weeks, including occasional lectures but mostly in the form of seminar-discussions; totalling 72-78 hours

II. ACADEMIC CONTEXT OF THE COURSE

York is a large (25,000 students) provincial university with a diverse student population. This course is offered in the Faculty of Arts and attracts mostly full-time students. As a third-year course it has a maximum size of 30 students. It generally closes registration at that number.

Students taking the course are often taking an elective to satisfy an interest or a distribution requirement, rather than fulfilling a requirement for the major. Others are Religious Studies or Humanities majors for whom this course does fulfill a major requirement. Any student in the course may--or may not--have taken other courses in modern Jewish history. The course, in other words, is designed for students with a variety of methodological backgrounds, who have not taken any related courses, although it is assumed that all students have some elementary acquaintance with the subject matter of the course. Most of the students, although not all, are Jewish. As a third-year course it may not be taken by first-year students.

III. OUTLINE OF THE COURSE

  A. The Setting

    1. Introduction: Europe, the Seedbed of the Holocaust
        Required Reading: "Emancipation" and "Europe" in the
        Encylopedia Judaica.

        Yehuda Bauer, A History of the Holocaust, (New York:
        1982), pp. 3-36.

        Suggested Reading: James Parkes, Antisemitism (Chicago:
        1969).

        Leon Poliakov, The History of Antisemitism (New York:
        1975).

        Jacob Talmon, "European History as the Seedbed of the
        Holocaust," in Holocaust and Rebirth: A Symposium on the
        Holocaust (Jerusalem: 1974), pp. 11-76.

    2. Jews as Outsiders

        Required Reading: Michael Marrus, "The Theory and Practice
        of Antisemitism," Commentary (August 1982), pp. 38-42.

        Bauer, pp. 39-48.

        Suggested Reading: Shmuel Ettinger, "Jew Hatred in Its
        Historical Context," Immanuel (Fall 1980), pp. 81-94.

        Jacob Katz, From Prejudice to Destruction: Anti-Semitism,
        1700-1933 (Cambridge: 1980).

    3. Jews in Germany

        Required Reading: Peter Gay, "German Jews in Wilhelmian
        Culture," in Freud, Jews and Other Germans (New York:
        1978), pp. 93-168 or in Midstream (February 1975), pp.
        23-65.

        Gershom Scholem, "Jews and Germans," in On Jews and Judaism
        in Crisis (New York: 1978), pp. 71-92.

        Suggested Reading: George Mosse, The Crisis of German
        Ideology (New York: 1964).

4. Jews in Germany (continued)

   Required Reading: Fred Uhlmann, **Reunion.**

   Suggested Reading: George Mosse, **Germans and Jews** (London: 1971).

   Sanford Ragins, **Jewish Responses to German Anti-Semitism, 1870-1914** (Cincinnati: 1980).

   Jehuda Reinharz, **Fatherland or Promised Land?** (Ann Arbor, Mich.: 1975).

5. Jews in Interwar Eastern Europe

   Required Reading: Bauer, pp. 48-64.

   Isaac Bashevis Singer, **The Family Moskat** (New York: 1950).

   Suggested Reading: Celia Heller, **On the Edge of Destruction** (New York: 1977).

   Robert Wistrich, **Revolutionary Jews from Marx to Trotsky** (London: 1976).

6. Jews in Europe on the Eve of Destruction

   Required Reading: Bauer, pp. 53-65.

   Aharon Appelfeld, **Badenheim, 1939** (New York: 1980).

   Suggested Reading: Norman Cohn, **Warrant for Genocide** (New York: 1981).

7. Jews and the Churches

   Required Reading: André Schwarz-Bart, **The Last of the Just** (New York: 1973).

   Suggested Reading: Seymour Cain, "The Holocaust and Christian Responsibility," **Midstream** (April 1982), pp. 20-27.

   Rosemary Radford Reuther, "Anti-Semitism and Christian Theology," in **Auschwitz: Beginning of a New Era,** Eva Fleischner (ed.), (New York: 1977), pp. 79-92.

Uriel Tal, **Christians and Jews in Germany** (Ithaca: 1975).

B.   The Event

8.   Hitler, the Man and the Leader

Required Reading: Bauer, pp. 79-138.

Film: "The Triumph of the Will."

Suggested Reading: Alan Bullock, **Hitler: A Study in Tyranny** (New York: 1962).

John Toland, **Adolf Hitler** (New York: 1979).

9.   The Nazi Seizure of Power

Required Reading: William S. Allen, **The Nazi Seizure of Power** (Chicago: 1965).

Bauer, pp. 73-79.

Suggested Reading: Wendelgard van Staden, **Darkness Over the Valley** (New Haven, Conn.: 1981), pp. 1-50.

10.   The Banality of Evil

Required Reading: Hannah Arendt, **Eichmann in Jerusalem** (London: 1964), pp. 1-34.

Kazimierz Moczanski, "Conversations with a Hangman," **Midstream** (November 1980), pp. 31-41.

Suggested Reading: Albert Speer, **Spandau: The Secret Diaries** (London: 1976).

11.   Responses of the Outside World

Required Reading: Irving Abella and Harold Troper, "'The Line Must be Drawn Somewhere': Canada and the Jewish Refugees, 1933-39," **Canadian Historical Review** (June 1979), or in **The Canadian Jewish Mosaic**, M. Weinfeld, W. Shaffir, and I. Cotler (eds.), (Toronto: 1981), pp. 49-78.

Suggested Reading: Yehuda Bauer, **American Jewry and the Holocaust** (Detroit: 1981).

Henry L. Feingold, **The Politics of Rescue** (New Brunswick, N.J.: 1981).

David Wyman, **Paper Walls** (Amherst, Mass.: 1968).

Irving Abella and Harold Troper, **None is Too Many** (Toronto: 1982).

Henry Kreisel, **The Rich Man** (Toronto: 1961).

12. Under Fire

Required Reading: Robert Weltsch, "The Yellow Badge, Wear It With Pride," [editorial] **Juedische Rundschau** (4 April 1933), reprinted in Ludwig Lewisohn, **Rebirth** (New York, 1935), pp. 336-341, and P. Mendes-Flohr and J. Reinharz (eds.), **The Jew in the Modern World** (New York/Oxford: 1980), pp. 488-489.

Moshe Flinker, **Young Moshe's Diary** (Jerusalem: 1976).

Suggested Reading: Jacob Presser, **The Destruction of Dutch Jewry** (New York: 1969).

Anne Frank, **The Diary of a Young Girl** (New York: 1953).

Leonard Baker, **Days of Sorrow and Pain** (New York: 1978).

13. In the Ghetto

Required Reading: Emanuel Ringelblum, **Notes from the Warsaw Ghetto** (New York: 1975).

Bauer, pp. 139-192.

Suggested Reading: John Hersey, **The Wall** (London: 1950).

Janusz Korczak, **Ghetto Diary** (New York: 1978).

Isaiah Trunk, **Judenrat: The Jewish Councils in Eastern Europe Under Nazi Occupation** (New York: 1977).

14. In Rebellion

Required Reading: Bauer, pp. 245-278.

Ringelblum, selections.

Yehuda Bauer, "Jewish Resistance During the Holocaust," in **The Jewish Emergence from Powerlessness** (Toronto: 1979), pp. 26-40.

Suggested Reading: Philip Friedman, **Martyrs and Fighters** (New York: 1954).

15. Responses of Non-Jews

Required Reading: Bauer, pp. 279-302.

Film: "The Sorrow and the Pity."

Suggested Reading: Michael Marrus and Robert O. Paxton, **Vichy France and the Jews** (New York: 1981).

Saul Friedlander, **Pius XII and the Third Reich** (London: 1966).

Philip P. Haillie, **Lest Innocent Blood Be Shed** (New York: 1979).

Rolf Hochhuth, **The Deputy** (New York: 1964).

Wendelgard von Staden, **Darkness Over the Valley** (New Haven: 1981), pp. 51-163.

Bernard Wasserstein, **Britain and the Jews of Europe, 1939-1945** (London: 1979).

C. The Camps

16. Life Within

Required Reading: Viktor Frankl, **Man's Search for Meaning** Part I (Boston: 1970).

Bruno Bettelheim, **The Informed Heart**, (Glencoe, Ill.: 1960), chs. 4-7.

Primo Levi, **Survival in Auschwitz** (London: 1961).

Suggested Reading: Terrence Des Pres, **The Survivor** (New York: 1976).

D. The Aftermath

  17. Christian Responses

  Required Reading: Gregory Baum, "Rethinking the Church's Mission," in Fleischner **op. cit.,** pp. 113-128.

  Norman Ravitch, "The Problem of Christian Anti-Semitism," **Commentary** (April 1982), pp. 41-52.

  Suggested Reading: Franklin Littell, **The Crucifixion of the Jews** (New York: 1975).

  18. God is Dead

  Required Reading: Adele Wiseman, **The Sacrifice** (New York: 1956).

  Suggested Reading: Richard Rubenstein, **After Auschwitz** (Indianapolis: 1976).

  19. Faith After the Holocaust

  Required Reading: Leo Baeck, "This People Israel," and

  Hans Jonas, "The Concept of God After Auschwitz," both in **Out of the Whirlwind,** Albert Friedlander (ed.), (New York: 1976), pp. 522-533, 462-476.

  Michael Wyschograd, "Some Reflections on the Holocaust," in **Living After the Holocaust,** Lucy Y. Steinitz (ed.), with David M. Szonyi (New York: 1979), pp. 65-68.

  Bauer, pp. 332-334.

  Suggested Reading: Eliezer Berkovits, **Faith After the Holocaust** (New York: 1973).

  20. The Memory

  Required Reading: Bernard Malamud, "The Lady of the Lake," in his **The Magic Barrel** (New York: 1971).

  Film: "Memorandum."

  Suggested Reading: Emil Fackenheim, **God's Presence in History** (New York: 1970).

21. The Survivor

Required Reading: Kalman Schulman, "Pan Janusz Kozicki."

Allen Gerson, "The World Gathering of Jewish Holocaust Survivors," **Midstream** (April 1982), pp. 28-31.

Dorothy Rabinowitz, **New Lives,** selections (New York: 1977).

Suggested Reading: Helen Epstein, **Children of the Holocaust** (New York: 1979).

Saul Friedlander, **When Memory Comes** (New York: 1979).

Edward Lewis Wallant, **The Pawnbroker** (New York: 1961).

22. Historical "Revisionism"

Required Reading: Arendt, pp. 135-256.

Bauer, pp. 303-330.

Suggested Reading: Yehuda Bauer, **American Jewry and the Holocaust** (Detroit: 1981).

23. Israel as Response

Required Reading: A.M. Klein, **The Second Scroll** (New York: 1952).

Bauer, pp. 337-350.

Suggested Reading: Gershon Mamlak, "A Speech That Wasn't Made," **Midstream** (April 1982), pp. 32-35.

Yehuda Bauer, "Zionism, the Holocaust and the Road to Israel," in **The Jewish Emergence from Powerlessness** (Toronto: 1979), pp. 41-78.

24. The New Anti-Semitism

Required Reading: Shlomo Avineri, "Aspects of Post-Holocaust Anti-Jewish Attitudes," and

Emil Fackenheim, "Post-Holocaust Anti-Jewishness," both in **World Jewry and the State of Israel**, Moshe Davis (ed.), pp. 3-10, 33-52.

David G. Dalin, "Jews, Nazis, and Civil Liberties," **American Jewish Yearbook** (1980), pp. 3-28.

Jack Nusan Porter, "Neo-Nazism, Neo-Fascism, and Terrorism: A Global Trend?" **Judaism** (Summer 1982), pp. 311-321.

Earl Raab, "The Insensitives - 'Neutral' on Anti-Semitism," **Midstream** (August-September 1978), pp. 59-63.

Suggested Reading: Arnold Forster and Benjamin R. Epstein, **The New Anti-Semitism** (New York: 1974).

Judith Plaskow, "Blaming Jews for Inventing Patriarchy," **Lillith** (Fall 1980), pp. 11-13.

25. Distortions and Misuses of the Holocaust

Required Reading: Edward Alexander, "Stealing the Holocaust," **Midstream** (November 1980), pp. 46-51

Robert Alter, "Deformations of the Holocaust," **Commentary** (February 1981), pp. 48-54.

Suggested Reading: William Styron, **Sophie's Choice** (New York: 1980).

George Steiner, **The Portage to San Cristobal of A.H.** (New York: 1981).

Jacob Neusner, "Wanted a New Myth," **Moment Magazine** (February 1976), pp. 34-35, 61, also in **Stranger at Home**, pp. 82-91 (Chicago: 1981).

26. Conclusion

<u>Requirements of the Course for Grading</u>:
1)   One book review (15% of grade), 5-8 pages in length.
2)   One longer research paper (30% of grade), 15-20 pages in length.
3)   A final examination (25% of grade).
4)   The remainder of the grade (30%) is based on class presentations
     and participation in class discussions.

IV.   CONCEPTUAL FRAMEWORK OF THE COURSE
Weeks 1-7:

     Placing the Holocaust in its European (especially, its German, but
also its East European), Christian and Jewish historical settings.
Introduction to two methodologies (historical and literary) used in the
course and to their complementary function.   Students are expected to
read both a history text and interpretative essays.

Weeks 8-15:

     An examination of the historical record regarding the behavior of
Jews and Germans during the Holocaust and the reactions of people
outside Nazi Europe to it, in an attempt to give an understanding of
the conditions of life in Nazi Europe and of the world-political
context of the Holocaust.

     Most of the readings are historical, but the study of primary
texts, both written and cinematic, is also introduced.

Weeks 12-16 (overlapping with the previous section):

     A consideration of the religious and psychological responses of
Jews and Gentiles in Europe during the Holocaust.

Weeks 17-21, 23-24:

The implications of the Holocaust for Judaism and Christianity and, in general, for the descendants of the perpetrators, the victims and the bystanders. A survey of the responses to the Holocaust, both religious and secular, and of the recrudescence of anti-Semitism.

Much of the reading in this section is theological. Literary texts are used to illustrate and elucidate theology.

Weeks 22, 25:

A consideration of the problematics involved in studying and discussing the Holocaust; indeed, of relating to it altogether.

Throughout, a goal of the course is to make evident the notion that the Holocaust poses different questions for different disciplines and, as a result, is better understood when different disciplines are used in its study. For their required book reports students are urged to choose one of the suggested readings. For their research paper, they are urged to work in a discipline in which they feel at home. The final examination demands a synthesis of the various subjects discussed, and methodologies employed, in the course.

I. THE COURSE

THE SOCIOLOGY OF AMERICAN MODERN ORTHODOX JEWRY

Samuel Heilman

Queens College, City University of New York; Department of Sociology

One semester for 3 hours per week, totalling 45 hours

Students are required to have completed at least one introductory course in sociology before taking this course

II. ACADEMIC CONTEXT OF THE COURSE

This course is an undergraduate elective in sociology; it is also offered as part of the interdisciplinary Jewish studies program. In most cases, the students who select this course come from the register of sociology, but occasionally those whose origins are in Jewish studies find their way to the course.

The course aims to provide some of the historical context in which contemporary Orthodoxy emerged; and focuses upon its place in the development of modern, post-emancipation and enlightenment Jewry. In sociological terms it outlines the demands of tradition versus those of modern secular society--the two contexts within which contemporary American Orthodoxy finds itself. Emphasis is upon ideological and behavioral elements of modern Orthodoxy, with particular attention to the ways that Orthodox Jews have found for handling the dual, often competing, demands of their Orthodoxy and contemporaneity.

III. OUTLINE OF THE COURSE

1. Background: The Character of American Jewry

Required Reading:

Nathan Glazer, **American Judaism**

David Sidorsky (ed.), **The Future of the Jewish Community in America**

Samuel Heilman, "The Sociology of American Jewry: The Last Ten Years," **Annual Review of Sociology** Vol. 5 No. 8, pp. 55-160

[Heilman plus either Glazer or Sidorsky]

2. Tradition, Modernity and Society

Required Reading:

Edward Shils, **Center and Periphery**, pp. 5-17

Alex Inkeles, **Becoming Modern**, ch. 1

3. Jewish Emancipation, Enlightenment and its Aftermath

Required Reading:

N. Rotenstreich, "Emancipation and its Aftermath," in Sidorsky (ed.), **The Future of the Jewish Community in America**

H. Kallen, "The Bearing of Emancipation on Jewish Survival," **Yivo Annual** 12 (1958), pp. 9-45

T. Veblen, "The Intellectual Pre-Eminence of Jews in Modern Europe," in his **Essays in Our Changing Order** (Viking, 1934), pp. 219-231

H. Greenberg, "Golus Jew," in Howe and Greenberg, **Voices from the Yiddish** (Schocken), pp. 270-276

4. The Situation of American Jewry: Acculturation vs. Marginality

Required Reading:

J. Teller, **Strangers and Natives**

E. K. Stonequist, "The Marginal Character of Jews", in Graeber and Britt (eds.), **Jews in a Gentile World** (Macmillan, 1942), pp. 296-310

Milton Goldberg, "A Qualification of Marginal Man Theory," **American Sociological Review** Vol. 6 No. 1, pp. 52-58

5. American Orthodoxy

Required Reading:

David Singer, "Voices of Orthodoxy," **Commentary** 58 (July 1974) pp. 54-60

C. Liebman, "A Sociological Analysis of Contemporary Orthodoxy," **Judaism** (Summer 1964), pp. 285-304

S. Heilman, "Inner and Outer Identity: Sociological Ambivalence Among Orthodox Jews," **Jewish Social Studies** Vol. 39 No. 3 (Summer 1977), pp. 227-240

S. Heilman, "Constructing Orthodoxy," **Society** Vol. 15 No. 4 (May 1978), pp. 32-40 or **In Gods We Trust**

S. Heilman, **Synagogue Life**

S. Heilman, "Prayer in the Orthodox Synagogue," **Contemporary Jewry** 6 (Spring 1982), pp.2-17

[and one of the following]

S. Poll, **The Hassidic Community of Williamsburg**

I. Rubin, **Satmar: Island in the City**

Additional Reading (optional):

M. Auerbach (1943), "Survey of Jewish History" in L. Jung (ed.), **The Jewish Library: 1st Series** (New York: Bloch), pp. 255-326

S. Berman (1972), "The Jewish Day School: A Symposium," **Tradition** Vol. 13 No. 1, pp. 96-99

J. T. Borhek and R. Curtis (1975), A **Sociology of Belief** (New York: John Wiley)

D. Eliach (1972), "The Jewish Day School: A Symposium," **Tradition** Vol. 13 No. 1, pp. 99-105

E. Erikson (1958), **Childhood and Society** (New York: Norton)

J. Fichter (1951), **Southern Parish** (Chicago: University of Chicago Press)

A. Fisher (1973), "The Outsider and Orthodox Judaism," **Tradition** Vol. 13 No. 3, pp. 48-66

S. Freud (1960/1919), "The Uncanny," **Collected Papers** 4 (New York: Basic Books), pp. 368-407

H. Gans (1953), "The 'Yinglish' Music of Mickey Katz," **American Quarterly** 5, pp. 213-218

C. Geertz (1973), **The Interpretation of Cultures** (New York: Basic Books)

E. Goffman (1961), **Encounters** (Englewood Cliffs, N.J.: Prentice-Hall)

E. Goffman (1963), **Behavior in Public Places** (New York: Free Press)

E. Goffman (1974), **Relations in Public** (Cambridge: Harvard University Press)

R. Gordis (1955), **Judaism for the Modern Age** (New York: Farrar, Straus and Cudahy)

Samuel Heilman (1976), **Synagogue Life: A Study in Symbolic Interaction** (Chicago: University of Chicago Press)

M. Himmelfarb (1968), "Secular Society? A Jewish Perspective," in W. McLoughlin and R. Bellah (eds.), **Religion in America** (New York: Houghton-Mifflin), pp. 282-298

S. R. Hirsch (1959), **Judaism Eternal** 2, I Grunfeld (ed.), (London: Soncino Press)

J. Hochbaum (1974), "American Orthodoxy," **Tradition** Vol. 14 No. 3, pp. 5-14

I. Jakobovits (1974), "Letter", **Commentary** Vol. 58 No. 5, p. 22

L. Jung (1930), "What is Orthodox Judaism?," **The Jewish Library: 2nd Series** (New York: Bloch)

C. Liebman (1973), **The Ambivalent American Jew** (Philadelphia: Jewish Publication Society), pp. 113-132

E. Mayer (1973), "Jewish Orthodoxy in America: Towards the Sociology of a Residual Category," **Jewish Journal of Sociology** Vol. 15 No. 2, pp. 151-165

W. McLoughlin (1968), "How is America Religious?" in W. McLoughlin and R. Bellah (eds.), **Religion in America** (New York: Houghton-Mifflin), pp. ix-xxiv

G. H. Mead (1934), **Mind, Self and Society** (Chicago: University of Chicago Press)

R. K. Merton and E. Barber (1963), "Sociological Ambivalence" in E. A. Tiryakian (ed.), **Sociological Theory, Values, and Sociocultural Change: Essays in Honor of Pitirim Sorokin** (New York: Free Press)

M. Novak (1973), "How American Are You If Your Grandparents Came From Serbia in 1888?" in S. TeSelle (ed.), **The Rediscovery of Ethnicity** (New York: Harper)

J. Ortega y Gasset (1961), **The Modern Theme** trans. J. Cleugh, (New York: Harper and Row)

S. Polgar (1960), "Acculturation of Mesquakie Teenage Boys," **American Anthropologist** 62, pp. 217-235

Philip Rieff (1970), "The Impossible Culture: Wilde as a Modern Prophet," in O. Wilde, **The Soul of Man Under Socialism**, pp. vii-xxxiv

Philip Rieff (1973), **Fellow Teachers** (New York: Harper & Row)

N. Rotenstreich (1973), "Emancipation and Its Aftermath," in D. Sidorsky (ed.), **The Future of the Jewish Community in America** (New York: Basic Books)

I. Rubin (1972), **Satmar: An Island in the City** (Chicago: Quadrangle)

G. Ryle (1949), **The Concept of Mind** (New York: Hutchinson)

R. H. Turner (1976), "The Real Self: From Institution to Impulse," **American Journal of Sociology** Vol. 81 No. 5, pp. 989–1016

L. Wirth (1928), **The Ghetto** (Chicago: University of Chicago Press)

Requirements of the Course for Grading:

Students are required to do the reading, and to take a midterm examination. Depending on the results of this examination, students either take a final examination or submit a paper.

IV.   CONCEPTUAL FRAMEWORK OF THE COURSE

The character of American Jewry. Giving students a sense of the major trends in American Jewish life, the assimilationist, accommodationist and contra-acculturative options are discussed.

Tradition, modernity and society. Definitions of the demands of tradition and those of contemporary society are presented and analyzed so that the modern Orthodox models will be placed in a larger context of adaptations of tradition to modernity and vice versa. The aim here is to see modern Orthodoxy in sociological terms as but one of many attempts at living simultaneously in both the past and the present, the particular and the universal, the cosmopolitan and the parochial.

Jewish emancipation, enlightenment and its aftermath. The historical context and background for the emergence of modern Orthodoxy, in particular, and American Jewry, in general, is reviewed. Here emphasis is on showing that contemporary Orthodoxy, even in its most traditionalist incarnation, is in fact a part of the modern world.

American Jewry: acculturation vs. marginality. The meaning and effects of acculturation and assimilation are discussed. The options of marginality are explored. The implications and possibilities of creating a marginal culture as a possible model for modern Orthodoxy are analyzed. The aim here is to evaluate the possibilities of maintaining the dualism of a modern Orthodoxy.

American Orthodoxy. A sociological map and "menu" of American Orthodoxy is provided here. These readings serve as a background against which empirical materials, gathered in an as yet unpublished survey of American Orthodoxy by Heilman and Cohen, are discussed and evaluated. The complexion and character of contemporary Orthodoxy is fleshed out by looking at behavior (a **mitzva** scale), belief (an **emuna** scale), communal affiliation (a **kehilla** scale) and social location and attitudes (a **chevra** scale).

I. THE COURSE

AMERICAN JEWRY: THE COMMUNITY

Paula Hyman

Jewish Theological Seminary; Department of History

One Semester (14 weeks) - 2 hours per week, totalling 28 hours

Knowledge assumed: Course in Medieval Jewish Communities and some
  background in Judaica

II. ACADEMIC CONTEXT OF THE COURSE:

This course is offered on the M.A. level as a required course for
students in a joint M.A. in Judaica-Master of Social Work program.
Undergraduates and regular M.S. students also may elect the course.
Because the Jewish Theological Seminary specializes in Judaica and
demands of its students course work in all areas of Jewish studies,
students have at least a basic knowledge of Jewish concepts and
historical development, although their familiarity with general history
may be limited.

This course focuses on American Jewry in the contemporary period
alone, as several other courses in American Jewish history are
available to JTS students. Moreover, the course emphasizes the
institutional context of American Jewry, since its primary students are
preparing themselves for communal service. Within that framework an
attempt is made to introduce students to a broad range of social and
intellectual developments within American Jewry as well as to a variety
of approaches for analyzing the community.

III. OUTLINE OF THE COURSE

   A. The Organizational Structure of American Jewry

      1. Historical introduction

          Suggested Reading: Lucy Dawidowicz, **On Equal Terms** (New York, 1982)

        * Aryeh Goren, **The American Jews** (Cambridge, Mass., 1982)

        * Henry Feingold, **Zion in America** (New York, 1974)

        * Ben Halpern, "America is Different," in Marshall Sklare (ed.) **American Jews: A Reader** (New York, 1983).

      2. A Map of the Community

        * Daniel Elazar, **Community and Polity** (Philadelphia, 1976), chs. 5, 6, 7, 9, 10

      3. The Leadership of American Jewry

        * Elazar, ch. 8

          Arthur Hertzberg, "The Changing American Rabbinate," **Midstream**, Jan. 1966.

          Jonathan Woocher, "The Civil Religion of Communal Leaders," **American Jewish Yearbook**, 1981.

          Suggested Reading: Charles Liebman, "Leadership and Decision-making in a Jewish Federation," **American Jewish Yearbook**, 1979.

      4. The Synagogue as Communal Institution

        * Samuel Heilman, **Synagogue Life** (Chicago, 1976)

        * Marshall Sklare, "The Sociology of the American Synagogue," in Jacob Neusner (ed.), **Understanding American Judaism**, Vol. 1 (New York, 1975), pp. 91-102.

          Conservative Judaism, Symposium on the Relationship between the Synagogue and the Center, Winter-Spring, 1962

          Additional reading on **Havurot**

* Available in paperback.

B. The Social Characteristics of American Jewry

    5. Demography and Identity

        Sidney Goldstein, "Jews in the U.S.: Perspectives from
        Demography," **American Jewish Yearbook**, 1981

     * Steven M. Cohen, **American Modernity and Jewish Identity**
       (New York, 1983), chs. 3, 4, 5

     * Chaim I. Waxman, **America's Jews in Transition**
       (Philadelphia, 1983), ch. 6

        Arnold Eisen, **The Chosen People in America** (Bloomington,
        Indiana, 1983), chs. 6, 7, 8

        Suggested Reading: Marshall Sklare and Joseph Greenblum,
        Jewish Identity on the Suburban Frontier, 2nd Edition
        (Chicago, 1979)

    6. Images of Jews in American Culture

        Charles Stember, **Jews in the Mind of America** (New York,
        1966), pp. 48-75.

        Xerox Material - recent survey of opinion polls regarding Jews.

C. The Religion of American Jews

    7. Reform and Reconstruction

     * Leonard Fein et al., "Reform is a Verb," in **American Jews**,
       pp. 275-300.

     * Eugene Borowitz, **Reform Judaism Today**, Vol. 1 (New York,
       1977), pp. XIX-XXv, 49-90.

        Charles Liebman, "Reconstructionism in American Jewish Life,"
        American Jewish Yearbook, 1970.

     * Suggested Reading: Mordecai Kaplan, **Judaism as a Civiliza-
       tion**, 3rd Editoin (Philadelphia, 1981)

        Michael Meyer, "Reform Judaism," in Bernard Martin (ed.),
        Movements and Issues in American Judaism (Westport,
        Conn., 1978)

8. Conservative Judaism

   * Marshall Sklare, **Conservative Judaism**, 2nd Edition (New York, 1972)

     Xerox handout of High Holiday message at Jewish Theological Seminary

   * Suggested Reading: **Understanding American Judaism**, Vol. II, chs. 25-27

9. Varieties of Orthodoxy

   Charles Liebman, "Orthodoxy in American Jewish Life," **American Jewish Yearbook**, 1965

   Egon Mayer, **From Suburb to Shtetl: The Jews of Boro Park** (Philadelphia, 1979)

   * Suggested Reading: **Understanding American Judaism**, Vol. II, chs. 19-22

   Egon Mayer and Chaim Waxman, "Modern Jewish Orthodoxy in America: Toward the Year 2000," **Tradition**, XVI (1977), pp. 98-112.

D. Contemporary Issues of Communal Concern

   10. Anti-Semitism and Defense Efforts

      Harold Quinley and Charles Glock, **Anti-Semitism in America** (New York, 1979), pp. 1-72, 158-183

      * Deborah Dash Moore, **B'nai B'rith and the Challenge of Ethnic Leadership** (Albany, 1981), ch. 5

      Naomi Cohen, **Not Free to Desist** (Philadelphia, 1972), ch. 13

   11. American Jewish Politics and Intercommunal Relations

      * Lucy Dawidowicz and Leon Goldstein, "The American Jewish Liberal Tradition," in Marshall Sklare (ed.), **The Jewish Community in America** (New York, 1974), pp. 285-300

* Seymour Martin Lipset, "Intergroup Relations/The Changing Situation of American Jewry," in Sklare, **Community**, pp. 312-338

* Cohen, ch. 7

   Charles Liebman, **The Ambivalent American Jew** (Philadelphia, 1973), chs. 2, 7

   Suggested Reading: Stephen Isaacs, **Jews and American Politics** (Garden City, N.Y., 1974)

   Arthur Liebman, **Jews and the Left** (New York, 1979)

   "Liberalism and the Jews: A Symposium," **Commentary**, Vol. 69, No. 1 (January, 1980)

12. The Contemporary Jewish Family

   Marshall Sklare, **America's Jews** (New York, 1971), ch. 3

* Cohen, ch. 6

* Waxman, ch. 7

   Egon Mayer, "Intermarriage and the Jewish Future," **American Jewish Committee** (New York, 1979)

13. The Impact of Feminism

   Anne Lapidus Lerner, "Who Hast Not Made Me a Man: The Movement for Equal Rights for Women in American Jewry," **American Jewish Yearbook**, 1977

* Susanah Heschel (ed.), **On Being a Jewish Feminist** (New York, 1983), pp. XIII-XXXVI, 152-166, 210-213, 223-233

* Waxman, pp. 215-221

* Suggested Reading: Blu Greenberg, On **Women and Judaism** (Philadelphia, 1982)

* Elizabeth Koltun (ed.), **The Jewish** Woman (New York, 1976)

14. American Jewry and Israel: Concord or Conflict

Liebman, ch. 4

* Cohen, ch. 8

Mervin Verbit, "Jewish Identity in the Israel-Diaspora Dialogue," **Forum** 48 (Spring 1983), pp. 63-74

Louis J. Walinsky (ed.), **The Implications of Israel-Arab Peace for World Jewry** (New York: World Jewish Congress, 1981)

Requirements of the Course for Grading:

1)   Students are expected to come to class prepared to discuss the reading assignment

2)   Final examination

3)   a 10-15 page paper, analyzing an aspect of Jewish organizational life or an issue of communal policy

IV.   CONCEPTUAL FRAMEWORK OF THE COURSE

Introduction: survey of historical development of American Jewry. Consideration of whether and how America is different.   American Jewish community as a post-emancipation, voluntary community. Ethnicity and religion in American life (with special reference to Will Herberg, **Protestant, Catholic, Jew**).

A Map of the Community: definitions of community.   The Institutional structure of American Jewry. How do individuals "fit" in the community?   Model of concentric circles.   Comparison of the "budget" of an American Jewish community with the budget of a 17th-century Polish **Kehilla.**

The leadership of American Jewry. Who are leaders of American Jewry?   What are their sources of authority, their social and ideological characteristics? As a pedagogic tool, draw up and discuss two lists of American Jewish leaders, one contemporary, the other from the pre-World War II period. With reference to John Higham's **Ethnic Leadership in America**, compare Jewish leadership with that of other American ethnic groups.

The synagogue as communal institution.   Its relationship to other communal institutions.   How the synagogue functions as a community.   The rise of **havurot.**   Refer back to Elazar's definition of community to test its adequacy and analyze its presuppositions.

Demography and identity: trends in Jewish patterns of identity and identification.   Introduce generational analysis.   Models of assimilation and their cogency.   Survey socio-economic structure of American Jewry and its social and geographic mobility.   Effect of mobility upon communal organizations and upon individual behavior. Adaptation of traditional Jewish concepts of self to the American milieu.

Images of Jews in American culture.   Use material from Museum of American Jewish Broadcasting.   How Americans perceive Jews. Evolution of images of Jews in American media. Relation between images and demographic data presented earlier.

Reform and Reconstructionism. Reform as first American version of Judaism. Evolution of Reform and Reconstructionist institutions and ideology. Discussion of elite and folk religion.

Conservative Judaism. Conservative Judaism as second-generation from of acculturation to American scene. Analysis of Sklare's model of relationship of social and residential mobility and religious acculturation. Institutional developments – JTS, the synagogue center, USY, Camp Ramah. Analysis of Conservative ideology of tradition and change.

Varieties of Orthodoxy. Ideological and institutional developments within Orthodoxy. What, in the American society, allows for greater religious/ethnic assertiveness. How an Orthodox community functions within the American environment.

Anti-Semitism and defense efforts. Analysis of nature and causes of anti-Semitism in America. Assessment of different theories of anti-Semitism (social and psychological). Significance of anti-Semitism in America, in comparison with Europe. Types of defense efforts, with reference to the American Jewish Committee and the Jewish Defense League. Role of defense in Jewish communal life.

American Jewish politics and intercommunal relations. Place of Jews within pluralist, liberal American democracy. Discussion of three Jewish political traditions and their legacies: medieval conservatism, modern liberalism and radicalism. Nature of Jewish political participation – as voters, contributors, professionals. How Jews define political interests.

The contemporary Jewish family. Why the family has become an issue of communal concern. Analysis of demographic data – late marriage, low fertility, significant level of intermarriage. Impact of changing family patterns on Jewish affiliation and identification.

The impact of feminism. Analysis of Jewish feminism and its impact upon religious and secular communal institutions; expanded roles for women in synagogue, in leadership; decline of volunteerism.

American Jewry and Israel: concord or conflict? Role of Israel in American Jewish identity and in political behavior of American Jewry. Nature of institutional relations between Israel and American Jewish community. Source of tension in relationship: political dissent, accountability of funds, Soviet Jewry. Alternative models of contemporary Jewish life: Israel as the center, or a multi-center model.

This course is essentially a sociology of contemporary Jewry with a particular communal focus. Since the teacher is a historian by training, historical comparisons are brought to each session. Frequent reference is made to European historical experience and the the nature of the pre-modern **kehilla** to illustrate elements of both change and continuity.

I. THE COURSE

RELIGION AND THE HOLOCAUST

Benny Kraut

University of Cincinnati; Judaic Studies Program

One Quarter (10 weeks), totalling 30 hours

Prerequisites: 1 course on the history of the Holocaust and/or 1 course in philosophy is preferred, but not required; sophomore standing at least; the reading of Elie Wiesel's Night.

II. ACADEMIC CONTEXT OF THE COURSE

This course is taught within the Judaic Studies Program which is an independent, B.A.-granting academic unit within the College of Arts and Sciences at the University of Cincinnati. There is no Department of Religion at the University, so that Judaic Studies appeals to students who are interested in religion as well as in Jewish history, Jewish sociology, Hebrew language and literature. The Program attracts Jewish and non-Jewish students, the proportions varying from course to course. There are majors in Judaic Studies who take this course, but the majority of students are seeking an elective to fulfill their college Humanities requirement and have never taken--and probably never will--another Judaic Studies course. From the points of view of ability, background, and purpose in taking this course, the student population is therefore extremely heterogeneous.

The ultimate aim of this course is to isolate, understand and evaluate the religious and theological responses to the Holocaust in the contemporary era, both by those who underwent the experience--whether they survived or not--and by the theologians and Jewish religious thinkers writing in the 1960s, 1970s and 1980s. This is done only after a review of Jewish literary, religious and theological reactions to Jewish national or group catastrophes in past history.

III. OUTLINE OF THE COURSE

Reading: Readings are all in English and are assigned from the books listed below as well as from xeroxed "hand-outs" distributed in class.

Required Reading:

Eliezer Berkovits - **Faith After the Holocaust**
Eliezer Berkovits - **With God in Hell**
Emil Fackenheim - **God's Presence in History**
Emil Fackenheim - **The Jewish Return into History**
Richard Rubenstein - **After Auschwitz**

Suggested reading:

Albert Alperin, "A Passover in the Ghetto," **Congress Bi-Weekly,** April 7, 1944, pp. 5-7.

Sholem Asch, "Exalted and Hallowed," **Jewish Frontier,** November 1942, pp. 17-20.

Eliot Dorff, "God and the Holocaust," **Judaism,** Winter 1977.

Mark Dworzecki, "Purim in the Vilna Ghetto," **Jewish Digest,** February 1956, pp. 9-10.

Mark Dworzecki, "A Yom Kippur Homily," **Jewish Frontier,** November 1946, pp. 10-14.

Richard Feder, "Religious Life in Terezin," in N. Katz (ed.), **Terezin.**

Moshe Flinker, **Young Moshe's Diary** (Jerusalem: 1976).

Zelig Kalmanowich, "A Diary of Life in Vilna," YIVO **Annual of Jewish Social Science,** Vol. 8, 1953.

Theodore Lewis, "From the Depths," **Jewish Spectator,** October 1959, pp. 18-20.

Alan Mintz, **Hurban,** 1985.

Leon Poliakov, "Human Morality and the Nazi Terror," **Commentary,** August 1950, pp. 111-116.

Moshe Preger, "A Chassidic Underground," **Yad Vashem Bulletin,** Vol. 6-7, June 1963, pp. 10-12.

Moshe Preger, "Reb Mendel of Pschanz Goes to Treblinka," **Jewish Spectator,** May 1950, pp. 29-31.

Irving Rosenbaum, **Holocaust and Halakhah.**

David Roskies, **Against the Apocalypse.**

Byron Sherwin, "The Impotence of Explanation and the European Holocaust," **Tradition,** Winter-Spring, 1972.

Pesach Schindler, "The Holocaust and **Kiddush Hashem** in Hassidic Thought," **Tradition,** Spring-Summer, 1973.

Charles W. Steckel, **Destruction and Survival.**

Isaiah Trunk, **Judenrat,** ch. 9.

Isaiah Trunk, "Religious, Educational and Cultural Problems in the Eastern European Ghettos under German Occupation," YIVO **Annual of Jewish Social Studies,** Vol. XIV, 1969.

Yosef Yerushalmi, **Zakhor: Jewish History and Jewish Memory.**

1. Introduction: the relationship between history and theology; the questions to be asked--old ones in new forms or radically new questions?

2. The Jewish **religious** response to Jewish catastrophe and suffering throughout history.

    (Bible) Book of Lamentations

    (Bible) Psalm 137

    Selections of **Kinot** (poetic elegies of medieval ages) taken from: Abraham Rosenfeld, (ed.), **Authorized Kinot for the Ninth of Av**, 2nd ed., 1970.
    i) pp. 125-126: R. Meir b. Yehiel (c. 1140)
    ii) pp. 161-162: R. Meir of Rothenburg (1215-1293)
    iii) pp. 168-170: Joseph of Chartres (c. 1170) – Elegy on the Martyrs of York
    iv) pp. 173-175: **Kinah** in Memory of Our Six Million Martyrs

    (handout) "The York Riots," in Jacob Marcus, **Jews in the Medieval World**, pp. 131-135. (To be read in conjunction with the above, pp. 168-170.)

    (handout) Extract of "The Chronicle of Salomon bar Simson," pp. 15-37, 142-151, from S. Eidelberg, **The Jews and the Crusaders.**

    Suggestion to the students: When reading this literature, examine what religious motifs and expressions of religious feelings find prominence in this literature.   Identify them by close literary analysis.
    On the use of Biblical models of suffering and faith that later Jewish generations adopted to link their own contemporary catastrophes and religious feelings, read:

    (Bible) Genesis: Ch. 22:1-9, Binding of Isaac **(Akeda)**

    (handout) Poem: "Akeda," pp. 142-512. Taken from Shalom Spiegel, **The Last Trial.**

(handout) Story of Hannah and her seven sons, from II Maccabees, pp. 463-465 (taken from the Apocrypha)

(Bible) Daniel - ch. 3, on Shadrak, Meshak, and Abednego.

On Biblical protest literature against unjust suffering, refer to:

(Bible) Genesis 18:16-33

(Bible) Exodus 32:7-14

(Bible) Jeremiah 12:1-4

(Bible) Habakkuk 1:1-4; 1:13

(Bible) Psalms 44:24-27

Compare with "Yossel Rackover's Appeal to God," in Berkovits, **With God in Hell**, pp. 128-131.

3. Jewish **theological** explanations of catastrophes throughout Jewish history: sin-punishment motif; Jews as suffering servants; no explanation, but silence; Lurianic kabbalah.

(Bible) Deuteronomy 28

(Bible) Deuteronomy 32:1-43

(Bible) Jeremiah 32:16-44

(Bible) Psalm 44

(Bible) Isaiah 52:13--53:12

Louis Ginzberg, **Legends of the Jews**, Vol. 1, on rabbinic interpretations of the Akedah;

Talmud Bavli, Menahot 29b; Makkot 24a-b;

Ismar Schorsch, "Holocaust and Jewish Survival," Midstream, January 1981, pp. 38-42.

On the midrashic mode as a rabbinic literary means to respond to catastrophe and on its dialectical faith posture--accepting the reality of evil yet affirming faith in God, see:

Fackenheim, **God's Presence in History**, ch. 1.

4. The dimensions and meaning of faith of the Jews living through the Holocaust; religious and theological reactions.

Berkovits, **With God in Hell**

Questions to ponder: Why are religious Jews true heroes according to Berkovits? How did they maintain their faith? What does this tell us of their values and orientation to life? What polemic does Berkovits browbeat assimilationists with? Why the great animosity to Bettelheim? What is religious faith according to Berkovits?

Suggested reading:

(handout) Bruno Bettelheim, "Freedom from Ghetto Thinking," Midstream, Spring 1962, pp. 16-25.

(handout) Responses to Bettelheim, **Midstream**, September 1962, pp. 84-88.

Also suggested that the student refer to any of the items listed in the beginning of the syllabus dealing with Jewish religious activities during the Holocaust.

(handout) Survivor accounts of religious behavior and theological feelings done in a social scientific account.
Selections taken from: Reeve R. Brenner, **The Faith and Doubt of Holocaust Survivors**, pp. 48-49; 52-55; 57-63; 67-75; 93-94; 96-121; 130-132; 210-211; 218-221; 224-227.
In their reading of the Brenner extracts, the students are asked to isolate the various kinds of religious reactions--religious practice, lack of practice, belief, unbelief, etc.; and the reasons given for them.

Suggested reading: Benny Kraut, "Faith and the Holocaust," Judaism, Vo. 31, no. 2, Spring 1982, pp. 185-201 (review essay of Berkovits and Brenner books).

Mid-term take-home examination: (10 double-spaced, typed pages; 50% of final grade.)

The religious response of Jews during the Holocaust as well as the reactions of survivors after the Holocaust reflect the basic patterns of religious and theological responses to catastrophes by Jews through-out the ages. Discuss and anaylze this assertion, relating Berkovits' **With God in Hell,** and the Brenner extracts to the motifs and models of religious and theological reactions of Jews in previous periods of Jewish history.

5.   The contemporary religious challenge: **Faith Denied;** why one may no longer believe in the God of history.

      Rubenstein, **After Auschwitz,** chs. 2-3, pp. 47-82; ch. 12, pp. 209-227.

6.   What to do as a Jew without God, and how to live Jewishly?

      Rubenstein, chs. 5, 6, 7, 13.

7.   **Faith Affirmed:** varieties of faith postures, including the Holocaust as a punishment for sins, by some traditional Orthodox respondents; Jews as suffering servants of mankind as exemplified in the thought of the religious Reformer Ignaz Maybaum.

      (handout) Rabbi Meisels, "God in Auschwitz," pp. 5-6.

      (handout) Thoughts of the Lubavitcher Rebbe, in Y.M. Kagan, ed., **A Thought for the Week,** Vol. 5, 1972, pp. 82-87.

      (handout) Bronznick, "A Theological View of the Holocaust: A Traditional Approach for Traditional Jewish Education," **Jewish Education,** Vol. 42, no. 4, Summer 1973, pp. 13-28.

      Suggested reading: Rabbi Hutner, "Holocaust," The Jewish Observer, October 1977, pp. 1-9.

      Letters re: Hutner and review of his talk, The Jewish Observer, January 1978, pp. 8-14.

      Lawrence Kaplan, "Rabbi Hutner's **Daat Torah** Perspective," **Tradition,** Vol. 8, no. 3, Fall 1980, pp. 235-248. (A vigorous critique of Rabbi Hutner's views.)

Ignaz Maybaum, **The Face of God After Auschwitz.**

Steven Katz, "Jewish Faith after the Holocaust: Four Approaches,"
Encyclopedia Judaica Yearbook, 1975-1976, pp. 92-105.

Pinchas Peli, "In Search of Religious Language for the Holocaust,"
Conservative Judaism, vol. 33, no. 2, Winter 1979, pp. 1-24.

8.   Rejection of "for our sins" and a facile religious affirmation--
Eliezer Berkovits, the free-will argument, and **hester panim**
(the hiding of God) as non-punishment concept.

Berkovits, **Faith After the Holocaust,** chs. 3, 4, 5, pp.
67-143.

Suggested reading: Katz, "Four Approaches;"

Marvin Fox, "Berkovits' Treatment of the Problem of Evil,"
Tradition, Vol.14, September 1974, pp. 117-124.

9.   The Commanding Voice of Auschwitz - the thought of Emil Fackenheim.

Fackenheim, **Jewish Return into History,** chs. 2, 3, 4, 5, pp.
19-57; and Ch. 7, pp. 81-102.

Fackenheim, **God's Presence in History,** Ch. 3, pp. 67-98.

Suggested reading: Seymour Cain, "E. Fackenheim's Post-Auschwitz
Theology," **Midstream,** May 1971, pp. 73-80.

Michael A. Meyer, "Judaism After Auschwitz," **Commentary,** June
1972, pp. 55-62.

Alan   Miller,   review   of   **God's   Presence,   Reconstructionist,**
November   1971,   pp.   7-10.

David   Biale,   review   of   **Return   into   History,   AJS   Newsletter,**
October 1980.

10.   Dialectical Faith - the thought of Irving Greenberg.

(handout) Irving Greenberg, "Cloud of Smoke, Pillar of Fire:
Judaism, Christianity and Modernity after the Holocaust," in Eva
Fleischner, (ed.), **Auschwitz: Beginning of a New Era?,** pp.
7-55.

(handout) M. Wyschograd, "Auschwitz: Beginning of a New Era?," **Tradition**, Fall 1977, pp. 63-78 (critique of Greenberg).

11.   Other theological approaches

(handout) M. Wyschograd, "Some Theological Reflections on the Holocaust," **Response**, Spring 1965, pp. 65-68.   (Critique of Fackenheim, Berkovits, Wiesel, plus religious formulation of his own).

(handout) S. Friedman, "God in Buchenwald," Jewish Spectator, December 1969, pp. 20-22. (Reinterpretation of God idea, and taking Berkovits' position to its logical conclusion.)

(handout) E. Wiesel, "Talking and Writing and Keeping Silent," pp. 269-277.

Suggested reading:

Marvin Fox, "Human Suffering and Religious Faith: A Jewish Response to the Holocaust," **Questions of Jewish Survival**, (University of Denver, 1980), pp. 8-19.

Walter Wurzburger, "The Holocaust – Meaning or Impact?" **Shoah**, Spring-Summer 1980, pp. 14-16.

Jacob Neusner, "The Implications of the Holocaust," in Neusner, (ed.), **Understanding Jewish Theology**, pp. 179-193.

12.   The Holocaust and the State of Israel: historic and/or religious relationship? Does Israel represent the beginning of the Messianic redemption? Does the creation of the State have religious significance, besides socio-political?

Fackenheim, **Jewish Return**, ch. 4, esp. pp. 53-57; ch. 10, pp. 129-143; ch. 13, pp. 188-209; ch. 17, pp. 273-286.

Berkovits, **Faith After**, ch. 6, pp. 144-169.

(handout) "Theological Implications of the State of Israel"
Walter   Wurzburger,   "The   Jewish   View,"   pp.   148-151;
Roy Eckardt, "The Protestant View," pp. 158-166;
Brother Marcel-Jaques Dubois, "The Catholic View," pp. 167-173.
These three articles appear in the Encyclopedia Judaica Yearbook 1974.

13.   Christian Theological Response to the Holocaust – is it of reli-
      gious importance to Christians as Christians? What kind of
      religious and theological reorientation is needed, if any?

      (handout) Franklin Littell, **The Crucifixion of the Jews**, chs.
      3-4, pp. 44-82.

      (handout) A. Roy Eckardt, **Your People, My People**, pp. 3-28.

      (handout) Alice Eckardt, "In Consideration of Yom Hashoah
      Liturgies," **Shoah**, vol. 2, no. 4, 1979, pp. 1-4.

      (handout) John T. Pawlikowski, "The Holocaust and Catholic
      Theology," **Shoah**, Spring-Summer, 1980, pp. 6-9.

      (handout) Michael Schwartz, "Are Christians Responsible?"
      National Review, Aug. 8, 1980, pp. 956-958. (A vigorous
      defense by a Catholic that Christians are not responsible. Cf.
      response by Friedlander.)

Requirements of the Course for Grading:

In addition to the mid-term take-home examination, there is a final
paper of ten to fifteen pages.

IV.   CONCEPTUAL FRAMEWORK OF THE COURSE

      This course is predicated on the assumption that in order to
understand contemporary Jewish theologians and religious thinkers on
the issues raised by the Holocaust one must perforce confront Jewish
religious and theological reactions to catastrophes in previous periods
of Jewish history.   The reasons for this are essentially three: First,
any phenomenon is always better understood when placed in historical
perspective.   Second, and far more significant, contemporary religious
writers on the Holocaust of necessity self-consciously link their
thought to classical religious ideals, symbols and models of Jewish
response to group or individual suffering, such as the biblical motif
of sin-punishment, the **Akedah** paradigm, etc. Hence, for the student

to really make sense of the writings of contemporary religious thinkers on the Holocaust, he must have access to their inherited religious ideas and worldviews, regardless of whether the theologian accepts, rejects, or modifies them in light of his perception of the religious challenges posed by the Holocaust.   Third, and equally important, a good number of the contemporary thinkers argue that the Holocaust in the context of Jewish history is a unique evil which raises unique questions that cannot be answered by the traditional faith postures or explanations of the past.   The student cannot evaluate the truth or falsity of this assertion unless he knows both what past evils befell the Jews and what religious and theological responses were elicited.

Hence, this course is organized into three units:
1.   Jewish religious and theological response to Jewish catastrophe from biblical up to modern times;
2.   Religious and theological reactions of the Holocaust victims;
3.   Religious and theological approaches of contemporary Jewish, and some Christian, thinkers and theologians.
This structure allows a full contextual overview of the fundamental motif.   It has the decided advantage of providing a comparative framework for the clash between historical evil and the historic belief in the God of history, and of self-consciously provoking historical comparisons.   Within section one, biblical and rabbinic responses to Jewish tragedy are crystallized; reactions to their own tragedies from later "contemporary" Jews in the medieval and early modern period are seen to invoke and modify classical religious responses.   Then the reactions of the Holocaust victims are compared to those in section 1: How do the victims appropriate the inherited religious traditions on the issue?   Are their responses similar or different, and in what way? Why?   Finally, the responses of the theologians can be compared with those of the classical Jewish tradition and pre-modern periods: Are

they the same or different?   Why?   How do contemporary thinkers
appropriate and/or modify or reject the classical religious postures?
Are we on the threshold of a requisite religious and theological break
with the past as some argue?   Also, how do the religious responses of
the theologians compare with those of the Holocaust victims?   Do the
former invent artificial categories of explanation and pervert the
experience of the victims, as they have been accused of doing by some
individuals?

Both the midterm and final papers reinforce the students'
grappling with these issues by demanding that they come to terms with
the material within each unit and then requesting that they compare
them. On the whole, the framework has proved successful; certainly by
the time students read the contemporary writers, they have acquired a
real appreciation for the reason the course is so concerned with the
earlier historical responses.   They find their understanding of the
contemporaries enhanced because they now can relate to the latter's
biblical and midrashic frameworks, reference points, and terminology.

Pedagogic Problems: The conceptual structure of the course is not
without some inherent difficulties.   First, pragmatically, students at
the outset are impatient with history--they don't want to begin with
the "past" but want to jump immediately into the "now." Their
restlessness has to be overcome.   Second, identifying Jewish religious
responses with past Jewish tragedies in effect demands the touching of
base with virtually every period in Jewish history, and that raises
enormous pedagogical questions.   Not only is the very limited time of
the course a crucial factor, but conceptually one must pause and ask:
how much of the Jewish and general historical background should and can
be effectively relayed in order to give the theme of Jewish response to

Jewish suffering an adequate historical context and perspective?   For example, how much should be taught--and with what, if any, readings--on the Crusades, on Marranos, and on Chmelniecki in order to give students an appreciation of the kinot, chronicles, and books of consolation? Moreover, by focusing on the critical theme of Jewish suffering and response to it, what conception of Jewish history is being transmitted, however subtly and unintentionally, to the students, most of whom will not take another Jewish history course?   Is there not a danger that students will come away with a "lachrymose conception of Jewish history," in Baron's words, with the sense that Jewish history is at best a story of "Kultur und Leidensgeschichte," as Graetz would have it? While there are no easy answers to these questions, clearly a supplementary role of the instructor in this type of course must be consciously to try to deflect some of these undesirable impressions.

I.   THE COURSE

ISSUES IN THE AFTERMATH OF THE HOLOCAUST

Ze'ev Mankowitz

Hebrew University, Jerusalem; School for Overseas Students

One semester, 4 hours per week, totalling 50 hours

Prerequisites: Previous completion of an academic course in the study
   of the Holocaust.

II.   ACADEMIC CONTEXT OF THE COURSE

The course is offered as part of the one-year program for overseas
students at the Hebrew University, for which credit is given at the
students' home universities. The students are from the USA, Canada and
Britain; generally liberal arts and social science majors. These
students are particularly well motivated because the one-year program
gives them an opportunity to pursue Judaic studies not offered at their
home university.

The course is designed for third-year B.A. students. It is
conducted as an honors seminar and the maximum number of students
accepted is 20. The seminar is largely based on class discussion which
focuses on short weekly papers prepared by the participants.

III. OUTLINE OF THE COURSE

1. Introduction:

   Course outline and goals

   The problematics of contemporary history

   The final stages of the Second World War

   Liberation:

   The Remnants of East European Jewry

   The Jewish Brigade

   Survivors in Germany

201

Background Reading:

Lucy S. Dawidowicz, **The War against the Jews,** Appendix B, The Final Solution in Figures.

Y. Bauer, **Flight and Rescue: Brichah,** "The Beginnings," pp. 3–42.

Source Reading:*

A. Kovner, "The Mission of the Survivors," Yad Vashem, **The Catastrophe of European Jewry, pp.** 671–683.

Y. Bauer, (ed.), **She-erit Hapleitah 1944–1947,** "A Detailed Report on the Liberated Jew ...," Abraham J. Klausner, pp. 6–9.

Reference:

Leo W. Schwarz, **The Redeemers,** (New York: 1953).

2. Germany: The Growth and Development of She-erit Hapleitah

Background Reading:

Bauer, **Flight and Rescue,** ch. 2, "The Survivors," pp. 43–47.

Source Reading:

"Declaration of Cinus Zioni Bavaria in Munich 25, 1945"

"Homecoming in Israel," in Leo Schwarz, **The Root** and **the Bough,** pp. 309–345.

Report by Mr. Ben Gurion on his visit to the Camps, 6.11.1945.

Leo Srole, "Why the DP's Can't Wait," **Commentary,** Jan. 1947, pp. 13–24.

Reference:

Leo W. Schwarz, **The Redeemers.**

* Source reading is available to the students at the library in files specially reserved for this seminar.

3. Ideology and Politics in **She-erit Hapleitah**

Background Reading:

Koppel S. Pinson, "Jewish Life in Liberated Germany," **Jewish Social Studies**, April 1947, pp. 101-126.

Source Reading:

S. Gringauz, "Jewish Destiny as the Dp's See It," in N. Glatzer, **The Dynamics of Emancipation**, pp. 127-128

U.S. Army Memorandum – Top Secret

Visit to Yad Vashem, exhibition of the newspapers and posters of She-erit Hapleitah; film "The Illegals" by Meyer Levin.

4. The Holocaust and the Creation of the State of Israel

Background Reading:

Y. Bauer, "The Holocaust and the Struggle of the Yishuv as Factors in the Establishment of the State of Israel," in Yad Vashem, **The Catastrophe of European Jewry**, pp. 611-632, or in Yad Vashem, **Holocaust and Rebirth.**

Source Reading:

The Harrison Report, August 1945, in Bauer, **She-erit Hapleitah 1944-1947**, pp. 10-14.

Leon Garfunkel, Memorandum to the Anglo-American Committee, Rome, 1946.

Minutes and Resolutions of Zionist Executive, Paris 1946.

Reference:

Zwi Ganin, **Truman, American Jewry and Israel 1945-1948**, (New York: 1979).

5. The Holocaust and the Creation of the State of Israel

Background Reading:

Michael Cohen, "Why Britain Left: the End of the Mandate," **Wiener Library Bulletin**, vol. XXXI, no. 45/46, 1978

Source Reading:

Exchange of Telegrams between Secretary of State and High Commissioner for Palestine, 11-12.10. 1947.

Menachem Begin, **The Revolt**, ch. 4., "We Fight Therefore We Are;" ch. 24, "Pathway to Victory."

Reference:

Walter Laqueur, **A History of Zionism**, ch. 11, "The Struggle for the Jewish State."

Christopher Sykes, **Crossroads to Israel**, chs. 12 and 13.

6. On Survivors and Surviving

Source Reading:

Primo Levi, **Survival in Auschwitz**, (New York: 1973).

Viktor E. Frankl, **Man's Search for Meaning**, Part One "Experiences in a Concentration Camp."

Jean Amery, **At the Mind's Limits**, (Indiana: 1980), pp. 1-20.

7. On Survivors and Surviving

Source Reading:

Bruno Bettelheim, **Surviving and Other Essays**, (New York: 1979) pp. 48-83, 84-99, 246-257, 284-298.

Terrence Des Pres, **The Survivor**, (New York: 1976), ch. 1, "The Survivor in Fiction;" ch. 5, "Life in Death;" ch. 6, "Us and Them," ch. 7, "Radical Nakedness."

8. Jews and Germans – The Reparations Debate

Background Reading:

Raul Hilberg, "Amends", in **Documents of Destruction**, (Chicago: 1971) pp. 237-242.

Source Reading:

H. Leivick, "No Blood Money from Germany," **Jewish Frontier,**
May, 1950.

S. Gringauz, "Germans Should Pay," **Jewish Frontier,** May 1950.

Nahum Goldmann and Joseph B. Schechtman, "Direct Israel-German
Negotiations?" **The Zionist Quarterly,** Winter, 1952.

Daniel Shabtain and M. Murock, "Shall We Demand Reparations From
Germany?" **The Jewish Horizon,** Jan. 1952.

Reference:

Nicholas Balabkins, **West German Reparations to Israel,** (N.J.:
1971), esp. ch. 4.

Nana Sagi, **German Reparations: A History of the Negotiations,**
(Jerusalem: 1980).

9. Consciousness of the Holocaust in Israel

Charles   Liebman   and   Eliezer   Don-Yehiya,   **Civil   Religion   in
Israel,**   (California: 1983),   chapter   5,   "The   New   Civil
Religion."

10. Consciousness of the Holocaust in Israel

Aharon Appelfeld, **The Age of Wonders,** (New York: 1981).

11. Hannah Arendt on the Eichmann Trial

Source Reading:

Hannah Arendt, **Eichmann in Jerusalem: A Report on the Banality
of   Evil,** (London: 1963).

Reference:

Ron Feldman, (ed.), **The Jew as Pariah,** (New York: 1978).

12. The Arendt Controversy and the Growth of Holocaust Awareness

Source Reading:

"Eichmann in Jerusalem" - An Exchange of Letters between Gershom Scholem and Hannah Arendt, in Feldman, **The Jew as Pariah**, pp. 240-251.

Daniel Bell, "The Alphabet of Justice," **Partisan Review**, vol. xxx, no. 3, 1963.

Marie Syrkin, "Miss Arendt Surveys the Holocaust," **Jewish Frontier**, May, 1963.

13. The Holocaust in the Mind of American Jewry

Source Reading:

Cynthia Ozick, "All the World Wants the Jews Dead: An Overwrought View from the Peak of the Bottom," **Esquire**, November 1975, esp. pp. 103-105.

Harold Schulweiss, "The Holocaust Dybbuk," **Moment Magazine**, February, 1976, pp 36-41.

"Debate: Ozick vs. Schulweiss," **Moment Magazine**, pp. 77-80.

Jacob Neusner, "Wanted: A New Myth," **Moment Magazine**, pp. 34-35, 61.

Irving Greenberg, "Confronting the Holocaust and Israel," 1975.

14. Trivializing the Holocaust

Background:

Yehuda Bauer, "Against Mystification," in **The Holocaust in Historical Perspective**, Vermont, 1979, pp. 34-49.

Source Reading:

Elie Wiesel, "Trivializing the Holocaust: Semi-Fact and Semi-Fiction," **The New York Times,** April 16, 1978.

Konrad Kellen, "Exploiting the Holocaust," **Midstream,** June, 1978, pp. 56-9.

Paula Hyman, "New Debate on the Holocaust," **New York Times Magazine,** September 14, 1980.

15. The Debate on the Uniqueness of the Holocaust

Source Reading:

Yehuda Bauer, **The Jewish Emergence from Powerlessness,** (Toronto: 1979). Foreword by Emil Fackenheim, p. vii-ix.

Irving Louis Horowitz, "Many Genocides, One Holocaust? The Limits of the Rights of States and the Obligations of Individuals," **Modern Judaism,** Volume 1, No. 1, 1981, pp. 74-89.

Steven T. Katz, "The 'Unique' Internationality of the Holocaust," **Modern Judaism,** Vol. 1, No. 2, 1981, pp. 161-183.

16. The Debate on the Uniqueness of the Holocaust (continued)

17. Rethinking Modernity - the Critique of Rationalism

Source Reading:

J.L. Talmon, **The Origins of Totalitarian Democracy,** (London: 1952), pp. 1-5.

Isaiah Berlin, **Two Concepts of Liberty,** (Oxford: 1958), pp. 52-54.

Leszek Kolakowski, "In Praise of Inconsistency," in **Beyond Marxism,** (London: 1969), pp. 236-237.

Richard Rubenstein, **The Cunning of History,** (New York: 1975), pp. 22-35.

Reference:

Daniel Bell, **The Cultural Contradictions of Capitalism,** (New York: 1976).

18. Rethinking Modernity – in Defence of Reason

Background Reading:

Dietrich Orlow, **The History of the Nazi Party 1919-1933,** (London: 1969), pp. 1-10.

George L. Mosse, **Nazism,** (N.J.: 1978), pp. 29-37, 126-129.

Peter Gay, **The Bridge of Criticism,** (New York: 1970), pp. 76-95.

Erich Goldhagen, "Obsession and Realpolitik in the Final Solution," **Patterns of Prejudice,** Jan-Feb. 1978, pp. 1-2.

Reference:

Peter Berger, et al., **The Homeless Mind,** (New York: 1973).

19. Re-evaluating Western Culture

Source Reading:

George Steiner, "A Season in Hell," In **Bluebeard's Castle,** (London: 1971), pp. 31-48.

Adin Steinsalz, "For Thy Sake Are We Killed."

Eliezer Berkovits, "The Vanishing West?" in **Faith After the Holocaust,** (New York: 1973), pp. 37-50.

Reference:

Emil Fackenheim, **Encounters Between Judaism and Modern Philosophy,** (New York: 1973)

20. Rethinking Christianity's Relationship to the Jews – Protestantism

Source Reading:

Rosemary R. Ruether, "Anti-Semitism and Christian Theology," in Eva Fleischner, (ed.), **Auschwitz: Beginning of a New Era?** (New York: 1977), pp. 79-92.

Roy A. Eckardt, "Introduction", **Elder and Younger Brothers: The Encounter of Jews and Christians,** (New York: 1967), pp. xv-xx.

Franklin H. Littell, "Christian Anti-Semitism," **The Crucifixion of the Jews,** (New York: 1975), pp. 24-43.

Reference:

Rosemary Ruether, **Faith and Fratricide,** (New York: 1974).

21. Christianity and the Jews - Catholicism

Gregory Baum, "Introduction," in R. Ruether, **Faith and Fratricide,** (1974), pp. 1-22.

John T. Pawlikowski, "Judaism in Christian Education and Liturgy," in Fleischner, **Auschwitz: Beginning of a New Era?,** pp. 155-178

Pinchas Lapide, "The Ecumenical Council's 'Jewish Schema' and Vatican II on the Jews," in **Three Popes and the Jews,** (New York: 1967), pp. 337-349.

22. Jewish Faith After the Holocaust

Source Reading:

Eliezer Berkovits, **Faith After the Holocaust,** (New York: 1973), ch. 3-5, pp. 67-143.

23. Jewish Faith After the Holocaust

Emil L. Fackenheim, **God's Presence in History,** (New York: 1970).

24. Anti-Semitism in the Aftermath of the Holocaust

Source Reading:

Shlomo Avineri, "Aspects of Post-Holocaust Anti-Jewish Attitudes," in Moshe Davis, (ed.), **World Jewry and the State of Israel,** (New York: 1977), pp. 3-10.

Edward Alexander, "Stealing the Holocaust," **Midstream** (November 1980), pp. 46-51.

"Holocaust 'Revisionism': A Denial of History," **ADL Facts,** June, 1980.

Patterns of Prejudice, Vol. 16, No. 4, October, 1982, "Anti-Semitism Today: A Symposium," contributions by Yehuda Bauer, Max Beloff, Immanuel Jakobovits, Stephen Roth, Bernard Wasserstein & Leon Wieseltier.

25. Summation: The Future of Memory

<u>Requirements of the Course for Grading</u>:

Active participation in the seminar discussions and presentation of a number of short papers.   The average achieved for these papers represents the final grade.

IV.   CONCEPTUAL FRAMEWORK OF THE COURSE

The seminar opens with a chronological consideration of the direct bridges between the Holocaust and its aftermath:

-the demographic situation of European Jewry, 1945

-survivors: their needs, organization, ideology and movements

-attempts at communal reconstruction in Europe

-reparations and relations with Germany from Nuremberg to the Eichmann Trial

Within this framework special attention is given to the period 1945-1948, where ongoing research is opening new perspectives on **She-erit Hapleitah** [the survivors], international responses to the Holocaust, the immediate impact of the Holocaust on world Jewry and the connections between the Holocaust and the creation of the State of Israel.

The second phase of the course focuses on the development of awareness of the Holocaust in the wake of the Eichmann Trial in three major Jewish communities: America, Israel and the Soviet Union.   In this context, the growth of historical awareness intersects with Jewish self-understanding and contemporary needs of the community in question. In   consequence,   the   discussion   proceeds   by   examining   the crystallization, spread, use and misuse of Holocaust awareness in each specific setting.   Thereafter, comparative study helps to underscore the differences and commonalities in the integration of the memory of the Holocaust into the lives of the communities under consideration.

The   third   phase   sets   out   to   probe   the   shared   structure   of Holocaust   awareness   in   more   substantive   terms   and   deals   with   the following:

-Jewish understanding of the uniqueness of the Holocaust

-the confrontation of the Holocaust with modernity and Western culture

-Jewish responses to modernity in the light of the Holocaust

-the implications of the Holocaust for Jewish faith

The organizing framework used to order this complex material is the transition from modernity into post-modernity.

The last part of the course looks briefly at the impact of the Holocaust on the non-Jewish world and focuses on the sustained and significant attempt to deal with it in various Christian settings. Finally, an examination is made of anti-Semitism in the aftermath of the Holocaust.

It should be indicated, in conclusion, that the attempt to achieve an integrated overview of the aftermath of the Holocaust has only just begun.   The students, therefore, are called upon to consult numerous source readings in the shared enterprise of mapping out a viable conceptual framework for this field of study.

I.   THE COURSE

ZIONISM: THE DEVELOPMENT OF A NATIONALISM

Aubrey N. Newman
University of Leicester, England; Department of History
Two lectures and one seminar a week for 20 weeks
There are are no prerequisites for students taking the course

II. ACADEMIC CONTEXT OF THE COURSE

The course is offered to final-year history students in the University of Leicester and to students studying history and politics. It aims to enable students following general historical studies to relate one of the most significant movements of modern times to their general history studies. Some of the students who take the course will have studied a second-year course on **Europe and the Jewish Problem, 1648-1948,** but this is not a necessary prerequisite. The overwhelming majority of these students are not Jewish and therefore no background of Jewish knowledge can be assumed.

The course studies Jewish nationalism within the framework of national movements in the late-nineteenth century as well as events in the Middle East. It is also necessary to relate Zionism to various aspects of Judaism through preceding generations.

III. OUTLINE OF THE COURSE

There is a basic book-list, and during the course of the lectures attention is drawn to specific titles. Tutors responsible for essay work also draw particular attention to books and articles of especial significance.*

In addition to the basic texts (see below) students are expected to read widely from the following:

A. Bein, **Theodore Herzl, A Biography** (Cleveland: World Publishing, 1962)

Isaiah Berlin, **The Life and Opinions of Moses Hess** (Cambridge: Heffer, 1959)

R. Chazan and M. L. Raphael, **Modern Jewish History: A Reader** (New York: Schocken, 1974)

Jonathan Frankel, **Prophecy and Politics** (Cambridge: Cambridge University Press, 1981)

Walter Laqueur, **A History of Zionism** (New York: Schocken, 1976)

Walter Laqueur, **The Israel-Arab Reader** (New York: Bantam, 1970)

Paul R. Mendes-Flohr and Jehuda Reinharz (eds.), **The Jew in the Modern World** (Oxford: Oxford University Press, 1980)

Lewis B. Namier, **Conflicts** (London: Macmillan, 1942)

Norman Rose, **Lewis Namier and Zionism** (Oxford: Clarendon, 1980)

H. M. Sachar, **The Course of Modern Jewish History** (New York: Delta, 1977)

Leonard Stein, **The Balfour Declaration** (London: Vallentine, Mitchell, 1961)

*Unlike the system customary in American universities, course outlines in British universities do not necessarily allocate exact reading lists for each lecture session.

Barbara Tuchman, **Bible and Sword** (London: Macmillan, 1982)

David Vital, **The Origins of Zionism** (Oxford: Clarendon, 1975)

David Vital, **Zionism: The Formative Years** (Oxford: Clarendon, 1982)

Chaim Weizmann, **Trial and Error** (New York: Schocken, 1972)

George Antonius, **The Arab Awakening** (London: Capricorn, 1965)

Elie Kedourie, **England and the Middle East** (London: Bowes and Bowes, 1956)

Christopher Sykes, **Crossroads to Israel** (Bloomington: Indiana University, 1965)

Students are reminded, however, that there is a very wide range of writing on many aspects of this subject and that further specialized titles will be mentioned during the course of the term.

Introduction

1. Introduction

2. Jewish communities in central and eastern Europe in the 19th century

3. The growth of Enlightenment

4. The growth of nationalism in Europe: Hess

5. The growing persecutions in the East; the emergence of Jewish self-consciousness; the emergence of BILU; Pinsker

6. The development of emigration from eastern Europe and its impact upon the rest of the world

7. The growth of anti-semitism in central and western Europe

8. France: the Dreyfus Case; Herzl

9. Reactions in Europe to the emergence of Zionism; Chovevei Zion, Herzlian Zionism, non-Jewish Zionism

Palestine

10. Settlements in Palestine before the first world war:
    a) early settlements before 1850
    b) the patterns of mid-19th century settlement
    c) interest in Palestine by the Western powers: political, archaeological, biblical
    d) Montefiore
    e) The first Aliyah
    f) The second Aliyah: the emergence of the Kibbutz

Modern Zionism

11. Splits in the Zionist movement: Chovevei Zion vs. Herzlian Zionism; Herzl v. Weizmann; the idea of Nacht-asyl

12. The Balfour Declaration, its emergence and significance

13. The political organization of Zionism

14. The third and fourth Aliyahs

15. The reactions of the Arabs to Zionism

16. The changes of the 1930s

17. Royal Commissions, Peel and Woodhead; partitions

The State of Israel

18. The fight for the State

19. The establishment of the State

20. Hopes, visions and fulfillment

Requirements of the Course for Grading:

The course is devised as a lecture course combined with a final examination. In addition, as an integral part of the course, all students are assigned to tutorial groups. Included within the course and incorporated as it proceeds are essays, seminars, and discussions of set texts. The particular titles of essays depend in part on the specific interests of the students, but each has to write four essays over the two terms in which the course is taught. The following are examples:

- Why should Herzl have involved himself in Zionism?
- How far is it possible to link philo-semitism and philo-Zionism?
- Did the Balfour Declaration create the National Home or did the National Home create the Balfour Declaration?
- Account for the strained relations between Jews and Arabs between 1920 and 1939.

The basic texts to be studied in seminar are: Moses Hess, **Rome & Jerusalem**; Leon Pinsker, **Auto-Emancipation**; Herzl, **The Jewish State**; Arthur Hertzberg, **The Zionist Idea**; and Jonathan Kaplan (ed.), **The Zionist Movement.** (This is a xeroxed volume specially produced by the Hebrew University for overseas students.)

IV. CONCEPTUAL FRAMEWORK OF THE COURSE

One essential consideration in the design and conduct of this course is that so far the students enrolling in it are not Jewish and therefore have little or no understanding of the basic facts of Jewish history. As a result, it is important to give them a comparatively substantial element of factual knowledge. Eventually it is hoped to make this a 'follow-up' course from one on general Jewish history in the period 1648-1948. If that develops it would be possible to reshape elements of this course.

The main organizing ideas and themes of the course are:

Introduction.   Outlines to the students the purpose of the course; the intellectual and religious origins and roots of the Zionist movement; the different concepts of Zionism; definitions of Zionism.

Jewish communities in central and eastern Europe in the 19th century.   An historical description of traditional communities and their non-Jewish background covering Germany and Russo-Poland.

The growth of Enlightenment.   The development of new philosophies in Central and Eastern Europe and the effect of new ideas upon traditional Judaism.

The growth of nationalism in Europe: Hess. The emergence in nineteenth- and twentienth-century Europe of concepts of national identity, both in historic Europe and amongst the submerged nationalities of Eastern Europe. This is linked with a study of Moses Hess, **Rome and Jerusalem.**

Persecutions/self-consciousness/BILU/Pinsker.   A description of the increasing governmental persecution of the Jews of Eastern Europe and the resultant pressure for self-recognition. Students are also introduced to the early Zionist movements and above all BILU. This is linked with Pinsker, **Auto-Emancipation.**

The development of emigration from Eastern Europe. An analysis of the patterns of migration out of Eastern Europe and the different routes by which the Jews moved; the impact of such movements upon the Jews of Western Europe, America, and the Eastern Mediterranean.

Anti-Semitism. A description of the growth of "racial" anti-semitism in Central and Western Europe; a contrast between this and "traditional" anti-semitism.

France: the Dreyfus Case; Herzl. A description and analysis of the France of the Dreyfus case and of its impact upon Herzl, **The Jewish State.**

Reactions in Europe to the emergence of Zionism. The growth of Zionist and quasi-Zionist movements in Western Europe. A description of the make-up of the Chovevei Zion movement in Britain.

Palestine. A description of the early settlements in Palestine since the middle of the sixteenth century, emphasizing the historical continuity of Jewish settlement in the towns and in the Galilee, and including the early settlements under the influence of the Rothschilds and Montefiore. Attention is also drawn to the ways in which the major European powers and the Americans developed an interest in the Holy Land. Thereafter, descriptions of the first two Aliyah movements and the emergence of their traditional concepts, such as the Kibbutz.

Splits in the Zionist movement. A discussion of the differences which emerged between the Chovevei Zion and the Herzlian organizations in, for example, Britain; above all the importance of the split over Uganda and the ways in which "popular" opinion insisted on maintaining Palestine as the only place for asylum.

The Balfour Declaration. How important was the Balfour Declaration? How did it arise in Great Britain? How did the English Zionist movement capture the institutions of Anglo-Jewry? What significance did it have for contemporaries?

The political organization of Zionism. How did the movement organize itself in relation to Palestine/the Mandate authority and in relation to the Jewish and non-Jewish communities in the outside world?

The third and fourth Aliyahs. The nature, numbers, and impact of the various immigrations into the Holy Land.

The reactions of Arabs to Zionism. The various ways in which Arabs in the Holy Land reacted to the growing Jewish presence, both favorably and unfavorably.

The changes of the 1930s. The changing patterns of the 1930s in Europe and in Palestine; the growth of new desperations; the closing of doors.

Royal Commissions, Peel and Woodhead; partitions. The abdication of responsibility by the Mandatory government; the growth of self-defense forces. Wingate.

The fight for the State. The destruction of European Jewry and the refusal of admission. The guilty conscience of Europe.

The establishment of the State of Israel. The fight with Britain; the Anglo-American Commission; the **Exodus**; the fight with the Arabs pre-May 1948; the United Nations vote. The wars of 1948-49; the armistice agreements; the ingathering of the exiles from Western and Arab lands.

Hopes, visions and fulfillment. An informal discussion on how far the State of Israel has met the wishes and ideals of the founding fathers, i.e., the early writers and the early settlers.

I. THE COURSE

THE   HOLOCAUST

Marc Lee Raphael
Ohio State University, USA; Department of History
One quarter (10 weeks) for 4 hours per week, totalling 40 hours
There are no prerequisites for students taking the course

II. ACADEMIC CONTEXT OF THE COURSE

Ohio State University has 60,000 students. This course is offered on the undergraduate level and is open to students in any department. It is an integral part of a large undergraduate program in Jewish history, and is usually included in the major program of students studying either military or European history.   The class is usually divided equally among Protestant, Catholic and Jewish students.

III. OUTLINE OF THE COURSE

1. Discussion of the syllabus and introduction:
   Racism, human nature, human prejudice, the question of evil and freedom of choice. [3 lectures]

2. Racism in the 18th, 19th and 20th centuries. [6 lectures]

   Required Reading:

   Blumenbach, **On the Natural Varieties of Mankind** (1798), pp. 229-235

   Lavater, **Essays on Physiognomy** (1781), pp. 464-491

   Kern, **Anatomy and Destiny**, pp. 45-55, 221-237

   Herder, **Reflections on the Philosophy of the History of Mankind** (1780s), pp. 43-51

   Gobineau, **The Inequality of the Human Race** (1853), pp. 122-123, 205-211

   Knox, **The Races of Man** (1850), pp. 130-131, 133, 137

   Galton, **Hereditary Genius** (1869), pp. 1-3, 325-337

   Blacker, **Eugenics, Galton and After**, pp. 103-123

   Poliakov, **History of Anti-Semitism**, Vol. 3, pp. 429-457

   The Third Reich, pp. 254-268

   Chamberlain, **Foundations of the Nineteenth Century** (1899), pp. v-xix

   Weininger, **Sex and Character** (1903), pp. 301-309

   Cohn, **Warrant for Genocide**, pp. 21-40, 126-148

3. The uniqueness of German culture and society. [2 lectures]

   Required Reading:

   Laqueur, **Young Germany**, pp. 3-38

   Erikson, "The Legend of Hitler's Childhood," in **Childhood and Society**, pp. 326-358

4. The impact of World War I on Germany. [1 lecture]

   Required Reading:

   Binion, "Hitler's Concept of **Lebensraum**: The Psychological Basis," and "Discussion," **History of Childhood Quarterly** 1 (1973), pp. 187-215, 216-258

5. Hitler. [4 lectures]

   Required Reading:

   Loewenberg, "The Unsuccessful Adolescence of Heinrich Himmler," **American Historical Review** 76 (1971), pp. 612-641

   "Discussion of Binion's **Hitler Among the Germans**," **Psychohistory Review** (Summer 1977), pp. 44-75

   Hitler, **Mein Kampf**, Ch. 11 pp. 389-455, Ch. 12 pp. 456-558

6. The destruction process:
   Definition; action; the Final Solution; the **Einsatzgruppen** and gas vans; the killing centers; euthanasia – prologue to the Final Solution. [6 lectures]

   Required Reading:

   Dawidowicz, **A Holocaust Reader**, pp. 35-53, 55-82, 83-104, 104-140, 141-170

   Sereny, **Into That Darkness**, pp. 13-18, 48-90, 145-250

7. The chances of survival:
   During concentration, deportation, selection and in the killing centers. [2 lectures]

   Required Reading:

   Dawidowicz, **A Holocaust Reader**, pp. 289-327

   Bettelheim, "Individual and Mass Behavior in Extreme Situations," **Journal of Abnormal and Social Psychology** 38, pp. 417-452

   Frankl, **From Death Camp to Existentialism**, pp. 1-91

8. Resistance. [3 lectures]

   Required Reading:

   Suhl, **They Fought Back**, pp. 7-84, 85-159

   Dawidowicz, **A Holocaust Reader**, pp. 329-380

9. The Jewish Councils. [1 lecture]

   Required Reading:

   Dawidowicz, **A Holocaust Reader**, pp. 235-287

10. Responses to the Holocaust:
    The Papacy; the Roosevelt Administration; American Jewry; the
    Nations. [4 lectures]

    Required Reading:

    Sereny, **Into That Darkness**, pp. 276-286

    Wyman, **Abandonment of the Jews**, pp. 61-206.

    Laqueur, **The Terrible Secret**, pp. 157-208

11. The relationship between the Holocaust and the birth of Israel.
    [1 lecture]

12. "The Dance of Genghis Cohn."

    Required Reading:

    Gary, **The Dance of Genghis Cohn**

13. Final Reflections. [2 lectures]

    Required Reading:

    Meyer, "If Hitler Asked You to Electrocute a Stranger, Would You?
    Probably!" **Esquire** (February 1970), pp. 140-144

    Kelman and Lawrence, "American Response to the Trial of Lt. William
    L. Calley," **Psychology Today** (June 1972), pp. 42ff.

    Redl, "The Superego in Uniform" in **Sanctions for Evil**, pp. 93-
    101

    Merton, "A Devout Meditation in Memory of Adolf Eichmann," 2 pp.

<u>Requirements of the Course for Grading</u>:

Students are expected to attend all lectures and to do the reading in advance of the lectures on the subject of the reading.

There are two hour-long midterm examinations, covering the lectures and especially the readings, two three-page essays (to be reviewed with the help of a "writing fellow"), and a comprehensive final examination of two hours.

The papers go through a three-stage process. First, the paper is handed in to a "writing fellow" for criticism and guidance. Second, it is returned to the student for revision. Finally, it is turned in to the lecturer for a grade. Examples of the papers required:

<u>Paper No. 1</u>:

Write an essay demonstrating how Hitler's ideas about the Jews might have been the consummation of more than a century of racial thought and anti-Semitism. Consider, especially, the passages from **Mein Kampf** distributed in class.

<u>Paper No. 2</u>:

Write an essay on Gary's **The Dance of Genghis Cohn** and consider some of the following: 1) ponder the differences between Cohn and Schatz as they reflect on the 1944 massacre in the Forest of Geist; 2) what does Schatz mean when he says, "I didn't know him [Cohn] and there was nothing personal about this ... I had my orders you understand; I was a soldier and I had to carry them out."; 3) how does the Dybbuk [Cohn] bring Schatz to a painfully slow recognition of his guilt?; 4) what does Cohn fear when he says that "With a little bit of luck and genius, even six million gassed Jews will become a major contribution to Culture."; 5) has Gary found the appropriate metaphor with which to transfigure actuality into fiction?

IV. CONCEPTUAL FRAMEWORK OF THE COURSE

Introduction. The course outline given to the students contains the following introductory statement:

> After a careful examination of the history of racism in European society from the 18th to the 20th century, we will combine the perspectives of history, psychology, literature, philosophy and religion in an attempt to understand how a bureaucracy could take time out from efficiently running a state to equally efficiently exterminate six million Jews, and we will attempt to understand the responses of individuals, groups, institutions and nations to the deliberate extermination of nearly a whole people.

> "Men have gained control over the forces of nature to such an extent that with their help they would have no difficulty in exterminating one another to the last man"
> Freud, **Civilization and its Discontents** (1929)

This raises (and preliminarily answers) the questions: why teach the Holocaust? How to (and not to) teach the Holocaust? And, what to teach?

Racism in the 18th, 19th and 20th centuries. To help understand how a nation could attempt the deliberate extermination of a whole people, the history of racism in modern Europe is discussed. This ends with a discussion of some of the traditional myths about Jews (ritual murder, wandering Jew curse, universal Jewish conspiracy) used for racial mysticism and political mobilization in the late 19th and early 20th centuries.

The uniqueness of German culture and society. Although nearly all Europeans were infected by racism, the main question raised is why in Germany--of all the countries in Europe where Jews had been the traditional victims of oppression--did the unparalleled genocide program develop? The discussion here envelops German culture, Germany's response to World War I, and Hitler's role as the embodiment of the darker side of German society.

The destruction process. This discussion explores the evolving pattern of Jewish oppression under the Nazis as well as the evolution of the killing program, and the historical realities that ultimately gave impetus to the Holocaust.

Euthanasia. Here euthanasia is discussed as both the necessary consequence of attempts to improve the race by doing away with its parasites and as a link in the eventual method of Jewish mass murder.

Chances of survival. Four phases of the SS killing operation are examined--concentration, deportation, selection, death--and the chances for survival in each phase.

Resistance. An exploration of Jewish resistance ideology and resistance itself--all over Europe--with an emphasis on the ghettos.

Jewish Councils. An analysis of the common features, but especially the local conditions, personalities and organizational structures of the several hundred Jewish Councils.

The responses to the Holocaust. Few any longer challenge the truth of the indifference of witnessing nations and agencies--including American Jewish institutions. The evidence for this indifference is delineated and an effort is made to understand it.

The Holocaust and the Birth of Israel. It is nearly everywhere written that the Holocaust triggered the birth of the Jewish state. Zionist thinking in the 20th century is therefore explored, as well as the UNSCOP, to understand better the relationship between these two events.

Final Reflections. Discussion of questions students have wanted to ask since the beginning: Could a holocaust happen on such a massive scale elsewhere? Can it happen again?

I. THE COURSE

SOCIOLOGY OF THE AMERICAN JEWISH COMMUNITY

Mervin F. Verbit

Brooklyn College of the City University of New York, Department of
    Sociology

One Semester (14 weeks), 3 hours per week, totalling 42 hours

Prerequisites: One course in sociology and one course in Judaic Studies,
    or equivalent background

II. ACADEMIC CONTEXT OF THE COURSE

Brooklyn College is one of the senior colleges in the City
University of New York. Although the college offers some graduate
programs (most CUNY doctorates are given by a central Graduate School)
and a number of special programs (e.g., a School of Education and a
Conservatory of Music), Brooklyn College is primarily a liberal arts
college with all of the standard majors. The college has about 13,000
students, most of whom are commuters. More than half are Jewish, with
backgrounds varying over the total range from nothing at all to twelve
years or more of intensive Jewish learning.

Brooklyn College has a Department of Judaic Studies, but there are
several courses in Jewish Civilization housed in the traditional
disciplinary departments as well. The present course is a regular
advanced elective in the Department of Sociology and is listed by the
Department of Judaic Studies as a "related course".

227

III. OUTLINE OF THE COURSE

Notes:

(1) Background readings for class discussions are drawn from several sources. Those used most fully are:

Steven M. Cohen, **American Modernity and Jewish Identity**, (New York: Tavistock Publications, 1983). "Cohen"

Arnold M. Eisen, **The Chosen People in America**, (Bloomington: Indiana University Press, 1983). "Eisen"

Charles Liebman, **The Ambivalent American Jew**, (Philadelphia: Jewish Publication Society, 1973). "Liebman"

Peter I. Rose, ed., **The Ghetto and Beyond**, (New York: Random House, 1971). "Rose"

David Sidorsky, ed., **The Future and the American Jewish Community**, (New York: Basic Books, 1973). "Sidorsky"

Marshall Sklare, **America's Jews**, (New York: Random House, 1971). "Sklare"

Marshall Sklare, ed., **American Jews: A Reader**, (New York: Behrman House, 1983). "Sklare Reader"

Chaim Waxman, **America's Jews in Transition**, (Philadelphia: Temple University Press, 1983). "Waxman"

(2) The starred (*) items are required reading. The other items are recommended, and every student is expected to read at least some of them.

(3) No dates are designated for specific topics, because the course moves through the outline at an uneven pace, depending on the interests of the class and the flow of class discussions.

A. Theoretical and Methodological Considerations (or, How to Study the Jews)

1. Brief history of the sociological study of Jewry

2. How to classify the Jews; a review of the options: race, nationality, ethnic group, culture, religion, people.

3. To whom we compare contemporary American Jewry:

   a. other American religious groups; other American ethnic groups; other Jewish communities in the past or present

   b. Jewry: "like everyone else" and "a unique people"

4. The factual basis: How "hard" are the data?

5. The meaning of objectivity in the study of Jewry

   Reading:

   *Marshall Sklare, "Introduction: The Sociology of Contemporary Jewish Studies" in **The Jews in American Society,** (New York: Behrman House, 1974)

   *Seymour Martin Lipset, "The American Jewish Community in Comparative Context" in Rose.

B. The Background of Contemporary American Jewry

   1. Historical Development: Antecedents in Europe and America

      Reading:

      *Sklare, chap. 1

      *Waxman, chap. 1

      *Gartner, "Immigration and the Formation of American Jewry, 1840-1925" in Sklare Reader

      *Halpern, "America is Different" in Sklare Reader

      Aryeh Goren, **The American Jews,** (Cambridge, Mass.: Belknap Press of Harvard University, 1982)

      Oscar and Mary Handlin, "The Acquisition of Political and Social Rights by Jews in the United States" in J. Blau et. al., **Characteristics of American Jews,** (New York: Jewish Education Committee, 1965)

      Eisen, Part One.

   2. Ideological Sources of Jewish Self-Definition: the confrontation of classical and modern notions of Jewishness

Reading:

*David Sidorsky, "Judaism and the Revolution of Modernity" in Sidorsky

*Natan Rotenstreich, "Emancipation and Its Aftermath" in Sidorsky

*Liebman, chap. 1

Cohen, chaps. 1-2

C. Contemporary Jewish Identity in America

1. The Nature of Jewish Identity

   Reading:

   Simon Herman, **Jewish Identity**, (Beverly Hills: Sage Publications, 1977). Part I

   Kurt Lewin, "Psycho-sociological Problems of a Minority Group" and "Bringing Up the Jewish Child" in **Resolving Social Conflicts**, (New York: Harper Bros., 1948)

2. The "First" Generation: Immigrants to a New World

   Reading:

   *Waxman, chap. 2

3. Marginality and its Children: the "Second" and "Third" Generations

   Reading:

   *Waxman, chaps. 3-4

   *Liebman, chaps. 2, 6

   *Charles Liebman, "American Jewry: Identity and Affiliation" in Sidorsky

   *Daniel Bell, "Reflections on Jewish Identity" in Rose

   *E. Digby Baltzell, "Jews and the Protestant Establishment" in Rose

Deborah Dash Moore, **At Home in America: Second Generation Jews in New York,** (New York: Columbia University Press, 1981)

C. Bezalel Sherman, **The Jew within American Society,** (Detroit: Wayne State University Press, 1960), chaps. 1, 2, 7, 12

Eisen, parts 2 & 3

Isidor Chein, "The Problem of Jewish Identification" in **Jewish Social Studies,** Vol. 17, pp. 219-222

Cohen, chap. 3

4. Mid-century Shocks and their Effects: the Holocaust, the State of Israel, the late Sixties

   Reading:

   *Sklare, chap. 7

   *Waxman, chap. 5

   *Liebman, chap. 4

   *Ben Halpern, "Zion in the Mind of American Jews" in Sidorsky

   *M. Sklare, "Lakeville and Israel/The Six-Day War and Its Aftermath" in Sklare Reader

   *B.Z. and M. Sobel, "Negroes and Jews: American Minority Groups in Conflict" in Rose

   "Introduction" to J. Sleeper and A. Mintz, eds., **The New Jews,** (New York: Vintage Books, 1971)

   C. Liebman, **Pressure without Sanctions,** (Rutherford: Fairleigh Dickinson University Press, 1977), chaps. 7 and 8

   Cohen, chap. 8

5. The "Fourth" Generation: Integration and Polarization

   Reading:

   *Waxman, chap. 6

   *Milton Gordon, "Marginality and the Jewish Intellectual" in Rose

6. Intermarriage as a Reflection of Changing Identity

   a. Intermarriage rates
   b. The meaning of exogamy--formerly and now
   c. The consequences of intermarriage:
      in individual families; for the Jewish community; for Jewish
      identity
   d. Conversion--changing attitudes and consequences

   Reading:

   *Sklare, chap. 6

   *Waxman, pp. 173-178

   *David Singer, "Living with Intermarriage" in Sklare Reader

   Erich Rosenthal, "Studies in Jewish Intermarriage in the United
   States" in **American Jewish Year Book** 1963

   I. Ellman, "Jewish Intermarriage in the United States of America"
   in B. Schlesinger, ed., **The Jewish Family: A Survey and
   Annotated Bibliography,** (Toronto: University of Toronto Press,
   1971)

   Egon Mayer, **Children of Intermarriage,** (New York: American
   Jewish Committee, 1983)

D. Jews as a Minority

   1. Internal and External Sources of Tension between Jews and
      Non-Jews

   2. Sources of Antisemitism

      a. the prejudiced personality
      b. structural and situational inducements to intergroup hostility
      c. ideological bases of antisemitism

   3. Jewish Responses to Antisemitism

      a. the "defense agencies" and their style
      b. individual reactions
      c. Jewish "self-hatred"

Reading:

*One of the following:

Larry Dinnerstein, ed., **Antisemitism in the United States,** (New York: Holt, Rinehart & Winston, 1971)

Arnold Forster & Benjamin Epstein, **The New Antisemitism,** (New York: McGraw Hill, 1974), chap. 1

Harold Quinley & Charles Y. Glock, **Anti-Semitism in America,** (New York: Free Press, 1979), chaps. 1, 2, 10

*Kurt Lewin, "When Facing Danger" and "Self-Hatred Among Jews" in **Resolving Social Conflicts, op. cit.**

*Marshall Sklare & J. Greenblum, "The Friendship Pattern of the Lakeville Jew" in Sklare Reader

*Peter Rose, "Strangers in Their Midst: Small Town Jews and Their Neighbors" in Rose

*Rodney Stark & Stephen Steinberg, "It **Did** Happen Here: An Investigation of Political Antisemitism: Wayne, New Jersey" in Rose

Larry Dinnerstein, ed., **Antisemitism in the United States, op. cit.**

Benjamin Ringer, "Jewish-Gentile Relations in Lakeville" in M. Sklare, ed., **The Jewish Community in America,** (New York: Behrman, 1974)

Charles Stember, ed., **Jews in the Mind of America,** (New York: Basic Books, 1966)

Maurice Samuel, **The Gentleman and the Jew,** (New York: Knopf, 1952)

Koppel Pinson, ed., **Essays in Antisemitism,** (New York: Conference of Jewish Relations, 1946)

E.   The Demographic Profile of American Jewry

Reading:

*Sklare, chap. 2

*Sidney Goldstein, "Jews in the United States: Perspectives from Demography" in Sklare Reader

Nathan Glazer, "The American Jew and the Attainment of Middle Class Rank: Some Trends and Explanations" in M. Sklare, ed., **The Jews,** (Glencoe: Free Press, 1958)

U.O. Schmelz, "Jewish Survival: The Demographic Factors" in **American Jewish Year Book** 1981.

Cohen, chaps. 4, 5.

F. "Institutional" Aspects of American Jewish Life

1. Religion

a. The "Movements" - differences in ideology and practice
b. organizational patterns
c. "official" and "popular" religion - the problem of mixed motivation
d. synagogues - religious and communal roles

Reading:

*Sklare, chap. 4, pp. 110-135.

*Charles Liebman, "The Religion of American Jews" in Sklare Reader

*Charles Liebman, "Orthodoxy in American Jewish Life" in Sklare Reader

*Marshall Sklare, "The Conservative Movement--Achievements and Problems" in Sklare Reader

*Leonard Fein et al., "Reform is a Verb" in Sklare Reader

Jacob Neusner, ed., **Understanding American Judaism,** (New York: Ktav Publishing House, 1975)

Nathan Glazer, **American Judaism,** (Chicago: University of Chicago Press, 1972)

Emanuel Rackman, **One Man's Judaism,** (New York: Philosophical Library, 1970)

Mordechai Waxman, ed., **Tradition and Change,** (New York: Burning Bush Press, 1970)

Bernard Martin, ed., **Contemporary Reform Jewish Thought,** (Chicago: Central Conference of American Rabbis, 1968)

Mordecai M. Kaplan, **Judaism as a Civilization,** (New York: Schocken, 1967)

Solomon Poll, **The Hasidic Community of Williamsburg,** (New York: Schocken, 1969)

Saul L. Goodman, ed., The Faith of Secular Jews, (New York: Ktav, 1976)

2. Communal Organization

   a. Meanings of "Jewish Community"
   b. Brief history of organized Jewish communities
   c. American voluntarism and group identity
   d. The "federal" character of the Jewish community
   e. Leadership in the American Jewish community – criteria and authority
   f. Federations vs. synagogues as the central organizations.

   Reading:

   *Sklare, chap. 4, exc. pp. 110-135

   *Waxman, chap. 9

   *Herbert Gans, "The Origins of a Jewish Community in the Suburbs" in Sklare Reader

   *Daniel J. Elazar, "Decision-Making in the American Jewish Community" in Sklare Reader or Sidorsky

   Herman Stein, "Jewish Social Work in the United States" in J. Blau et al., **Characteristics of American Jews, op. cit.**

   Abraham Karp, **To Give Life: The UJA in the Shaping of the American Jewish Community,** (New York: Schocken, 1981)

Philip Bernstein, **To Dwell in Unity: The Jewish Federation Movement in America since 1960,** (Philadelphia: Jewish Publication Society, 1983)

Jonathan Woocher, "The 'Civil' Judaism of Communal Leaders" in **American Jewish Year Book,** 1981

Daniel J. Elazar, **Community and Polity: The Organizational Dynamics of American Jewry,** (Philadelphia: Jewish Publication Society, 1976)

Aryeh Goren, **New York Jews and the Quest for Community, The Kehilla Experiment 1908-1922,** (New York: Columbia University Press, 1970)

3. Jewish Family Patterns

   a. Classical Jewish family norms
   b. Contemporary trends and their basis

   Reading:

   *Sklare, chap. 3

   *Waxman, chap. 7, exc. pp. 173-181

   *Chaim Waxman, "The Threadbare Canopy: The Vicissitudes of the Jewish Family in Modern American Society: in Rose

   *Zena Smith Blau, "In Defense of the Jewish Mother" in Rose

   William Mitchell, "Descent Groups among New York City Jews" in M. Sklare, ed., **Jews in American Society, op. cit.**

   Jack Balswick, "Are American Jewish Families Closely Knit?" in B. Schlesinger, ed., **The Jewish Family, op. cit.**

   Cohen, chap. 6

4. Jewish Education

   a. The relationship of educational systems to society
   b. Varieties of Jewish education and Jewish identity

Reading:

*Sklare, chap. 5

*Lloyd Gartner, "Jewish Education in the United States" in Sklare Reader

*William Ackerman, "The Jewish School System in the United States: in Sidorsky

*Seymour Fox, "Toward A General Theory of Jewish Education" in Sidorsky

James Sleeper, "A Radical View of Jewish Culture" in Sidorsky

5. The Politics of American Jewry

    a. The Jewish role in American politics
    b. Jewish "liberalism" – theories about its causes
    c. Are Jews becoming more "conservative?"

Reading:

*Liebman, chaps. 7, 8

*Daniel J. Elazar, "Jewish Political Theory and the Political Notions of American Jews" in Rose

*Louis Ruchames, "Jewish Radicalism in the United States" in Rose

Stephen D. Issacs, **Jews and American Politics,** (Garden City: Doubleday, 1974)

Arthur Liebman, **Jews and the Left,** (New York: John Wiley, 1979), chaps. 1, 2, 4, 8, 9

Lucy Dawidowicz & L. Goldstein, "The American Jewish Liberal Tradition" in M. Sklare, ed., **The Jewish Community in America, op. cit.**

Cohen, chap. 7

G. On Predicting the Future

    1. "If present trends continue..."

2. But will they?

   Reading:

   *Waxman, chap. 10

JOURNAL LITERATURE

Students should become generally familiar with the kinds of material that can be found in the following periodical publications:

American Jewish Year Book, CCAR Journal, Commentary, Conservative Judaism, Contemporary Jewry, Jewish Journal of Sociology, Jewish Social Studies, Journal of Jewish Communal Service, Judaism, Midstream, Moment, Present Tense, The Reconstructionist, Response, Tradition, YIVO Journal

Requirements of the Course for Grading:

Each student is required to write a term paper on one of the following themes:

1. Choose a sub-group of American Jews (e.g., Southern Jews, Sephardim, rural and small-town Jews, Hasidim, poor Jews). Compare the sub-group with more "typical" American Jews, citing both major similarities and significant differences. Explain the differences.

2. Several local Jewish communities have been studied in historical or sociological works. (Baltimore, Rochester, Cleveland, Los Angeles, Boston and Providence are a few of the many communities on which books have been written). Choose one such work, and show how the community in question reflects general American Jewish patterns, as well as how it has its own special character. Account for both.

3. Read a book-length work on a contemporary diaspora Jewish community other than that of the United States. Compare that Jewish community with American Jewry, and account for the differences.

4. In 1950 Eli Ginzberg wrote **Agenda for American Jews.** Choose two or three chapters from that work. Discuss the changes that have taken place over the three and a half decades since Ginzberg wrote with regard to the content of the chapters you choose. Analyze how those changes have come about, and write a contemporary "Agenda" for the issues considered in those chapters.

Before writing the paper, the student must submit a proposed outline and bibliography for the instructor's suggestions and approval. It is possible to also submit a first draft for the instructor's comments. The paper is due at the final meeting of the class.

Final grades are based on a mid-term examination (30%), a final examination (40%), and the term paper (30%). Active and constructive participation in class discussions may raise the grade.

IV. CONCEPTUAL FRAMEWORK OF THE COURSE

The basic premise of the course is that human behavior responds not only to the situations in which people find themselves, but to their definitions of those situations and of themselves. Accordingly, after a few preliminary considerations of a general and methodological nature, the sources of contemporary American Jewish self-definition, their content, and their interrelationships are explored in some detail. These include: classical Jewish notions, the ideology of "modernity," the Emancipation and its implications, and American cultural definitions of the place of the Jews in the society. American Jewish responses to these sets of ideas are traced from the major Jewish immigration around the turn of the twentieth century to the present. Each "generation's" dominant responses are examined, with special reference to the impact of the preceding generation and of the sociocultural conditions of the time. Theories about the influence of the Holocaust, the re-establishment of the Jewish state, and the events of the late 1960s are also reviewed. The first part of the course thus deals with changing patterns of "Jewish identity" in twentieth-century America. The earlier period in American Jewish history is dealt with briefly, largely through assigned background reading.

The bridge to the second major part of the course comprises two themes: (1) demographic patterns of American Jewry, and (2) anti-semitism: its sources, changing manifestations, and Jewish responses.

The second major part of the course deals with the "institutional" aspects of American Jewry and analyzes them in light of the identity patterns that have already been examined. Reviewed here are religious organization and behavior (the "movements" and synagogue role and structure), communal organization, family trends, Jewish education, and the political behavior of Jews in America. In all of these, changes are traced over the last half-century or so, and alternative hypotheses to explain the changes are examined in light of their theoretical implications and empirical evidence.

Such sociological issues as the logic of hypothesis testing, scale construction, the relationship of concepts and indicators, and ways of assessing the relative impact of simultaneous antecedent conditions are explicitly considered where the material lends itself to an examination of these elements of sociological analysis.

I.   THE COURSE

SOCIOLOGY OF THE AMERICAN JEWISH COMMUNITY

Chaim I. Waxman

Yeshiva University, USA; Graduate Program in Jewish Education

One semester of 14 weeks, 2 hours per week, totalling 28 hours

II.   ACADEMIC CONTEXT OF THE COURSE

This course is offered on the graduate level for students in the graduate program in Jewish education. The course may be taken on either the masters or doctoral level. In certain cases, students in other graduate programs of the University, or upper-level undergraduates, may be admitted to the course with the permission of the instructor.

The purpose of this course is to deepen the student's knowledge and understanding of the American Jewish community. By "community" is meant both America's Jews as a group and the organized institutional structure of the group.

III. OUTLINE OF THE COURSE

The core book for the course is Chaim I. Waxman, **America's Jews in Transition** (Temple University Press, 1983). Three other books which are central to the course are: Steven M. Cohen, **American Modernity and Jewish Identity** (Tavistock, 1983); Daniel J. Elazar, **Community and Polity** (Jewish Publication Society, 1976); and Marshall Sklare (Ed.), **American Jews: A Reader** (Behrman House, 1983).

The Formative Period, 1654 – 1880

Waxman, AJIT, ch. 1

1. The Sephardi Pioneers.

Required Reading:

C. Roth, **A History of the Marranos** (Philadelphia, 1941)

H. B. Grinstein, **The Rise of the Jewish Community of New York, 1654-1860** (Philadeplphia, 1945)

E. Wolf and M. Whiteman, **The History of the Jews of Philadelphia** (Philadelphia, 1975)

2. The Central Europeans.

Required Reading:

S. Hertzberg, **Strangers Within the Gate City** (Philadelphia, 1978)

C. Reznikoff and U. Z. Engleman, **The Jews of Charleston** (Philadelphia, 1950)

S. G. Mostov, "A Sociological Portrait of German Jewish Immigrants in Boston: 1845-1861", **AJS Review** Vol. 3 (1978), pp. 121-152

3. Religious Developments.

Required Reading:

L. A. Jick, **The Americanization of the Synagogue, 1820-1870** (Hanover, 1976)

4. Communal Developments.

Required Reading:

B. W. Korn, **The American Reaction to the Mortara Case** (Cincinnati, 1957)

A. Tarshish, "The Board of Delegates of American Israelites (1859-1878)", **PAJHS** Vol. 44, pp. 16-32

D. D. Moore, **B'nai B'rith and the Challenge of Ethnic Leadership** (Albany, 1981), ch. 1

The Eastern European Immigration

Waxman, **AJIT**, ch. 2

5. Background.

Required Reading:

L. Dawidowicz (ed.), **The Golden Tradition** (New York, 1967), "Introduction"

I. Howe, **World of Our Fathers** (New York, 1976)

S. Kuznetz, "Immigration of Russian Jews to the United States", **Perspectives in American History** Vol. 9 (1975), pp. 35-124

M. Wischnitzer, **To Dwell in Safety** (Philadelphia, 1949)

6. Building a Community.

Required Reading:

L. P. Gartner, **History of the Jews of Cleveland** (Cleveland, 1978)

A. Goren, **New York Jews and the Quest for Community** (New York, 1970)

N. W. Cohen, **Not Free to Desist** (Philadelphia, 1972), chs. 1-7

Y. Shapiro, **Leadership of the American Zionist Organization, 1897-1930** (Urbana, 1971)

M. Soltes, **The Yiddish Press** (New York, 1969)

M. Davis, **The Emergence of Conservative Judaism** (Philadelphia, 1963)

G. Klaperman, **The Story of Yeshiva University** (New York, 1969)

L. Wirth, **The Ghetto** (Chicago, 1928)

7. The Acculturation of the Second Generation

Required Reading:

Waxman, **AJIT**, ch. 3

D. D. Moore, **At Home in America** (New York, 1981)

M. Sklare, **Conservative Judaism** (New York, 1972)

N. Goldberg, **Occupational Patterns of American Jewry** (New York, 1947)

Editors of **Fortune, Jews in America** (New York, 1936)

K. Lewin, "Leaders from the Periphery", in his **Resolving Social Conflicts** (New York, 1948)

Y. Bauer, **My Brother's Keeper** (Philadelphia, 1974)

8. The Third Generation Community

   Required Reading:

   Waxman, AJIT, ch. 4

   H. J. Gans, "The Origin and Growth of a Jewish Community in the Suburbs", in M. Sklare (ed.), **The Jews** (New York, 1958), pp. 205-248

   M. Sklare and J. Greenblum, **Jewish Identity on the Suburban Frontier** (Chicago, 1979)

   J. R. Kramer and S. Leventman, **Children of the Gilded Ghetto** (New Haven, 1961)

   S. Goldstein and C. Goldscheider, **Jewish Americans** (Englewood Cliffs, 1968)

   C. S. Liebman, **The Ambivalent American Jew** (Philadelphia, 1973)

9. The Pendulum Shifts, 1965 - 1975.

   Required Reading:

   Waxman, AJIT, ch. 5

   A. Liebman, **Jews and the Left** (New York, 1979)

   N. Glazer, "The Jewish Role in Student Activism", **Fortune** (Jan, 1969), pp. 112ff

   N. W. Cohen, **American Jews and the Zionist Idea** (New York, 1975) ch. 9

   S. M. Russ, **The Zionist Hooligans** (Ann Arbor, 1981)

   C. I. Waxman, "The Centrality of Israel in American Jewish Life", **Judaism** (Spring 1976), Vol. 25 No. 2, pp. 175-187

   E. Mayer, **From Suburb to Shtetl** (Philadelphia, 1979)

10. The Contemporary Community: A Demographic Overview.

   Required Reading:

   Waxman, AJIT, ch. 6

11. The American Jewish Family.

   Required Reading:

   Waxman, AJIT, ch. 7

   M. Himmelfarb and V. Baras (eds.), **Zero Population Growth – For Whom?** (Westport, 1978)

   E. Mayer and C. Sheingold, **Intermarriage and the Jewish Future** (New York, 1979)

   C. I. Waxman, **Single Parent Families: Challenge to the Jewish Community** (New York, 1980)

   S. M. Cohen, **American Modernity and Jewish Identity** (New York, 1983), ch. 6

12. Denominational Patterns, Jewish Education, and Immigration

   Required Reading:

   Waxman, AJIT, ch. 8

   B. Lazerwitz and M. Harrison, "American Jewish Denominations," **American Sociological Review** 44 (August 1979), pp. 656-666

   C. S. Liebman, "The Future of Conservative Judaism in the United States," **Jerusalem Newsletter: Viewpoints** 11, (31 March 1980)

   D. Elizur, "Israelis in the United States," AJYB 80, pp. 53-67

   Z. Gitelman, "I Didn't Collect Baseball Cards: Soviet Immigrant Resettlement in the United States," **Soviet Jewish Affairs** (forthcoming)

13. The Organized Community: Consensus and Conflict.

Required Reading:

Waxman, AJIT, ch. 9

D. J. Elazar, **Community and Polity** (Phildelphia, 1976)

B. Reisman, **The Chavurah** (New York, 1977)

A. L. Lerner, "'Who Hast Not Made Me a Man': The Movement for Equal Rights for Women in American Jewry," **AJYB** 77, pp. 3-38

C. I. Waxman, "The Impact of Feminism on American Jewish Communal Institutions," **Journal of Jewish Communal Service** Vol. 57 No. 1 (Fall, 1980), pp. 73-79

A. Mintz, "The People's Choice?: A Demurral on Breira," **Response** 32 (Winter, 1976/77), pp. 5-10

14. Outlook and Prospects for the Future.

Required Reading:

Waxman, AJIT, ch. 10

Requirements of the Course for Grading:

Each student is expected to prepare a term paper which concentrates on a significant issue in, or aspect of, the contemporary American Jewish community. By the third session, the student should submit a proposal, including a suggested outline and suggested bibliography, to the instructor for approval. The instructor, in turn, returns the proposal along with content suggestions and further bibliographic recommendations. The term paper serves as the primary basis upon which a grade is given.

IV.   CONCEPTUAL FRAMEWORK OF THE COURSE

The course begins with a brief historical overview of the development of the organized American Jewish community during the 18th and 19th centuries.   Special attention is paid to the massive wave of immigration of Eastern European Jews at the turn of the 19th and 20th centuries.   An in-depth comparative sociological analysis of developments in each subsequent generation is provided, the primary focus being upon the contemporary American Jewish community. Topics such as socio-economic status, geographic patterns, family, relationship with Israel, anti-Semitism, political values and behavior, Jewish education, social welfare, religious patterns, recent Jewish immigration, leadership and challenges, are explored in depth.

A basic assumption underlying the entire course is that one cannot understand the contemporary American Jewish community without an understanding of both its historical development and the nature of American society in which it has developed. The American Jewish community is an ethno-religious community, that is, America's Jews are both a religious group and an ethnic group, and the manner in which both of these components are intertwined appears to make for the uniqueness of this group. While there have been periods in which the group emphasized one of these components more so than the other-- sometimes the religious, sometimes the ethnic--both continue to play a role in its development. To understand the community in perspective requires a knowledge of Jewish history in various societies, American Jewish history, American social history, and the experiences of other ethnic and religious groups in American society. It is insufficient to compare and evaluate the state of American Jewry solely by comparing it with a Jewish community in a different society with different experiences, just as it is insufficient to compare it solely with a contemporary American ethnic or religious group. It must be viewed in terms of the total dynamic.

When viewed dynamically, both the weaknesses and strengths of the contemporary American Jewish community take on a different light. While its weaknesses, both in comparison to past Jewish communities and even the American Jewish community in earlier times, are serious, the contemporary community also manifests strengths which were not apparent in earlier decades. The extent to which it will be able to build on these strengths and maintain itself in the future is its greatest challenge.

Since this course is expressly designed for future Jewish educators and other Jewish communal workers, the student requires to learn the nature of the American Jewish communal structure in which he or she will function, and to understand the variety of ways in which different segments of the community conceive of themselves as Jews. The student will need to move beyond his or her preconceived notions of what Jewish identity is and understand the diverse ways in which different segments of American Jewry consciously or unconsciously express their Jewish identity.

PUBLICATIONS OF THE STUDY CIRCLE ON WORLD JEWRY

IN THE HOME OF THE PRESIDENT OF ISRAEL*

Moshe Davis, editor

FIRST SERIES – 1966/1967

(1) Roberto Bachi: **Demography of World Jewry – Methods of Research;**
(2) Benjamin Akzin: **The Political Status of Diaspora Jewry;**
(3) Jacob Robinson: **The Jewish Community Councils during the Nazi Era
– Severance or Continuity;** (4-5) Nathan Rotenstreich: **"Galut" in
Contemporary American Jewish Thought;** (6) Julius Gould: **Changing
Patterns in British Society; Their Impact on the Jewish Community;
Anglo-American Jewish Life.**

SECOND SERIES – 1967/1968

(1-2) **Diaspora Jewry and Eretz Yisrael** – Iyar-Sivan 5727 – June
1967; (3-4) Shmuel Ettinger: **The Conventional and the New in Modern
Anti-Semitism;** (5-6) Alexander M. Dushkin: **Jewish Education in the
Diaspora – The Problems of Teachers and Teaching;** (7) Hayyim J.
Cohen: **20th Century Aliya from Asia and Africa.**

THIRD SERIES – 1968/1969

(1) Andre Neher: **The Jewish Community in France in Light of the New
Political Policy;** (2) Haim Beinart: **The Jewish Community in Spain
Today – Background and Evaluation;** (3) Binyamin Eliav: **Jews in the
Soviet Union;** (4) Haim H. Cohn: **Jewish Issues at the United Nations
Council on Human Rights;** (5) Uriel Tal: **Patterns in the Contempo-
rary Jewish-Christian Dialogue;** (6-7) Ben Halpern and Israel Kolatt:
Changing Relations Between Israel and the Diaspora.

FOURTH SERIES – 1970/1971

(1) Shlomo Avineri: **University Protest Movements and their Implica-
tions for the Jewish Communities;** (2) Ezra Spicehandler: **Contempo-
rary Iranian Jewry;** (3) Ernst Stock with Daniel Elazar, Gabriel Cohen
& Marie Syrkin: **American Jewry Confronts Black Anti-Semitism;** (4)
Isadore Twersky: **Jewish Studies in American Universities;** (5) S. Z.
Feller: **Recent Rumanian Legislation and its Influence on the Jewish
Community;** (6) Haim Avni: **Jewish Students and the Argentinian
Jewish Community.**

*These publications are available in Hebrew only. However, a revised
English version of the tenth, twelfth and thirteenth series has
appeared in consecutive issues of **Forum** (W.Z.O., Info. Dept.,
Jerusalem) vols. 41-55, 1981-1985.

FIFTH SERIES - 1971/1972

(1) Ben Halpern, Israel Kolatt, Nathan Rotenstreich: **The Zionist Idea in Today's Jewish World**; (2) Eli Ginzberg: **Notes for the Study of the Economic Life of Jews in the Diaspora**; (3) Simon Kuznets: **Economic Structure of U.S. Jewry - Recent Trends**; (4) Emil L. Fackenheim: **The Impact of the Holocaust on Contemporary Jewish Life**; (5) Yehuda Bauer: **The Holocaust Today - An Attempt at a New Evaluation**; (6) Haim Avni, Edward B. Glick, Moshe Lazar & Netanel Lorch: **Latin American Jewry in a Changing Era.**

SIXTH SERIES - 1972/1973

(1-2) Chone Shmeruk and Michael Zand: **Jewish Culture in the Soviet Union**; (3) Joshua A. Fishman: **The Sociology of Yiddish in America - Past, Present and Future**; (4) Mordecai Altshuler, Jakob Pinhasi and Michael Zand: **Bukharan and Mountain Jews - Two Communities of the Southern Soviet Union**; (5) Simon N. Herman and Gideon Shimoni: **The Jewish Community in the Apartheid Society of Southern Africa**; (6) Eliezer Schweid: **Identification with the Jewish People in Israeli Education**; (7) Menachem Elon: **Halachic Problems in Israel State Law.**

SEVENTH SERIES - 1974/1975

(1) Ephraim E. Urbach: **Center and Periphery in Historic Jewish Consciousness**; (2) Nathan Rotenstreich: **State and Diaspora in Our Time**; (3) Moshe Ma'oz: **Anti-Jewishness in Official Arab Literature and Communications Media**; (4-5) Zvi Gitelman: **Patterns of Jewish Identification and Non-Identification in the Soviet Union**; (6) Zalman Shazar: **Reflections on the Jewish Present.**

EIGHTH SERIES - 1975/1976

(1) Abraham S. Halkin: **The Relevant Elements of Basic Zionist Ideologies**; (2) Yehuda Nini: **Early Aliyah from Yemen: Immigration without Organization**; (3) Haim Avni: **Zionism in Latin America**; (4) David Sidorsky: **"The End of Ideology" and American Zionism**; (5) Mordechai Altshuler: **Soviet Jewry: Zionism and Aliya Today**; (6) **Zionism Considered: A Global Review** (Symposium).

NINTH SERIES - 1977/1978

(1) Jacob Katz: **The Jewish Nature of Israeli Society**; (2) Samuel N. Eisenstadt: **Comments on the Continuity of Some Jewish Historical Forms in Israeli Society**; (3) Shimon Agranat: **The Jewish Component in Israeli Society: Its Reflection in Judgements of the Supreme Court**; (4) Aharon Yadlin: **The Jewish Component in Israeli Education**; (5) Bezalel Amir: **The Jewish and Zionist Components of the Israel Defense Forces**; (6) Elihu Katz: **The Use of Leisure in**

Israel; (7) Nathan Rotenstreich, Zalman Abramov, Yehuda Bauer: Israel's Responsibility to the Diaspora.

TENTH SERIES - 1978/1979
(1) Benjamin Akzin: **Assimilation in the Post-Emancipation Period;** (2) Yaakov Rabi: **Assimilation in Western and Eastern Europe;** (3) Roberto Bachi: **The Demographic Crisis of Diaspora Jewry;** (4) Emanuel Rackman: **Approaches to Combating Assimilation in the United States Today;** (5) Jose Itzikson, Nathan Lerner, Haim Avni: **The Struggle Against Assimilation in Latin America;** (6) Mordechai Altshuler: **Trends and Counter Efforts in Soviet Jewish Assimilation;** (7) Yehuda Nini: **Western Cultural Assimilation Among Jews of the Mediterranean Basin.**

ELEVENTH SERIES - 1980/1981
(1-2) Elazar Leshem: **Immigration and the "Drop-Out" Phenomenon Among Soviet Jews: Main Findings and Recommendations;** (3) Amnon Netzer: **The Jews of Iran Today;** (4) Itzhak Minerbi: **Change and Development in French Jewry;** (5) Michel Abitbol: **Contemporary North African Jewry;** (6-7) Seymour Fox: **Is Jewish Education a Bulwark Against Assimilation?** (8) Moshe Davis: **University Teaching of Jewish Civilization.**

TWELFTH SERIES - 1981/1982
(1) Michel Abitbol: **Manifestations of Jewish Group Identity in France;** (2) Gideon Shimoni: **Jewish National Identification in the Diaspora: The South African Community;** (3) Itzhak Harkavi: **Jewish National Identity in Latin America;** (4) Louis Jacobs: **Jewish National Consciousness in the Anglo-Jewish Community: An Analysis;** (5) Shmuel Ettinger: **Jewish Re-awakening in the Soviet Union;** (6) Nathan Rotenstreich: **The United States of America: Expressions of Jewish National Identity;** (7) Hedva Ben-Israel Kidron, Israel Kolatt: **Expressions of Jewish National Identity in the Diaspora: Analysis and Conclusions.**

THIRTEENTH SERIES - 1982/1983
(1) Avraham Harman: **Israel's Place in American Jewry Today;** (2) S. Z. Abramov: **The Relationship to Israel of Jewish Religious Groups: Reform Judaism;** (3) Aharon Lichtenstein: **The Relationship to Israel of Jewish Religious Groups: Orthodoxy;** (4) Lloyd P. Gartner: **Israel's Place in American Jewry Today: Conservative Jewry;** (5) Mordechai Altshuler, Vadim Meniker, Juri Stern: **Israel and Soviet Jewry Today;** (6) Israel Finestein: **The Place of Israel in the Life and Thought of Anglo-Jewry: Changing Perspectives;** (7) Daniel J. Elazar: **The Place of the Zionist Vision and the State of Israel in**

the Sepharadic World; (8) Peter Medding, Simon Herman, Shulamit Nardi: The Place of Israel in Three English-Speaking Communities: Australia, South Africa and Canada; (9) Ernest Stock: The Israeli Branches of Diaspora Religious Movements: Indigenous Developments and Potential Influence on the Diaspora.